In this book, Dr. Allen provides a thoughtful and nuanced empirical discussion of children with problematic sexual behavior (PSB), a very poorly understood phenomenon. Dr. Allen is a leader in this area, and this work clearly summarizes our current theory and research. Moreover, Dr. Allen also puts forth a flexible phase-based individual treatment for PSB, a significant innovative contribution to this field, which is sure to help effectively mitigate children's PSB.

—**Rachel A. Wamser, PhD,** University of Missouri, St. Louis, MO, United States

This volume is an indispensable resource for clinicians who encounter children with problematic sexual behavior. Dr. Allen's approach is based on standard child psychotherapy principles and expands existing expertise so that referral to a specialist is not required. It can be flexibly delivered as a standalone intervention or embedded within a broader course of therapy. The extremely informative case scenarios walk clinicians through assessment and the phases of treatment.

—**Lucy Berliner, LICSW,** University of Washington, Seattle, WA, United States

This book represents a substantial contribution to the field, successfully bridging research and practice while correcting long-standing misconceptions about childhood problematic sexual behavior. It offers an empirically grounded, developmentally sensitive, and clinically practical approach to assessment and treatment that is feasible for real-world settings. Its clear structure, strong assessment framework, and thoughtfully integrated case material make it an invaluable resource for clinicians, trainees, and advanced students in psychology and related disciplines.

—**Kelly M. Babchishin, PhD,** Assistant Professor and Director, Sexually Harmful Behaviours Research Lab, Carleton University, Ottawa, ON, Canada

Children With Problematic Sexual Behavior

Children With Problematic Sexual Behavior

Theory, Research, and Evidence-Based Practice

Brian Allen

AMERICAN PSYCHOLOGICAL ASSOCIATION

Published by
American Psychological Association
750 First Street, NE
Washington, DC 20002
https://www.apa.org

Order Department
https://www.apa.org/pubs/books
order@apa.org

Typeset in Charter and Interstate by Circle Graphics, Inc., Reisterstown, MD

Cover Designer: Gwen J. Grafft

Library of Congress Cataloging-in-Publication Data

Names: Allen, Brian, 1979- author
Title: Children with problematic sexual behavior : theory, research, and evidence-based practice / Brian Allen.
Description: Washington, DC : American Psychological Association, 2027. | Includes bibliographical references and index.
Identifiers: LCCN 2026018813 (print) | LCCN 2026018814 (ebook) | ISBN 9781433847387 paperback | ISBN 9781433847394 epub | ISBN 9781433851780 pdf
Subjects: LCSH: Children--Sexual behavior--United States | Child psychology--Methodology | Sex (Psychology)--United States | Child development--United States
Classification: LCC BF723.S4 A45 2027 (print) | LCC BF723.S4 (ebook)
LC record available at https://lccn.loc.gov/2026018813
LC ebook record available at https://lccn.loc.gov/2026018814

https://doi.org/10.1037/0000516-000

Printed in the United States of America

10 9 8 7 6 5 4 3 2 1

This book is dedicated to Lucy Berliner, William Friedrich, Barbara Bonner, David Finkelhor, and all the other pioneers of the field of child maltreatment who blazed a trail toward a better tomorrow for children.

Contents

Preface

Josiah was a 9-year-old boy brought into treatment after his mother overheard him asking a younger sister to perform oral sex. Shocked, the caregivers questioned the sister and discovered this was not the first incident; it happened several times in the past, and sexual contact between the two had occurred on multiple occasions. Josiah was too young to prosecute in his jurisdiction, so Child Protective Services (CPS) referred him for therapy. The clinician assigned to assess and treat Josiah was at a loss. She believed the severity of the behavior required a clinician with specialized training, although she could not find a provider in the area with such expertise. Even though she had over 20 years of experience as a clinician and believed herself to be a competent provider for children, she felt unprepared and unqualified to treat the case.

The story of Josiah is reflective of a countless number of cases relayed to me over the years.[1] Sometimes, they involved the types of interpersonally intrusive behavior ascribed to Josiah, while other times, they involved significant self-focused behavior (e.g., inserting objects into oneself). A more recent concern involves preteen children accessing internet pornography, and schools are increasingly being called upon to address sexually inappropriate comments and behaviors occurring through digital means (e.g., social media, texting). Considering these concerns to be behavioral problems, various sources refer such children to a mental health professional. However, like the clinician

[1]The cases in this book are composites and identifying details have been changed to protect client confidentiality.

asked to treat Josiah, many providers lack the experience and training to serve such children, leading to a significant shortage of available services. Various service brokers and policymakers have undertaken concerted efforts to improve access to services, often by training mental health clinicians in the available interventions. Over the past few years, I have delivered numerous year-long, intensive training programs in the treatment of preteen children with problematic sexual behavior (PSB), and in each case, the uncertainty and hesitation of some attendees is clearly visible, if not outright discussed. I have found it helpful to share a brief story of how I came to focus my research and clinical practice on the topic of childhood PSB.

In the spring of 2010, I taught a graduate-level course in developmental psychology to mostly PhD students within a forensically oriented clinical program. Understandably, many of the students chose to write their term papers on some topic related to criminal behavior or juvenile justice. One particularly exceptional student, Alexandra Tellez (now with her PhD), wrote her paper on preteen children exhibiting PSB. Given my training and experience in the field of child maltreatment, I expected her paper to largely confirm my existing perspective on the etiology of this behavior, specifically, its origins in the experience of childhood abuse. However, her paper explored a much wider range of factors and emphasized the developmental context in which those factors operate. It was intriguing and made me realize that research and clinical practice related to PSB were greatly underdeveloped.

Wanting to learn more, I made a concerted effort to read all the literature I could find on PSB, using Dr. Tellez's reference list as my starting point. Within a week, I read every peer-reviewed journal article I could identify and located two books on the topic through the university's library. With few exceptions, these resources constituted the whole of the published literature on PSB in 2010. With a wonderful team of graduate students, I launched into a new field of research with several different avenues to explore, all the while maintaining a focus on the clinical relevance of our findings. That research took on many forms, including developmental and etiological studies, systematic reviews and meta-analyses, and the validation of new assessment techniques. In addition, these research efforts coalesced into the evidence-informed treatment model that is highlighted in this book, phase-based treatment (PBT) for problematic sexual behavior.

I often share this story with clinicians participating in PBT training for three reasons. First, many clinicians working in the child maltreatment field who commonly treat children presenting with PSB share the belief that a child presenting with PSB likely experienced some form of child sexual abuse (CSA). We now know that many children with PSB do not have a CSA history, and learning this can leave some clinicians feeling defensive or discouraged, especially those who previously delivered treatment in such cases with the presumption that CSA occurred. I find this story is helpful for letting those clinicians know they are not alone. There was a period of time when CSA was considered the primary etiological mechanism of PSB, a view promoted by the most knowledgeable minds in the field, and it is not surprising that many clinicians learned this perspective through their training, as I did.

Second, this anecdote underlines that there are many different findings related to PSB that clinicians may find surprising. For instance, girls display PSB just as frequently as boys, and younger children (e.g., preschoolers) are more likely to display PSB than 11 or 12-year-olds on the cusp of entering adolescence (e.g., middle schoolers; Allen et al., 2025). For some, these results fundamentally conflict with their understanding of (and, potentially, training in) sexual behavior or sexual dysfunction, where men are more commonly expected to display such problems, and difficulties are most likely to occur at the time when pubertal hormones affect the body and mind. This is often an appropriate time to reframe PSB away from a view of sexual deviancy and highlight that many times, these behaviors have nothing to do with sexual arousal, desire, or any other adult-oriented concept of sexual behavior. In short, these behaviors rarely represent the same thing for a child as they do for an adult.

Third, it is heartening for some to hear that the most evidence-based techniques for treating PSB are the same ones many of them already have experience implementing, typically, through training in other treatment models. In effect, the barrier is not a lack of clinical knowledge or skill but, rather, a lack of experience and confidence in applying those techniques with the somewhat intimidating population of children with PSB. As a reflection of this, the PBT protocol constitutes practical steps, distilled from the research literature and constructed based on clinical experience, that provides the clinician with a sort of road map that offers scaffolding for implementing techniques when a child with PSB presents for treatment. In this way, the final goal of sharing the story of how I came to work with this specific population is to impart a sense of self-confidence in the trainees. As I find myself often telling clinicians, "You know how to treat PSB; you just don't know that you know how to treat PSB."

Acknowledgments

The first published paper I ever wrote on the topic of treating problematic sexual behavior (PSB) was a case study. Wanting to have a more seasoned and respected clinician or researcher review it, I sent an email to an individual I had never met, Lucy Berliner, MSW. She quickly agreed to read the draft and later wrote the discussion for that paper. Since then, Ms. Berliner and I have become frequent collaborators, writing several papers together, and she was one of the three authors of phase-based treatment for PSB (PBT), offering exceptional clinical wisdom and always maintaining a focus on the applicability of the techniques in general practice. She has my enduring gratitude for her gracious collegiality and her decades of service working to improve the lives of children.

The other coauthor of PBT is Chad Shenk, PhD, a colleague and long-time collaborator. Dr. Shenk and I have worked on numerous clinical trials and developmental studies and, with each collaboration, I learn more from him about our field and how to study it in a rigorous way. His prior training in dialectical behavior therapy for adolescents lent a special expertise to the development of PBT that enriched both its empirical basis and effectiveness. Although we now work at different institutions, I look forward to continuing our collaborations for years to come and thank him for all of his patience, effort, and insight in the development of PBT, as well as our other endeavors.

It is appropriate to also acknowledge the considerable work of pioneers in the field whose research and clinical experience paved the way and allowed an intervention like PBT to be built on a solid empirical foundation. Foremost among these individuals is William N. Friedrich, PhD. Dr. Friedrich's influence is pervasive as he not only researched typical sexual development but also conducted the first studies on the etiology of PSB, developed the most widely used assessment measure of PSB, and explored different treatment options for the problem. Indeed, without his work, our understanding of and response to PSB would be decades behind where it is today. Other influential figures in this field deserve recognition for their amazing efforts at changing the perception of children with PSB and creating an environment where treatment is not only available but also effective. These include Barbara Bonner, PhD; Mark Chaffin, PhD; Judith Cohen, MD; Esther Deblinger, PhD; David Finkelhor, PhD; Toni Cavanaugh Johnson, PhD; David Kolko, PhD; Anthony Mannarino, PhD; and Jane Silovsky, PhD.

I would be remiss if I did not thank my family for the incredible support they provide every day and in every way. The countless days spent on the road can take a toll on those who love and support you. I have missed soccer games, school concerts, and my turns tucking my daughters into bed and making dinner. My remarkable wife, Kristen, picks up the slack when I am out of town, makes sure the house does not fall apart, and gets our girls where they need to go, all while continuing her own career as a school psychologist. It is not always easy, I realize that, but I hope she views accomplishments such as this book as being as much hers as mine. The same can be said for my daughters, Ashlyn and Linnea. Through no choice of their own, they share their dad with people they will never know in the service of helping children they will never meet. I thank them both so very much and look forward to all of the amazing things they will accomplish. To my wife and daughters, I love you more than words can express.

Lastly, I wish to recognize and express deep appreciation for the countless children and families, and practicing clinicians who provided valuable feedback, participated in clinical research, and helped craft PBT into its current form.

Children With Problematic Sexual Behavior

INTRODUCTION

Improving the Care of Children With Problematic Sexual Behavior

As mentioned in the preface, there are several misconceptions regarding children with problematic sexual behavior (PSB) that restrict the implementation of research-supported approaches to assessment and treatment. Although much of this relates to a historical lack of training and resources, another source of disconnect is the difficulty of translating often complex research findings into clinically practicable recommendations. Clinicians typically report accessing more books than academic journal articles and prefer reading case material over the results of research studies laden with statistical analyses (Allen & Armstrong, 2014). Although understanding of children with PSB and how to best provide clinical care has advanced considerably over the past 2 decades, much of that literature is found in academic sources and fails to provide clinical demonstrations. This book attempts to address these concerns by providing an empirically based, practical manual geared toward mental health clinicians.

https://doi.org/10.1037/0000516-001
Children With Problematic Sexual Behavior: Theory, Research, and Evidence-Based Practice, by B. Allen

GOALS AND APPROACH TO CONTENT

PSB among children is one of those topics rarely discussed in mental health training or in continuing education programs. This creates a significant problem in the dissemination and implementation of evidence-based practices as clinicians often report being unsure what types of training to attend or whether they are sufficiently qualified to provide services in such cases. However, it is often encouraging for many clinicians to learn that children with PSB are not particularly dissimilar from other cases treated in typical child-serving programs, and that experienced clinicians typically possess all of the necessary skills to effectively treat these children. This book aims to provide a suitable introduction to the topic of PSB, discuss how this research-derived understanding can translate into effective clinical practice, and provide a treatment protocol based in the current empirical evidence that can be implemented in practice.

Several aspects of this book were specifically designed to achieve these goals. First, this book's approach is decidedly scientific in nature. In other words, while several ideas and theoretical propositions are available and discussed in various publications, this book relies on content derived from empirical research. Second, the presentation of all material in this book is practical in orientation. In-depth discussions of statistical analyses are avoided in preference to practical descriptions of how the empirical findings relate to clinical practice. Citations are clearly provided throughout, and readers interested in exploring the more technical aspects of the research can easily identify the studies on which the discussions are based. In this spirit, Chapter 1 provides a practical introduction to the current knowledge base related to the development (i.e., etiology), maintenance, assessment, and treatment of PSB. Chapter 2 proposes an assessment protocol that logically flows from the material covered in the first chapter and provides clear treatment implications. Chapter 3 reviews phase-based treatment for PSB (PBT) and discusses how the intervention was developed on this knowledge base, the current evidence for its effectiveness, and training options.

Third, a central focus of this book is clinical demonstration. Case studies are used heavily throughout to demonstrate the techniques of the intervention. In the chapter focused on the assessment of PSB (Chapter 2), three disguised cases are introduced to the reader, Lydia E., Maria A., and Alex J. The background, assessment data, and conceptualization of each case is discussed to demonstrate the diversity of presentations that fall under the umbrella of PSB and the different etiological mechanisms that may be operative. These three cases are then revisited in each chapter describing the treatment techniques of PBT (Chapters 4, 5, and 6) to demonstrate the application of the protocol to such varied presentations and backgrounds. This method also reveals the flexibility of the protocol to cultural, familial, and practical differences. Chapters 7, 8, and 9 provide full length unified descriptions of the treatment of three cases (Alyssa P., Alvi L., and Jamar W.) with presentations and challenges different from those of the three cases presented in the earlier chapters.

Lastly, this book is meant to boost the confidence of clinicians treating children with PSB by anticipating and answering questions and providing appropriate resources. Throughout the three chapters specifying the protocol (Chapters 4, 5, and 6), "Clinical Tips" are inserted that provide suggestions on how to improve implementation and avoid commonly experienced difficulties. A common question asked is when to use PBT as opposed to another treatment approach or if PBT can be integrated into another model. This topic is addressed in its own chapter, Chapter 10, by discussing how PBT's structure can result in a clinician thoughtfully integrating PBT techniques within another form of treatment. Other frequently asked questions are answered in Chapter 11. Through years of practice with PBT and consulting with clinicians, several pitfalls were identified and solutions tested. Some of these are discussed in Chapter 11. Finally, several resources that clinicians might find useful when implementing PBT, including fact sheets, books, and online videos, are provided in an appendix and categorized based on topic. Also, measures that clinicians may use free of charge in their clinical practice are provided in the appendix.

A NOTE ON TERMINOLOGY

There are countless terms related to sexuality and sexual behavior, many of which are quite familiar and imply certain experiences or behaviors. For instance, terms such as voyeurism, exhibitionism, and masturbation require no definition for most adults. However, these terms are often associated with the experience of sexual arousal and denote a desire to achieve some level of sexual gratification. In this respect, and as will be discussed in detail in Chapter 1, these terms are not directly applicable to many preteen children who exhibit PSB. In short, attempting to apply adult-focused terms related to mature sexual behavior and interests to children is inherently misdirected and likely counterproductive in efforts to apply the current empirical knowledge. As such, terms will be used throughout this book that are self-explanatory and avoid applying adult concepts to the behavior of children. To complete the example just provided, terms to be used within this book include *looking behaviors* (instead of voyeurism), *showing behaviors* (instead of exhibitionism), and *self-stimulation* (instead of masturbation).

Even the term “problematic sexual behavior” is a more recent innovation in terminology. Not long ago, the umbrella term used to describe these concerns was “sexual behavior problems.” Unfortunately, this latter term was used in several instances to suggest that sexual behavior from children itself was problematic; developmentally typical behaviors sometimes were identified as potential targets of clinical intervention. It is important to recognize that sexual behavior, just as with social behavior or language acquisition, displays a developmental progression and certain behaviors are to be expected, a topic reviewed in Chapter 1. These issues led various experts to restructure the term to more clearly identify “problematic sexual behavior” as qualitatively different from “typical sexual behavior.”

One particularly concerning form of PSB is interpersonal, intrusive behavior that involves direct contact with another individual or animal. Over the decades of research and discussion on this topic, these acts have been described as “sexually abusive” or “molestation,” with the children themselves being labeled as “children who molest other children” or “child perpetrators.” These terms imply a level of sexual deviancy and criminal intent that is not typically present with children who display these behaviors. Also, use of these terms may suggest that the risk of future sexual offending is high, when the current evidence suggests that such risk is actually quite low (see Chapter 1). Throughout this book, the term *intrusive behavior* is used to describe behavior that involves interpersonal contact and the term *initiator* is employed to identify the child primarily responsible for introducing the behavior.

Lastly, a number of different terms are commonly utilized in clinical practice to describe PSB, although they are not typically employed in the research literature. These phrases include “sexual acting out” and “sexually reactive.” The problem with these terms is that they suggest an etiological cause for the PSB, namely, that some factor internal to the child is being expressed in an external way, which leads to the conclusion that effective treatment must resolve this presumed underlying issue. As will be discussed in the first three chapters, the current empirical evidence suggests the most effective intervention for PSB focuses on helping caregivers implement behavioral change techniques and not on processing a child’s unconscious motivations. These terms are avoided throughout this book.

CONCLUSION

PBT was the result of years of empirical research and clinical practice, combined with expert deliberations, pilot testing, and clinician feedback. In a sense, it was designed to provide a trained clinician with a clear treatment plan for a child presenting with PSB. However, it was not designed to be a one-size-fits-all approach to treatment. As will be seen in the pages that follow, PBT is flexible and tailored to the unique needs and aspects of a given case. As such, the use of the protocol is not meant to replace clinical experience and judgment but rather to direct a clinician to utilize their skills in an evidence-informed approach to the issue of childhood PSB. In this manner, therapists can provide their young patients with the best possible care, making use of both a skilled and knowledgeable clinician and the current empirical evidence of how to best treat PSB.

PART I UNDERSTANDING CHILDREN WITH PROBLEMATIC SEXUAL BEHAVIOR

1 CHILDREN WITH PROBLEMATIC SEXUAL BEHAVIOR

A Practical Overview

Before discussing problematic sexual behavior (PSB) of children, it is important to first define the types of sexual behavior considered normative. This can be a challenging task for many mental health clinicians, as well as allied professionals, given the relative lack of training on the topic. In addition, childhood sexual behavior is a politically charged topic in the current environment and engenders strong feelings within some circles, further complicating any discussion of the topic. Nonetheless, there are certain behaviors that even those who find the topic objectionable surely concede happen in the typical course of development. For instance, at some point, children learn that men and women possess different forms of genitalia, even if not specifically instructed in anatomical differences by a caregiver or teacher. Similarly, most people will acknowledge that very young children, toddlers or preschoolers, for example, are not ashamed or embarrassed by appearing naked in front of others, although these emotions are typically ingrained by the beginning of the grade school years.

https://doi.org/10.1037/0000516-002
Children With Problematic Sexual Behavior: Theory, Research, and Evidence-Based Practice, by B. Allen

Part of the challenge in defining normative sexual behavior among preteen children is the diversity of topics included in the category, such as *sexual knowledge and interest-related behaviors* (e.g., knowing about genital differences), *looking behaviors* (e.g., peeking at someone in the bathroom), *showing behaviors* (e.g., exposing oneself to others), *self-focused behaviors* (e.g., self-stimulating), and interpersonally *intrusive behaviors* (e.g., touching the genitalia or breasts of others). Many of these behaviors are relatively common at some points in childhood while rarer, and potentially problematic, at other points (Okami et al., 1997). For instance, a recent nationally representative study of 1,400 caregivers across the United States found that 43.5% reported their child (ages 3–12) had either asked a question about or directly performed a sexual behavior in the prior month (Allen, Silovsky, Kolko, et al., 2026). Using these same data, Table 1.1 shows how frequently different types of sexual behaviors were reported as having occurred over the prior 6 months across different age groups. Some behaviors appeared fairly common regardless of the age of the child, such as "Asks questions about private parts or sexual acts to a trusted adult." Other behaviors occurred more frequently among preschoolers and school-age children before all but disappearing among preteens (e.g., "Touches or rubs own private parts when around other people"), while other behaviors were more common among preteens than among younger children (e.g., "Uses sexual words in an insulting, disrespectful, and/or suggestive way"). Clearly, the knowledge and display of sexual behavior follow a developmental course, and evidence suggests that such normative behaviors do not predict future problems of sexual, behavioral, and/or emotional functioning (Okami et al., 1997).

There is a biological and evolutionary basis for childhood sexual development. Comparative psychologists observe that juvenile nonhuman primates, such as chimpanzees and bonobos, often engage in sexual play, even though they have not reached sexual maturity and display many of the same behaviors discussed above that are commonly observed from prepubescent humans (de Waal, 2007; Hashimoto & Furuichi, 1994). In addition, anthropologists document similarities in the display of childhood sexual behavior across diverse global cultures, even if the meanings assigned to these behaviors differ (Nieto, 2004). As such, sexual curiosity and behavior among children appears to have an innate basis that can be seen across species and cultures. From an evolutionary perspective, if one accepts that humans instinctively have a propensity toward reproduction and genetic survival, then it can be argued that development prepares the individual for productive sexual activity once procreation is possible (i.e., puberty). In this manner, childhood sexual behavior merely reflects a natural learning process

TABLE 1.1. Frequency of Sexual Behaviors in a Normative U.S. Sample

Behavior	Preschool (3–5 years) *f* (%)	School-Age (6–9 years) *f* (%)	Preadolescent (10–12 years) *f* (%)
Knowledge and interest-related			
1. Asks questions about private parts or sexual acts to a trusted adult	64 (18.5)	135 (23.2)	82 (17.4)
2. Talks about private parts, sexual topics, or toileting behaviors at inappropriate times	27 (7.8)	47 (8.1)	27 (5.7)
3. Uses sexual words in an insulting, disrespectful, and/or suggestive way	2 (0.6)	12 (2.1)	20 (4.2)
4. Uses the internet to seek out information on sexual topics	0 (0.0)	14 (2.4)	31 (6.6)
Looking behaviors			
5. Looks at or tries to look at others who are nude, undressing, and/or toileting	26 (7.5)	48 (8.2)	8 (1.7)
6. Looks at pictures or videos that show nudity and/or sexual acts	4 (1.2)	18 (3.1)	21 (4.4)
Showing behaviors			
7. Shows own private parts to others	16 (4.6)	14 (2.4)	5 (1.1)
8. Sends sexual messages, pictures, and/or videos to others (such as through texts or social media	0 (0.0)	2 (0.3)	2 (0.4)
Self-focused behaviors			
9. Touches or rubs own private parts when alone	35 (10.1)	66 (11.3)	31 (6.6)
10. Touches or rubs own private parts when around other people	24 (6.9)	27 (4.6)	3 (0.6)
Intrusive behaviors			
11. Touches or tries to touch the breasts of others	17 (4.9)	28 (4.8)	6 (1.3)
12. Touches or tries to touch the private parts of others	5 (1.4)	10 (1.7)	4 (0.8)

Note. Preschool *n* = 346, school-age *n* = 582, preadolescent *n* = 472.

with the goal of acquiring adaptive sexual knowledge by the time of sexual maturity (Frayser, 2003; Heiman et al., 2003).

Even with an apparent biological underpinning for childhood sexual behavior, development occurs within a cultural milieu and few topics in human behavior are more laden with cultural meanings and mores than sex and sexuality. The types of sexual behavior considered appropriate and the education children receive regarding these topics varies widely.

For example, in a series of studies comparing American preschoolers to their counterparts in the Netherlands and Sweden, two countries noted for being more sexually liberal than the United States, the Dutch and Swedish children demonstrated a significantly greater frequency of looking, showing, and self-stimulatory behaviors than American children (Friedrich et al., 2000; Larsson et al., 2000). However, these behaviors are not generally considered troubling nor even discouraged within the Dutch and Swedish samples but were rather viewed as natural curiosity and likely healthy (Jonkman et al., 2019; Larsson & Svedin, 2002). Differences in the normative sexual behavior of children are reported among other cultures as well, such as in Finland (Sandnabba et al., 2003) and South Korea (Choi & Song, 2022), and among Latino populations in the United States (Kenny & Wurtele, 2013). In short, cultural values and standards dictate the types of childhood sexual behavior that are acceptable and those in need of correction and, therefore, childhood sexual behavior is at least partially culturally determined.

PROBLEMATIC SEXUAL BEHAVIOR AMONG CHILDREN

Understanding typical sexual development allows for the definition of problematic sexual behavior (PSB), which then guides research on etiology, assessment, and treatment. The following sections provide a suitable introduction to these topics for clinicians working with PSB.

Definition

The definition of PSB most commonly used in current practice was provided by a task force of the Association for the Treatment and Prevention of Sexual Abusers, chaired by Mark Chaffin et al. (2008): "Children ages 12 and younger who initiate behaviors involving sexual body parts (i.e., genitals, anus, buttocks, or breasts) that are developmentally inappropriate or potentially harmful to themselves or others" (p. 200). Using this characterization, there are two ways that a sexual behavior can be termed problematic. The first is that the displayed behavior is outside of developmental expectations for a given social or cultural context. This may be the result of a singular behavior that is generally considered common for a given age (e.g., preschoolers touching their private parts) occurring with atypical frequency. Many times, this can be determined if the repetitiveness of the behavior causes functional impairment (e.g., reduced interest in other activities, school problems, social consequences). However, the accumulation of multiple discrete sexual behaviors of different types within a relatively brief period of time (e.g., looking behaviors, self-stimulating behaviors) may also go beyond developmental expectations and collectively qualify as PSB.

The second way a behavior may qualify as PSB is if the behavior is harmful, or potentially harmful, to the child or another person or animal. Many of these types of PSB are easy to identify. For example, invasive or sustained behavior that may cause physical damage is clearly a PSB (e.g., inserting objects in oneself or another, self-stimulating to the point of injury). Any behavior that is coercive and seeks to trick or force others to engage in sexual behavior is also generally considered a PSB. A single incident of these behaviors is typically sufficient to qualify as problematic. Nonetheless, harm can be a difficult standard to apply in some situations. For instance, a singular occurrence of two preschool-aged children "playing doctor" and touching each other's genitals may be within normal limits and it is unlikely that either child is harmed in this experience, even if one child clearly presented the idea. However, if the initiating child coerced or repeatedly hassled the other child to join in the play, then this type of behavior seemingly went against the wishes of the other child and harm is plausible. In this instance, the behavior of the initiating child would be considered problematic. It is not possible to define all of the different types and frequencies of behaviors that may qualify as PSB, but the use of a validated assessment measure can aid in this process (see Chapter 2).

Recent years have seen significant concerns voiced about children accessing sexually explicit media online and/or using technological devices (e.g., smartphones, tablets) to request, send, and/or receive sexually explicit media (i.e., "sexting"). However, relatively little is known about these electronic and online sexual behaviors (EOSB) in the preteen period. There is general consensus, however, that the intentional and sustained use of electronic devices for sexual purposes among the preteen population falls under the general definition of PSB (Allen, Silovsky, Ferrer Pistone, et al., 2025). It is important in such cases to distinguish problematic EOSB from other types of technology-mediated exposure, such as accidental exposure (e.g., an adult inadvertently leaves a device open that shows sexual content), intentional sexualization of the child (e.g., an adult forcing the child to watch pornography), and limited information seeking by the child (e.g., performing a web search of an unknown term or phrase heard at school). Assessing whether an EOSB qualifies as PSB will be highlighted in Chapter 2.

Prevalence and Persistence

The prevalence of PSB is difficult to establish as such behaviors historically were minimized either through dismissal (e.g., "boys being boys") or an unwillingness to report the behavior to anyone outside of the home. Nonetheless, recent studies provide some useful data. Lussier et al. (2018) reported that 17% of preschoolers in their sample displayed some form of sexual behavior in the prior 6 months, while 12% of these same children continued to display such behavior in the 6 months prior to being assessed between the ages of 6 and 8. However, they included several different types of sexual behavior in their definition (e.g., looking behaviors, intrusive behaviors) and it was not possible to distinguish between typical and problematic behavior. In a sample of 8-year-old children ($n = 1{,}112$) experiencing some form of psychosocial risk (e.g., maltreatment, poverty), Allen (2017) documented that 22% displayed PSB over the prior 6 months. Perhaps the best data on current prevalence of PSB in a normative sample comes from Allen, Silovsky, Kolko, et al. (2026). In their sample of 1,400 caregivers across the United States, 4.7% reported their child displayed PSB over the prior month and 5.5% displayed PSB over the prior six months.

A few studies provide estimates of the prevalence of the specific subtype of intrusive sexual behavior (ISB). Allen, Silovsky, Kolko, et al. (2026), when limiting their consideration only to clearly problematic intrusive behaviors within a normative sample, found ISB among 3.8% of preschoolers (age 3–5), 3.6% of school-aged children (ages 6–9), and 2.3% of preteens (ages 10–12) over the prior month. When looking at a 6-month timeframe, the prevalence was between 2.5% (preteens) and 4% (preschoolers and school-aged children). Allen's (2017) study of 8-year-old children from "at-risk" populations identified slightly higher rates of ISB (6.9%).

Attempts to identify the prevalence of EOSB in the preteen years yield widely different results, depending on the methodology used. For instance, one study that surveyed 10 and 11-year-olds found that less than 2% disclosed intentionally accessing sexual content online, although 17% disclosed unintentionally finding such material (Wolak et al., 2007). However, in another survey, nearly 33% of 18 and 19-year-olds acknowledged internet pornography use prior to the age of 13 (Astle et al., 2020). Allen, Silovsky, Ferrer Pistone, et al. (2025) found that nearly 7% of caregivers reported knowing of their child performing an EOSB, whether normative or problematic, in the prior 6 months, with the most common behaviors involving information-seeking attempts. This last study is notable for exclusively including children between the ages of 7 and 12 years.

The persistence of PSB is understudied. The few reports that are available suggest that the presentation of PSB may be stable in many cases. For instance, Ensink et al. (2018), in a study of sexually abused children with PSB, found that 56.7% of the sample continued to display PSB 2 years later. Lévesque et al. (2012) followed a small sample of children displaying ISB and involved in the child welfare system over the course of a year; 43% continued to display ISB at follow-up. Lussier et al. (2018), in their longitudinal study, discerned four different trajectories in the data. Two courses were marked by low levels of sexual behavior both earlier and later in development, one course demonstrated initial moderate levels of sexual behavior that steadily persisted over time (48.3% of the sample), and the last was a pattern of increasing sexual behavior through age 8 (13.4%). This last trajectory was noted to display the highest rate of intrusive behavior, with over 65% of the group performing at least one such behavior during the 6 months prior to the last assessment (age 8). These results suggest that PSB does dissipate or cease in many cases, but persistence is also common, including for ISB, and that an escalation in both the frequency and severity of behavior is possible.

Demographic Characteristics

PSB occurs among children from diverse backgrounds. Attempts to identify demographic risk factors have met with limited success, but it is worth reviewing these findings.

Age

Several studies document that normative sexual behavior, broadly conceived, is more readily observed among younger children (Friedrich, 2003; Schoentjes et al., 1999; see Table 1.1 for examples). This is likely a result of typical developmental progression. For instance, younger children have more rudimentary emotion and behavior regulation skills, are less aware of social boundaries and cultural mores, and are less likely to experience complex emotions such as embarrassment or shame. By the same token, PSB is more likely to occur among younger children, with a recent meta-analysis finding a correlation of −0.21 between PSB and age (Allen, Wamser, et al., 2025). However, singular behaviors that generally suggest a more mature interest in sex and sexuality (e.g., using the internet to seek out information, making sexually suggestive comments or gestures) are more common among older children (see Table 1.1).

Gender

Many often assume PSB is more common among boys, likely as a result of the clear overrepresentation of males among adolescents and adults who commit sexual offenses (Cortoni et al., 2017). However, studies of childhood PSB generally fail to identify gender differences within their samples (e.g., Kenny & Wurtele, 2013; Meyer-Bahlburg et al., 2000), including studies that focus specifically on ISB (Friedrich et al., 2003; T. J. Smith et al., 2019). Similarly, meta-analytic results show that gender is weakly related to PSB ($g = 0.12$), with boys only slightly more likely to display PSB than girls (Allen, Wamser, et al., 2025).

Race and Ethnicity

Several studies examining the relationship of racial and ethnic status to the display of PSB have failed to find a relationship (e.g., Allen, 2023a; Allen et al., 2015; C. L. Campbell & Wamser, 2024; Meyer-Bahlburg et al., 2000; Wamser-Nanney & Campbell, 2022), while one study showed higher scores among White participants (Cale & Lussier, 2017). However, much of the available research on PSB did not examine potential differences based on race or ethnicity, and examinations of specific cultural practices or beliefs that may influence the emergence of PSB are rare. One notable exception is the work of Jeffry Thigpen with African American families. He showed that sexual behavior and PSB seemingly occurred with less frequency among Black families than among White families (Thigpen, 2009), but cultural values may have impacted reporting and that parental attitudes and responses to a child's sexual behavior are likely the critical factor shaping the child's behavior and beliefs about sex and sexuality (Thigpen & Fortenberry, 2009). The implication is that cultural beliefs may largely influence a child's sexual behavior through their impact on parenting practices and the larger family context.

Socioeconomic Status

Socioeconomic status is linked to a host of developmental and clinical outcomes, although its relationship to PSB is unclear. Friedrich et al. (2003) found family income to be one of the best predictors of PSB, but Lussier et al. (2018) failed to replicate this finding. When clinical samples are used instead of general population samples, studies generally fail to find a relationship between PSB and socioeconomic status (e.g., Allen, 2023a; T. J. Smith et al., 2019; Wamser-Nanney & Campbell, 2020), although exceptions are present (e.g., Gray et al., 1997). In short, there is little evidence that PSB is directly related to socioeconomic status. However, certain familial and parental factors more common in lower socioeconomic strata (e.g., parenting stress, physical discipline) are linked to PSB, as discussed later.

Biological and Neurocognitive Substrates of PSB

It is commonly believed that youth do not develop sexual attraction, arousal, identity, or interests until reaching an age when sexual reproduction is possible (i.e., puberty). In the past few decades, however, cross-cultural and biological evidence has shown that these activities begin much earlier. Adrenarche, when the adrenal glands begin producing hormones that may result in secondary sex characteristics (e.g., body odor, pubic and underarm hair), frequently begins between the ages of 6 and 7 years and exerts a significant impact on neurological, physical, and cognitive development (B. C. Campbell, 2011; Remer et al., 2005). Adrenarche appears to portend the rise of sexual arousal and attraction, even if children do not fully understand these new feelings and physiological sensations (see Herdt & McClintock, 2000, for a review). Recent research on sexual identity formation likewise shows that sexual orientation may emerge in observable ways during the preteen years (Calzo et al., 2011; Feinstein et al., 2024; Oginni et al., 2024). In brief, the physical aspects of sexual development begin long before the onset of gonadarche between 10 and 12 years of age, a phase marked by the development of breasts and menarche in girls and the enlargement of testicles in boys.

Given physical development, it is expected that preteen children may explore their own bodies, display increasing interests in the bodies and genitalia of others, and seek out information about sexual topics. Sometimes, however, these behaviors exceed the bounds of what is considered normative in a given context (i.e., PSB), and limited research points to potential biological causes. In the only known study of its kind, researchers in Sweden assessed twins to explore a potential genetic influence on problematic self-stimulating sexual behavior among children aged 7 to 9 years (Långström et al., 2002). They found the degree of behavioral concordance was significantly higher amongst monozygotic twins than dizygotic same-sex twins and concluded that 77% of the variability in self-stimulating PSB was attributable to genetic factors.

Neurocognitive factors have received greater attention, but few definitive conclusions can be drawn. The currently available studies do not find a relationship between PSB and verbal ability and/or other proxies of intelligence (e.g., Bonner et al., 1999; Silovsky & Niec, 2002; T. J. Smith et al., 2019). However, these studies typically report mean scores below the population average (i.e., 88–98) and compare the PSB sample to another clinical sample without PSB. As such, the conclusion that PSB is not related to verbal ability or intelligence is tentative. It should be mentioned that studies examining PSB among preteen children often exclude those with significant cognitive impairments (i.e., intellectual disabilities), as these individuals may display elevated rates of sexualized behaviors related to impaired neurological functioning and/or an inability to understand societal rules governing such behavior (Davis et al., 2016). Readers interested in sexual behavior among individuals with intellectual and/or severe developmental disabilities are referred to McLay et al. (2015).

The most examined neurocognitive correlate of PSB is the cluster of hyperactivity, impulsivity, and attentional deficits. Such concerns are commonly related to the display of PSB when using caregiver report measures and/or a clinician diagnosis of attention-deficit/hyperactivity disorder (ADHD; Allen, 2017; Gray et al., 1997; Jonkman et al., 2019; Lengua et al., 2001; Lepage et al., 2010; Wamser-Nanney & Campbell, 2019). Also, several reports show a significant correlation between PSB and dissociation among children with a sexual abuse history (Allen et al., 2015; Ensink et al., 2020; Jonkman et al., 2019; van Duin et al., 2018). Given that dissociation is often conceptualized in these studies as a posttraumatic symptom of distractibility and involuntary cognitive withdrawal, these findings appear to support the hypothesis that attentional deficits are related to PSB.

The Relationship of PSB With Emotional and Behavioral Problems

As is the case with many emotional and behavioral concerns, PSB tends to co-occur with an assortment of other problems. Most common among these is externalizing difficulties (e.g., oppositionality, lying), as the association between PSB and general externalizing problems is quite strong ($g = 0.95$; Allen, Wamser, et al., 2025). This relationship is robust, as studies document PSB and externalizing problems continue to be related after controlling for several other factors, including socioeconomic status, gender, age, and maltreatment and trauma histories (Friedrich et al., 2003; Lévesque et al., 2010). There is also a significant relationship between PSB and internalizing difficulties (e.g., depression, anxiety; $g = 0.63$; Allen, Wamser, et al., 2025). This relationship, too, continues to be observed after controlling for a variety of other influences (Friedrich et al., 2003). As discussed later on, many children with PSB previously experienced traumatic events and several studies have tested whether PSB may be associated with posttraumatic stress (PTS) symptoms. Indeed, a recent meta-analysis confirmed a significant relationship between the two outcomes ($g = 0.75$; Allen & Ferrer Pistone, 2025). In short, there is compelling evidence that PSB often presents alongside a multitude of other emotional and behavioral difficulties.

Parental and Familial Correlates of PSB

As with other behavioral problems, several parental and familial characteristics are linked to the display of PSB among children. Caregivers experiencing mental health challenges and stress are more likely to have a child with PSB (Bonner et al., 1999; Hall et al., 1998; Pithers et al., 1998). One possible reason for this relationship is that caregivers experiencing mental illness and stress are more likely to employ physical discipline techniques (e.g., spanking) and less likely to provide an emotionally supportive environment (S. H. Goodman et al., 2020; MacKenzie et al., 2011), and these parenting techniques may predict the onset of PSB. For instance, some evidence suggests that lower levels of parental emotional support and involvement are associated with an increased risk of PSB (Wamser-Nanney & Campbell, 2019). Following discovery of child sexual abuse, caregiver emotional support is related to a lower risk of PSB (Wamser-Nanney et al., 2019), while physical discipline (e.g., spanking) may increase the risk for PSB (Latzman & Latzman, 2015). Alternatively, parents experiencing stress and mental illness are less likely to monitor the activities of their children (Racz & McMahon, 2011), potentially resulting in more opportunities to perform problematic behavior. In addition, children of distressed parents spend a greater amount of time on electronic devices, increasing the likelihood of exposure to sexually explicit media (Pulkki-Råback et al., 2022).

One of the most common family experiences linked to the display of PSB is exposure to nudity and sexual behavior in the home. Studies repeatedly demonstrate that children displaying PSB are more likely to reside in homes marked by cobathing, witnessing sexual behavior among adults or teens, and lax rules around in-home nudity (Allen, Silovsky, Kolko, et al., 2026; Bonner et al., 1999; Friedrich et al., 2003; Hall et al., 2002; Lévesque et al., 2010). There is also limited evidence that exposure to sexual coercion, within the context of interpartner violence, increases the risk for PSB (Cale & Lussier, 2017). One analysis including youth between the ages of 4 and 18 displaying PSB found that the majority reported exposure to some form of sexually explicit media (DeLago et al., 2020). There is now meta-analytic evidence that exposure to sexual content, either in the home or online, increases the risk for displaying PSB by at least 82% (Mori et al., 2023).

Of course, exposure to sexuality or sexual content is practically unavoidable given the multitude of ways children may be exposed, and longitudinal evidence suggests that the risk for negative long-term outcomes is relatively low in the majority of cases (Okami et al., 1998). There is also an argument that it is not helpful to prevent all exposure given normative developmental progression and the need to learn about values and boundaries. However, fears about corrupting a child's "innocence," anxieties about what information to share, and uncertainty about how to teach it in an effective way interferes with many caregivers' ability to discuss the topic with their children (C. Davies & Robinson, 2010). Also, gender differences emerge when examining the type of sexual education that caregivers provide to their children, with girls more likely to learn the basic elements of reproduction, be told to remain abstinent, and instructed to guard against the sexual advances of others (Kuhle et al., 2015; Martin & Luke, 2010). This creates an unfortunate circumstance where many children will be exposed to sexual content, either at home or elsewhere, but their caregivers fail to help them understand these experiences and/or neglect to teach helpful knowledge and skills. Although untested, this combination of exposure to sexual content without education on what is being observed may be more powerful in predicting PSB than exposure to sexuality alone.

The Relationship of Maltreatment and Trauma to PSB

One of the most frequently examined correlates of PSB is a history of trauma and maltreatment. Given the common belief that these experiences underlie the display of PSB, it is important to understand the nature of these relationships.

Childhood Sexual Abuse

Many of the earliest investigations into childhood PSB hypothesized that these behaviors were likely the result of child sexual abuse (CSA), and research designs commonly compared a group of children with CSA histories to another group without such exposure. Indeed, a significant amount of research documents that PSB is more common among children who experienced CSA (e.g., Allen, 2017; Ensink et al., 2020; Friedrich et al., 2001). However, several studies finding such a relationship also show that the majority of children exhibiting PSB do not have a CSA history (e.g., Allen, 2017; Bonner et al., 1999), and some reports fail to find any relationship between the two variables (e.g., Silovsky & Niec, 2002; Tremblay et al., 2020; van Duin et al., 2018). A recent meta-analysis showed the relationship between PSB and CSA is moderate in strength ($g = 0.64$–0.71) and that older studies tended to find a stronger relationship (Allen, Wamser, et al., 2025). This is likely the result of newer studies examining a broader assortment of potential influences, while older studies focused more intently on CSA.

Nonsexual Forms of Maltreatment and Trauma

After CSA, childhood physical abuse is the most common form of maltreatment examined for a relationship to PSB. Results generally demonstrate that physical abuse increases the likelihood of a child displaying PSB (e.g., Allen, 2017; Bonner et al., 1999; Wamser-Nanney et al., 2019). Interestingly, the magnitude of the relationship is stronger when only ISB is considered, as opposed to a broader concept of PSB (e.g., Allen, Wamser, et al., 2025; Friedrich et al., 2003). Other forms of nonsexual maltreatment are less frequently studied; however, there is some limited evidence linking PSB to exposure to interpartner violence (Cale & Lussier, 2017), physical neglect (Allen, 2017), and emotional/psychological maltreatment (Merrick et al., 2008). One difficulty with this line of research is that different types of maltreatment typically co-occur, and the experience of several forms of maltreatment and trauma (i.e., polyvictimization) is common among children with PSB (Lussier et al., 2019). Nonetheless, when multiple forms of maltreatment are examined concurrently, CSA and/or physical abuse typically emerge as the types most strongly related to PSB (see Allen, 2023b, for a review).

PSB and Preschool Settings

Limited research has examined the display of childhood sexual behavior in preschool settings. S. L. Davies et al. (2000) interviewed 58 preschool teachers in the United Kingdom and found that the majority reported commonly seeing some sexual behaviors from children within this setting, such as touching one's own genitals, attempting to touch breasts, and showing their genitals to others. However, two separate reports from Sweden that asked preschool teachers similar questions, found that such behaviors in preschool were much less common in that country (Larsson & Svedin, 2002; Lindblad et al., 1995). More severe behaviors (e.g., inserting objects, performing sexual acts) were exceptionally rare in all of these studies. Looking across these reports, it is difficult to say whether the preschool environment impacts the development of PSB. Certainly, it is possible that exposure to sexual behavior may occur in day care and preschool settings, but the types of behaviors observed are typically within the normative range for this age (see earlier sections). Friedrich and Trane (2002) found some evidence that more time spent in a day care or preschool per week correlated with an increased risk of showing, looking, self-focused, and intrusive sexual behaviors. However, the effects were remarkably small and were likely statistically significant only because the sample was exceptionally large ($n = 2{,}370$). In short, it is unclear what effect, if any, day care or preschool attendance has on the etiology or maintenance of PSB. It should also be noted that most of this research occurred in the early 2000s, and it is unclear how well these findings generalize to the present day.

Long-Term Outcomes of Children With PSB

The long-term outcomes of preteen children displaying PSB are rarely studied, but the available evidence does suggest cause for concern. In a 10-year follow-up to a clinical trial, Carpentier et al. (2006) found that 10% of children displaying ISB and receiving a supposedly innocuous treatment were charged with a sexually based offense at follow-up. This suggests that a small minority of children may continue to display intrusive behavior into adolescence. However, only one child in the study (2%) who received a cognitive-behavioral intervention was charged with a sexually based offense at the 10-year assessment, suggesting hope for effective treatment. More to the point, this latter rate was similar to a group of comparison children originally receiving services for nonsexual behavioral problems, such as ADHD or oppositional behavior. The conclusion was that properly treated children are at no greater risk for committing sexually based criminal offenses during adolescence than children displaying nonsexual behavioral difficulties. Some limited evidence from reviews of child protective services records indicated that the children with PSB most susceptible to continuing such behavior into adolescence were those that experienced out-of-home placement, neglect, and who had a parent with a criminal record (Chouinard-Thivierge et al., 2022).

Other long-term consequences are documented for children with PSB. Primary among these are other forms of concerning conduct behaviors, such as affiliating with negative peer groups and being charged with nonsexual forms of crime (Merrick et al., 2015; Negriff, 2018). In addition, there are personal consequences associated with childhood PSB. For instance, preteen children displaying concerning sexual behavior are at increased risk for engaging in consensual sexual activity and sexual risk-taking behaviors throughout their teenage years (Negriff, 2018). Allen (2025) demonstrated that a cascade effect was likely, as children displaying PSB at age 8 were more likely than their peers to report preoccupation with sexual topics and behaviors at age 12, which, in turn, increased the likelihood of engaging in consensual sexual intercourse by age 14. Taken together, these findings on the long-term consequences of PSB underscore the importance of increasing accessibility to effective interventions.

THEORETICAL MODELS: A FRAMEWORK FOR ASSESSMENT AND TREATMENT OF PSB

The most eminent theoretical perspective on the topic of childhood sexual development and its clinical implications was offered by Freud (1966/1920) in his famous psychosexual stages. Freud's hypothesis was that largely unconscious impulses for pleasure evolved during the childhood years and consequently manifested in different parts of the body. The manner in which caregivers responded to these behaviors was thought to impact the development of one's personality through the formation and effectiveness of the ego. Much of Freud's theory on psychosexual development is directly refuted by contemporary research. For instance, as discussed at the beginning of this chapter, studies do not "observe a halt and retrogression in sexual development" (i.e., latency) between the ages of 6 and 12 as Freud (1966/1920, p. 404) proposed, as childhood sexual development is clearly continuing in important and multifaceted ways. Nor are PSB and other forms of emotional and behavioral problems believed to be the result of sexual repression established in childhood, regression to an earlier stage of childhood sexual development, or a fixation of libidinal impulses. Rather, contemporary scientific research and theory provide more viable perspectives on the etiology of PSB. Three of the most prominent contemporary approaches to understanding the development of PSB, each of which holds important clinical implications, are discussed here.

Developmental Psychopathology

A central tenet of developmental psychopathology is that an understanding of how typical development unfolds can lead to an understanding of how emotional and behavioral problems emerge. In other words, this perspective argues that the maladaptive development of core developmental competencies (e.g., emotion regulation, social skills, identity formation) underlie various forms of psychopathology (Cicchetti & Toth, 1995). Numerous types of adverse and/or traumatic events (e.g., CSA, neglect, parental depression) can lead to the same outcome (e.g., aggression) because each of these experiences can adversely impact the development of the child's ability to regulate emotions and behaviors (i.e., equifinality), for example. In addition, a single form of negative experience (e.g., CSA) can lead to several different outcomes (e.g., aggression, anxiety, depression) because each of these outcomes is related to the maladaptive development of the same core competencies (i.e., multifinality; Cicchetti & Rogosch, 1996). A developmental psychopathology approach explains why so many different distal factors (e.g., CSA, physical abuse, neglect, parental stress, parenting techniques) appear linked to the display of PSB and why PSB appears to co-occur with so many other outcomes (e.g., externalizing problems, internalizing problems, PTS; see Elkovitch et al., 2009).

A developmental mechanism receiving significant attention in recent years is the construct of self-regulation. Nigg (2017) described self-regulation as "the ongoing, dynamic, and adaptive modulation of internal state (emotion, cognition) or behavior by central and peripheral physiology" (p. 361). Within this broader term are the subtypes of emotion regulation (i.e., ability to identify, tolerate, and modulate positive and negative emotions), behavior regulation (i.e., inhibiting and initiating behaviors to promote effective responding), and cognitive regulation (i.e., modifying and implementing attentional and memory resources to improve adaptation). Implicit in Nigg's definition is that self-regulation may be modified based on experience and training. This makes self-regulation a useful construct for understanding the etiology of emotional and behavioral concerns, as well as a target for intervention efforts. Indeed, a significant literature now demonstrates the relationship of self-regulation to myriad emotional and behavioral problems among children (see Beauchaine, 2015; Robson et al., 2020) and several interventions with significant empirical support are found to improve child self-regulation (e.g., Luby et al., 2018; Reid et al., 2005; Shenk et al., 2022).

The question that remains is whether problems with self-regulation can explain the emergence of PSB. Allen (2023a) showed that difficulties with self-regulation significantly mediated the relationship between experiences of CSA and physical abuse and the display of PSB. However, this study exclusively utilized measures that were collected at a single point in time. Allen and Wamser (2025) used a longitudinal design and showed that CSA and physical abuse experienced in the first 6 years of life predicted greater problems with self-regulation at age 6, which then predicted the display of PSB at age 8. This is the most direct evidence yet that problems with self-regulation, resulting from abusive experiences, may underlie childhood PSB.

Another developmental mechanism that may be linked to the display of PSB is aberrant social development. Several studies converge on the finding that children with PSB display poorer social competence (Allen, 2017; Baker et al., 2008; Tarren-Sweeney, 2008; Wamser-Nanney & Campbell, 2019). Various developmental experiences shape children's social cognitions and skills, but whether social competence mediates the relationship between adverse and/or traumatic experiences and PSB is unknown. More research is needed to determine the nature of this relationship. Studies that consider the role of self-regulation and social competence concurrently within the same model may be particularly helpful in understanding the etiology of PSB.

Clinically speaking, a developmental psychopathology framework argues for a focused assessment of various developmental abilities of the child (e.g., self-regulation, social competence) as well as associated caregiver factors (e.g., stress, discipline techniques; see Chapter 2). This perspective also suggests that interventions should target the improvement of childhood developmental outcomes and recommends achieving this goal through changing the child's environment, most commonly performed through direct training of and assistance to the caregivers. Indeed, several parent-training interventions appear effective at improving child self-regulation (see Morawska et al., 2019), and there is limited evidence that these interventions are capable of improving PSB as well (Allen et al., 2016; Friedrich, 2007; Shawler et al., 2018). Similarly, studies suggested that parent-focused interventions are capable of prompting improvements in child social competence (Hukkelberg et al., 2019; Menting et al., 2013).

Social Learning

Decades ago, Bandura and colleagues (1961) demonstrated that children exposed to adult models of aggressive behavior were more likely to subsequently display aggressive behavior than children not exposed to such models. Since that time, research has clearly established that observational learning of aggression may come from various sources. For instance, substantial evidence links childhood aggression to experiences such as physical abuse and witnessing interpartner violence (Gershoff et al., 2018; Labella & Masten, 2018), as well as other forms of violence exposure, such as violent video games (Prescott et al., 2018). These studies suggest that children naturally imitate what they see in the world and those initial attempts can lead to further learning experiences, elicit formative responses from those around them, and impact the development of beliefs and attitudes.

Social learning mechanisms also may account for the link between exposure to sexual modeling and the display of PSB. As discussed previously, there is considerable evidence that exposure to sexual content, whether in reality or through online or electronic means, increases the risk of a child displaying PSB (e.g., Friedrich et al., 2003; Mori et al., 2023). In addition, it is likely the case that CSA provides a social learning experience for impacted children that itself can lead to the display of PSB (Allen, 2023a; Wamser-Nanney & Campbell, 2019).

Although the mechanisms through which this type of exposure may lead to PSB are unclear, beyond the obvious imitation of observed behavior, several hypotheses are evident. First, evidence suggests that children commonly possess limited information regarding sex and sexuality (Brilleslijper-Kater & Baartman, 2000), and it is likely in many cases that children do not understand the rules and mores governing the behaviors to which they are exposed. The result may be children mimicking behavior without understanding the purposes of it. Alternatively, exposure to sexual behavior may result in a ruminative process. For instance, Noll et al. (2011) showed that CSA can lead to later preoccupation with sexual topics. Current theory suggests that rumination on a topic may serve as an emotion regulation strategy that helps the individual avoid troublesome situations (Nolen-Hoeksema et al., 2008). Unfortunately, in such instances, it also means the child continues to think about sexual topics and behaviors, which may increase the risk for acting in sexual ways.

Another approach that deserves investigation is the development of sexual schemas and scripts (Astle et al., 2025; Wiederman, 2015). Just as with other social constructs, youth develop cognitive representations of themselves as sexual beings, scripts of how to engage in sexual relationships, and the behaviors involved in sexual encounters. Social modeling experiences may exert a profound impact on the development of the child's sexual understanding, including on topics such as consent, relationship dynamics, sexual self-image, and how to interpret social situations and environmental cues. This approach may explain why some preteen children willfully engage in sexual behaviors or attempt to coerce other children to engage in them. Consider, for instance, a child exposed to CSA in which the perpetrator attempted to gain compliance by telling the child that these behaviors are common when people love each other. Then, this same child encourages a sibling to engage in sexual contact and believes such behavior is appropriate given that the siblings love one another. In this case, the child's CSA experience resulted in the development of a maladaptive sexual schema that led to the display of PSB.

There is some evidence that social learning mechanisms may be a key factor discriminating children with PSB from children with other concerns. For instance, Cale and Lussier (2017) studied preschool children and found that exposure to interpartner violence did not itself predict PSB; however, if that violence included sexual coercion, then the children were significantly more likely to display PSB, including interpersonally intrusive PSB. Similarly, Lévesque and colleagues (2010) parceled out externalizing problems and found that exposure to sexual modeling in the home was the most predictive factor of whether a child displayed PSB. However, sexual modeling did not predict the display of general externalizing problems, leading to the conclusion that modeling of sexual behavior is specifically related to the display of PSB and not to behavioral problems in general.

Given that it is not possible to remove previous modeling or induce forgetting of memories, the social learning perspective argues primarily for providing new learning experiences that can supplement, if not replace, the lessons of prior experiences. While clinicians may teach more adaptive information directly to children with PSB, treatment is time-limited and sexual development occurs throughout adolescence and into adulthood. This suggests greater benefit in helping caregivers directly discuss these topics with their children and facilitating a supportive relationship between the parent and child related to these topics. Although caregivers often recognize the importance of teaching their children healthy information about sex, many are uncomfortable and unsure how to proceed (C. Davies & Robinson, 2010). There is some evidence that caregivers are more willing to teach their children age-appropriate sex education material when they have an accurate understanding of typical sexual development, are presented with effective strategies and helpful materials for teaching this information, and when such discussions can utilize religious and cultural teachings or supports (Wilson et al., 2010).

This suggests directions for clinicians working with children displaying PSB and their caregivers. Specifically, it stresses the importance of helping caregivers clarify their own beliefs regarding sex, providing psychoeducation on childhood sexual development, and integrating a family's cultural and moral values into the material presented to the child.

Traumatic Sexualization

One of the earliest theories about the etiology of PSB, traumatic sexualization, emphasized the impact of CSA through social learning mechanisms (see previous sections) and the development of PTS symptoms (Finkelhor & Browne, 1985). A primary mechanism highlighted by this viewpoint is PTS intrusive symptoms (i.e., reexperiencing symptoms), where memories of one's traumatic event (e.g., CSA) involuntarily intrude into conscious awareness. Commonly described intrusive symptoms include nightmares, thinking about the trauma when not wanting to, and posttraumatic play. For example, a child playing with dolls may begin thinking about their CSA experience, which then results in the child undressing the dolls and using them to simulate sexual acts. Similarly, these intrusive thoughts of sexual abuse can result in the child displaying other forms of sexual behavior, such as self-focused behaviors, drawing sexual pictures, talking about sexual topics at inappropriate times, and possibly introducing sexual content to other children.

As mentioned earlier, a recent meta-analysis clearly established a significant relationship between PTS symptoms and PSB (Allen & Ferrer Pistone, 2025). However, this same meta-analysis also demonstrated that the strength of this relationship was not moderated by whether the child had experienced CSA. In other words, the relationship between PTS and PSB did not differ based on whether the child experienced CSA or some other form of traumatic event (e.g., physical abuse, witnessing interpartner violence). Given that intrusive memories of a traumatic event are not typically sexual if the trauma itself was not sexual, this finding argues against the idea that intrusive symptoms are the cause of a relationship between CSA and PSB. Some studies have directly tested the hypothesis that intrusive symptoms mediate the relationship between CSA and PSB. For instance, in a group of children presenting for treatment of PSB and experiencing at least one traumatic event, Romero et al. (2025) found no relationship between intrusive symptoms and scores on a measure of PSB. Similarly, Jonkman et al. (2019), in a sample of children displaying PSB and/or experiencing CSA, found intrusive symptoms were weakly related to scores on a measure of PSB. There is also some indication that post-CSA anxiety and avoidance of sexual topics (i.e., posttraumatic stress avoidance) may reduce the likelihood of a child displaying PSB (Simon & Feiring, 2008). In short, while there is evidence that PTS and PSB co-occur, there is little evidence that PSB is a sign or direct result of CSA-related PTS symptomatology.

Nonetheless, many children with a CSA history do ruminate on sexual topics, exhibit sexually based posttraumatic play, and display significant anxiety or avoidance in response to sexual cues. This led to the suggestion that a trauma-focused intervention targeting PTS symptoms may reduce the occurrence of sexualized behaviors among children. Indeed, several studies show a reduction of caregiver-reported child sexual behaviors and sexual anxiety following trauma-focused cognitive behavior therapy (TF-CBT; e.g., Allen & Hoskowitz, 2017; Cohen et al., 2004). However, in each of the studies identified, the average participant child did not display elevated scores for PSB at the beginning of treatment, making it difficult to assert that the intervention was effectively treating PSB. These studies also show that TF-CBT significantly reduces externalizing behavior problems and any change in PSB may be attributable to these mechanisms of behavior change as opposed to the amelioration of PTS symptoms. Regardless, it is clear that PSB is a common concern among children experiencing CSA and presenting for treatment with concomitant PTS symptoms; recommendations on how to integrate PSB-focused treatment techniques into TF-CBT are available (Allen, 2018).

An Integrated Understanding of PSB

While some cases of PSB may be explained by the application of one of the perspectives discussed in this chapter, such as a child imitating something seen in the home or online (i.e., social learning), it is likely the case that the majority of PSB instances are the result of a more complex etiology. Given the strong relationship between PSB and a multitude of other emotional and behavioral concerns, it appears evident that self-dysregulation is a prime causal factor in many cases of PSB, which seemingly explains the association of PSB with various forms of adverse events (e.g., maltreatment, parental stress and mental illness). When a dysregulated child is exposed to some form of social learning, whether through CSA or digital media or exposure to sexual behavior in the home, it may be difficult for the child to effectively refrain from engaging in the modeled behavior. As such, the child's behavioral concerns then include a sexual element alongside the other presenting concerns. Alternatively, exposure to sexual content may precede the development of self-dysregulation. For instance, in some cases, the child may experience CSA as an initial adverse event and a cascade of factors after the fact (e.g., parental divorce, untreated PTS, maladaptive sexual self-concept) result in a poor developmental trajectory, ending in the same outcome of a dysregulated child with sexual interests. A particularly risky situation may present itself when self-dysregulation and social learning of sexual behavior are combined with the modeling of coercion (e.g., domestic violence, physical abuse). This mixture of factors appears to significantly increase the likelihood for a child to display coercive, intrusive forms of PSB. By considering these forms of interactive effects among these different etiological perspectives, clinicians can develop a more sophisticated understanding of the experiences and challenges of the children with whom they work.

COMMUNITY EFFORTS AND PUBLIC POLICY

Preteen children with PSB rarely received public attention before the 1990s, when a focus on the perceived crises of youth (e.g., gang involvement, pregnancy, drug use) combined with several high-profile cases of child abduction and sexual assault to place a spotlight on juvenile-perpetrated sexual crime. Little research at the time had examined children with PSB, and no studies were available to discern the long-term risk of such children. However, interviews with adult sexual offenders suggested that many of them first developed deviant fantasies and began their sexually perpetrative behavior in their teenage years, if not younger (Abel et al., 1987; Marshall et al., 1991). This led some to the conclusion that children displaying PSB (particularly intrusive forms of PSB) should be subjected to strict criminal justice sanctions, intensive treatment, and various forms of social control, in the belief this would protect the public by preventing future sex offenses. Chaffin and Bonner, writing in 1998, sounded an alarm about these public policy approaches:

> We have been concerned to see children as young as 10 or 12 subject to sex-offender registration laws and neighborhood notification; to have seen a 10-year-old coercively interrogated by police without parents or attorneys present . . . to see parents told that their 7-year-old child could never return home again after two incidents of genital fondling of a 5-year-old sibling—all in the name of controlling sex offenders . . . (p. 315)

Chaffin and Bonner argued strenuously that such responses were not based in scientific research or clinical experience. Rather, they concluded these ideas were the result of an uncritical application of adult sex offender concepts to young children.

Despite a lack of scientific support, the heavy-handed response to children with PSB continues in many ways. In the United States, the Adam Walsh Child Protection and Safety Act of 2006 required states to identify individuals convicted of certain sexually based crimes and to transmit their names to a national sex offender registry. Further, the bill specified that individuals at least 14 years of age must be included, but states could set their own minimum age requirements and report younger perpetrators if they chose. Given that many states allow for prosecution of children as young as 10 years, it is not uncommon to hear of preteen children being included on a sex offender registry (Pickett et al., 2020). Chaffin (2008) examined the rationale behind such policies and concluded that they are primarily the result of (a) inaccurate perceptions of risk for future sexual offenses; (b) a mistaken belief that children with PSB are unique in some way when compared with other groups of children with behavioral concerns; (c) a lack of appreciation for the diversity of presentations, motivations, and risk factors inherent among children with PSB; and (d) a faulty assumption that PSB is resistant to effective intervention.

Chaffin applied his list of common misunderstandings not only to criminal justice public policy, but to mental health policy as well. Within the United States, several states developed policies that require individuals adjudicated for a sexual offense to be treated by specially trained and certified sex offender treatment providers. These clinicians, commonly trained in adult-focused techniques that emphasize identifying and controlling sexual fantasies, are often deemed the only appropriate professionals for preteen children displaying PSB. Despite findings that adult sex offender treatment techniques are ineffective for preteen children (St. Amand et al., 2008), it is not uncommon for adjudicated children in some states to be legally bound to receive treatment from a qualified sex offender treatment provider.

There are indications, however, that public policy related to children with PSB is changing to more closely align with the current empirical and clinical knowledge. In 2010, the U.S. National Institute of Justice (NIJ) established and funded a program focused on building community supports for youth with PSB (ages 10–18), which included dissemination of evidence-based interventions. Program evaluations of these efforts show that the implementation of a cognitive-behavioral treatment program within community agencies is cost effective, particularly when compared to more traditional and intensive treatment approaches (Dopp et al., 2020). In addition, stakeholders were generally satisfied with these services and believed they were beneficial, with the most noted concerns related to funding and sustainability (Mundey et al., 2021). After several incidents of high-profile cases on U.S. military bases involving youth with PSB, the Department of Defense (DoD) partnered with the NIJ to increase access to effective services in these settings. In addition, the DoD took several steps to improve prevention and intervention efforts for youth with PSB, including developing a standardized reporting process, a multidisciplinary team response (Department of Defense, Office of the Inspector General, 2020), and a tool designed to facilitate case management decision making (Schulte et al., 2023).

Several states and nonprofit agencies have allocated funding to improve services for children with PSB and their families. For example, the National Children's Alliance (2017), which coordinates and accredits child abuse investigation and treatment centers across the United States (i.e., child advocacy centers), undertook concerted efforts to integrate evidence-based services for children with PSB into their programs. These efforts have resulted in reduced stigma and fear of children with PSB and a greater awareness that appropriately trained child-serving mental health clinicians can effectively treat the problem (Harris et al., 2023). In addition, there is now evidence that clinical services provided within these settings can effectively ameliorate the display of PSB (Allen et al., 2025).

Efforts outside of the United States similarly are making strides to improve the understanding of and quality of care for children with PSB. For instance, the availability of treatment services has increased significantly in the United Kingdom since 2010 and been the subject of several reports from academics and nonprofit agencies (e.g., Hackett, 2014; C. Smith et al., 2014). Concerted efforts are underway to enhance assessment and treatment services in a host of other European countries, including the Netherlands, Norway, Poland, and Sweden. Outside of the Western context, several reports have emerged since 2018 examining the normative and problematic sexual behavior of children in South Korea, including attempts to improve assessment of PSB (e.g., Choi & Song, 2022; Hong et al., 2018). Indeed, addressing PSB among children has become a global effort.

CONCLUSIONS

PSB among children is a multifaceted and complex behavioral phenomenon attributable to several biological, cognitive, emotional, familial, social, and cultural influences. Clinicians working with these children and their families must be cognizant of these various factors and how they may impact treatment planning and delivery. The chapters that follow will help clinicians achieve that goal. However, before implementing a treatment for PSB it is important to conduct an effective assessment, which identifies how these different factors present with a given child and family.

2 ASSESSMENT OF CHILDREN WITH PROBLEMATIC SEXUAL BEHAVIOR

Historically, the assessment of problematic sexual behavior (PSB) occurred within one of two contexts. In the first case, children displaying PSB were presumed to have experienced child sexual abuse (CSA), which resulted in a number of assessment techniques designed to elicit an allegation or otherwise provide evidence that the abuse did, in fact, occur. In the second case, children displaying intrusive forms of PSB were subjected to a "risk assessment" in which the goal for the clinician was to determine the likelihood the child would repeat the behavior. As research evolved, PSB was increasingly treated as a behavioral problem in its own right, and the recommended assessment techniques correspondingly changed. This chapter focuses on assessing PSB for the purposes of treating the problematic behavior and does not presume that PSB is a sign of undisclosed CSA or a criminal act that requires determining a child's "risk." The scientific background provided in Chapter 1 serves as the basis for the assessment procedures described in this chapter, and it is recommended that clinicians are familiar with the content of Chapter 1 before beginning an assessment of PSB. Also, this chapter assumes that the child is being accompanied to the assessment session by a caregiver

https://doi.org/10.1037/0000516-003
Children With Problematic Sexual Behavior: Theory, Research, and Evidence-Based Practice, by B. Allen

who lives in the same home. It is recognized that this will not be the situation for all children (e.g., a caseworker accompanies the child), but it is typically important to assess the child's home life and to have an active caregiver involved in treatment.

CLINICAL INTERVIEW

There is no substitute for a good clinical interview. Many, if not most, clinicians learn how to conduct an effective assessment interview during their training and standard topics should be assessed in cases of PSB (e.g., developmental history and milestones, family medical and mental health history, general functioning across settings). However, there are some important considerations worth mentioning when conducting an interview in cases of PSB. First, it is recommended to conduct the interview with the caregiver alone. It is not uncommon that children and caregivers experience significant negative emotions following PSB, which can carry forward into the clinical setting. Children may be embarrassed, ashamed, or sad when discussing the sexual nature of the behaviors and, in a small number of cases, they may be fearful of a caregiver who displayed a particularly angry response when the PSB was discovered. As for caregivers, they may display similar emotions, as well as question their competence as a caregiver, believe they have failed their child in some way, or blame themselves for the behavior. Discussing any of these emotions and thoughts in an open and honest manner can be difficult when the child and caregiver are together, and the child's presence may prevent the caregiver from clearly describing the PSB. These topics will be addressed during treatment, but for the purposes of the assessment, it is best to efficiently gather the needed information by seeing the child and caregiver separately. Nonetheless, observing the child and caregiver interacting is important and will be discussed in this chapter.

Second, when discussing the PSB with the caregiver, it is critical to gain an understanding of the entire sequence of events. This includes knowing the exact nature and extent of the behavior, the setting(s) where it occurred, if it involved other people, its frequency, when it first began, and how the caregiver responded after learning of it. Many caregivers are excellent reporters, but some may omit important pieces of information because they are unsure of what happened or may not view certain aspects as relevant. On rarer occasions, caregivers may be presenting for treatment of PSB, but deny any PSB occurred. This is most likely to occur when caregivers are receiving services at the direction of law enforcement or Child Protective Services (CPS). As such, clinicians should be attuned to the completeness of the information relayed and ask necessary questions to fill in the gaps (see Clinical Tip 2.1: Responding to Incomplete Information). This process can be aided by the completion of a measure assessing childhood sexual behavior.

Third, throughout the clinical interview, the clinician should proceed with an eye toward ensuring safety within the home. For example, if the PSB was intrusive, it will be critical to identify whether the caregiver is actively monitoring the child around others, particularly if the PSB involved other children. As another example, if the PSB involved the child inserting objects into genitalia or the rectum, the child's access to these objects and/or their unsupervised use of them should be restricted. Some caregivers will already have taken these precautions before the assessment session, but others will not have taken such steps. Safety planning is a focus of the first session of treatment and is discussed in more detail in Chapter 4, but safety concerns should be addressed as they are identified, including in the assessment.

Fourth, clinicians should be aware of the multitude of factors related to the display of PSB (see Chapter 1), and the clinical interview should correspondingly include a discussion of several of these factors. At the top of this list is identifying other individuals living in the home who might have an influence on the child or be involved in the PSB in some way. Of particular note is clarifying those who have a caregiving or supervisory role over the child. It is typically advantageous to learn whether these individuals will actively participate in treatment, or at least adhere to changes in caregiving techniques and home structure that might occur as a result of treatment. Other areas to be assessed include broader child emotional and behavioral

CLINICAL TIP 2.1. Responding to Incomplete Information

There are many situations when a reporter will not provide desired information during the assessment. Sometimes, this is due to circumstance, such when the caregiver is a foster parent that has limited knowledge of the child's background, while other times, this is a deliberate choice on the part of the caregiver. This latter situation can be difficult for clinicians, as the caregiver may deny that PSB occurred or be actively hostile as a result of being compelled to participate in treatment (e.g., court ordered). In these moments when the information appears incomplete, or possibly inaccurate, it is important to remember that the goals of treatment services are to improve current functioning and reduce future risk. Instead of focusing on the concept of treating a problem, it can be helpful to reframe the purpose of services to those goals the caregiver may find less objectionable, such as promoting safety and well-being. It is also advised that the clinician take care to maintain rapport with the caregiver by not pushing for a rationale, explanation, or specific detail the caregiver is not willfully providing. After all, other sources may yield additional information, including assessment measures and other reporters. In situations when little information is provided, the clinician is typically aware of the alleged PSB if they are considering a PSB-focused treatment. It is often possible for the clinician to proceed with the assumption that the behavior did occur, even if the caregiver does not provide confirmatory evidence.

problems (i.e., self-regulation), exposure to sexual modeling, the discipline techniques used in the home, and the caregiver's own level of stress.

Lastly, once the caregiver interview is complete, the clinician can determine whether or not, and how, to interview the child. Interviewing children can be difficult depending on the age and development of the child. There are many situations where the clinician may decide to forgo speaking individually with the child, at least for the purposes of the assessment. The clinician must remember that children often have been disciplined in some way after PSB, and it may be an unpleasant topic for the child. The child's sexual behavior will be discussed during the treatment process, but asking the child about the behavior is not generally necessary for conducting an assessment to determine the nature of the problem. If the clinician decides to proceed with interviewing the child, it is advised that they use caution. At this point in services, clinicians typically know very little, if anything, about the caregiver's cultural or moral perspectives regarding sex and sexuality. Asking questions about these topics to the child risks endangering therapeutic rapport with the caregiver if the clinician transgresses the caregiver's beliefs. The clinician should limit the interview with the child to other topics that might be germane to treatment, such as preferred activities, their relationships with caregivers and siblings, peer relationships, and school. Alternatively, the clinician may use this time to develop rapport with the child, which is discussed in more detail in Chapter 4.

ASSESSMENT MEASURES

Principles of evidence-based practice promote the use of validated measures to improve the quality and utility of an assessment. Clinicians should implement measures with acceptable psychometric properties for assessing the construct being examined. In today's mental health field, there is a particular focus on the development and dissemination of brief measures that minimize the amount of time required for completion and that are low cost or free, to respect the limited financial resources of many programs. The different constructs suggested for assessment are discussed below and a recommended assessment protocol is provided in Table 2.1.

Problematic Sexual Behavior

Only a handful of measures are available that specifically assess for the presence of PSB. The current "gold standard" measure is the Assessment of Sexual Behavior-Child version (ASB-C; Allen, Silovsky, Berliner, et al., 2026).

TABLE 2.1. Recommended Assessment Protocol

Domain/construct	Assessment measure
Child Sexual Behavior	Preferred: Assessment of Sexual Behavior-Child version (ASB-C) Acceptable: Child Sexual Behavior Inventory (CSBI)
Broadband Emotional/ Behavioral Problems	Preferred: Child Behavior Checklist (CBCL), Behavior Assessment System for Children (BASC), Strengths and Difficulties Questionnaire (SDQ)
Trauma Exposure and Posttraumatic Stress	Preferred: Child and Adolescent Trauma Screen (CATS), Child PTSD Symptom Scale (CPSS), UCLA PTSD Reaction Index (UCLA-PTSD-RI) Acceptable: Trauma Symptom Checklist for Young Children (TSCYC)
Sexual Modeling*	Preferred: Exposure to Sexuality Scale (ESS) Acceptable: Family Sexuality Inventory (FSI)
Caregiver Mental Health	Preferred: Patient Health Questionnaire-9 (PHQ-9)
Caregiver Stress	Preferred: Parenting Stress Index-Short Form (PSI-SF) Acceptable: Parental Stress Scale (PSS)

*The clinician may want to withhold assessing sexual modeling until (a) it is clear the child displays problematic sexual behavior and (b) the clinician can adequately preface the implemented measure for the caregiver (see Chapter 4).

The ASB-C was designed to remedy the shortcomings of previous measures and was developed specifically to assess normative sexual behaviors and PSB of children ages 3 to 12. Caregivers report the frequency with which the child displayed 38 separate behaviors over the prior month and scoring directions allow the clinician to quickly recognize cases that exceed developmental expectations. In addition, several "critical items" allow for identification of behaviors that are exceptionally rare in the normative population and may signal the potential for harm. The items on the measure cover the entire range of behaviors subsumed under the broad definition of PSB, including self-focused, looking, showing, and intrusive behaviors. Also, the ASB-C is the first measure that includes items specifically designed to assess electronic and online sexual behaviors. The measure was standardized with a nationally representative sample of 1,400 children and psychometric analyses demonstrated its ability to discriminate children displaying PSB (Allen, Silovsky, Kolko, et al., 2026). An extended version of the ASB-C is available that assesses whether the behaviors have occurred over the prior 6 months, which makes it more suited to initial assessments. Use of the measure may facilitate the assessment process as the clinician is able to review endorsed items with the caregiver. All forms of the ASB-C are freely available. The full measure is provided in Appendix B; other versions of the measure, translations, scoring sheets, and a training video can be accessed through the phase-based treatment for problematic sexual behavior (PBT) resource site and the National Center on the Sexual Behavior of Youth (see Appendix A for websites).

Another measure, the Child Sexual Behavior Inventory (CSBI; Friedrich, 1997), was developed in the early 1990s with the initial goal of assessing behaviors that might discriminate sexually abused from nonabused children. Indeed, a large body of evidence demonstrates that children with CSA histories score higher on the CSBI than children without such histories (e.g., Friedrich et al., 2001). However, it was controversial whether PSB, and the CSBI in particular, should be used for the purpose of identifying CSA, as studies showed that many children with PSB did not have a CSA history (Drach et al., 2001; see Chapter 1, this volume). The developer of the CSBI, William Friedrich (2007), later conceded that a clinically significant score on the CSBI identified unusual and problematic sexual behaviors but was not necessarily an indication of CSA. Nonetheless, given its original intent, the CSBI includes several items that assess presumed manifestations of posttraumatic stress and forms of anxiety that occur with greater frequency among CSA samples. Also, the CSBI is a product of its time, as it includes several items written with heterotypical language and some items that assess behaviors more common among transgender children, and the available norms are now decades old. Although the CSBI contributed in a profound way to the advancement of research on and treatment of PSB, it is no longer recommended as a frontline assessment tool.

Several other attempts over the years have been made to develop measures that might assess PSB. Previous versions of the Child Behavior Checklist (CBCL; Achenbach & Rescorla, 2001) included a "sex problems" subscale, as well as norms used for determining clinical cases. However, more recent versions of the CBCL no longer include directions for scoring this subscale, and some items of the original subscale are no longer included on the measure. The Trauma Symptom Checklist for Young Children (TSCYC; Briere, 2005) is a popular measure in some trauma-related settings, as it includes subscales assessing posttraumatic stress, depression, anxiety, and "sexual concerns." However, of the nine items on this last subscale, four of them assess forms of sexual anxiety or emotional reactions to sexual topics. As such, this subscale of the TSCYC is designed primarily to assess behaviors or concerns that are commonly experienced after sexual forms of trauma and not PSB itself. Several other attempts to assess PSB are scattered throughout the literature, but these measures have not typically been subjected to psychometric evaluation.

Emotional and Behavioral Concerns

Oftentimes, children with PSB display other emotional and/or behavioral concerns, which can complicate treatment progress if not sufficiently considered. Several valid and reliable caregiver-reporting tools for assessing broader concerns among children are available, such as the CBCL or the Behavior Assessment System for Children (BASC; Reynolds & Kamphaus, 2015). If a particular clinic already uses those instruments, they can effectively provide the needed information. However, these measures are relatively long and require an appreciable amount of time for the caregiver to complete. They also are proprietary, and the cost may be prohibitive for low-resource settings. An alternative is the Strengths and Difficulties Questionnaire (SDQ; R. Goodman, 1997), which provides a handful of scales assessing emotional and behavioral concerns, but it is much briefer in time and freely available. The psychometric qualities of the SDQ are generally considered acceptable (Stone et al., 2010).

Trauma Exposure and Posttraumatic Stress

As is standard practice in contemporary mental health settings, and particularly important when assessing PSB, a screen for traumatic experiences is recommended. Several options are available. The Child and Adolescent Trauma Screen (CATS; Sachser et al., 2017) is one possibility. It can be administered as an interview or a caregiver-report form and asks about the occurrence of 15 different types of traumatic events a child may experience. Separate forms are available for the preschool (ages 3–6) and school-age (7–12) periods, and it is available free of charge. Another option is the Child PTSD Symptom Scale (CPSS; Foa et al., 2018), which also asks about 15 different forms of trauma and is free to use. For a longer trauma screen that asks about more forms of traumatic events, the UCLA PTSD Reaction Index (UCLA-PTSD-RI; Kaplow et al., 2020) is available. However, there is a charge for using the UCLA-PTSD-RI. Each of these three measures (i.e., CATS, CPSS, UCLA-PTSD-RI) include a scale assessing posttraumatic stress symptoms that follow the traumatic event screen. This allows the clinician to administer one tool to assess exposure to trauma and to determine whether the child is experiencing posttraumatic-stress disorder (PTSD) symptoms. Another option is the TSCYC, which is popular in many child maltreatment settings. The TSCYC includes a posttraumatic stress subscale, as well as several other subscales (e.g., anger, depression), but it has not been updated to coincide with the current fifth edition of the *Diagnostic and Statistical Manual of Mental Disorders* (*DSM-5*), and it does not include a trauma history screen. Also, there is a charge to use the TSCYC.

Sexual Modeling

An assessment of the child's ongoing exposure to the modeling of sexual behavior is important. However, many caregivers and clinicians report that it can be an uncomfortable conversation, as it inherently involves discussing a caregiver's own sexual behavior, if it is occurring in such a manner that the child is exposed to sexual content. Although most children are not exposed to graphic sexual acts in the home, it is more common for a child to witness consenting adults touching one another in a sexual way (e.g., slapping buttocks, touching breasts). Sexual conversations also are often overheard by a child. An alternative to directly discussing these types of behaviors is to ask the caregiver to complete a brief questionnaire. This provides some distance between the clinician and caregiver but allows the clinician to follow up by reviewing with the caregiver any endorsed items. Friedrich (2007) provided one option, termed the Family Sexuality Index (FSI), which asks the caregiver to answer 16 questions. However, several of the items inquire about the caregiver's own comfort with sexual topics and their sexual history, and the FSI does not ask about exposure to electronic or online content. A more recent tool is the Exposure to Sexuality Scale (ESS), which is provided in Appendix C. The ESS asks only about the child's exposure to sexual content, including via electronic or online means, and does so in a way that does not confuse the child's PSB (e.g., the child asking for sexual pictures) with the child's exposure to sexual behavior (e.g., caregivers watching pornography in a common area). Neither the FSI or ESS should be scored; rather, clinicians can use the item-level content to spur a conversation with a caregiver. Note that it may be advantageous for the clinician to withhold assessing sexual modeling until such time, as the clinician can prepare the caregiver for the measure and it is clear that the child displays PSB. This will be discussed in greater depth in Chapter 4.

Caregiver Stress and Mental Health

Effective treatment for PSB requires active caregiver participation and, thus, caregiver mental health and their capacity to effectively parent the child is an important assessment consideration. Several measures are available for assessing a range of mental health outcomes; experience and empirical research suggest focusing specifically on the factors of caregiver depression and parenting stress. As for depression, several brief measures are available that may be accessed free of charge, such as the Patient Health Questionnaire-9 (PHQ-9; Kroenke & Spitzer, 2002). The PHQ-9 is easy to administer and score, and the information provided can alert a clinician to potential caregiver depression that deserves further attention during the assessment. Similarly, several measures are available to screen for parenting stress. The most popular measure, the Parenting Stress Index-Short Form (PSI-SF; Abidin, 2012), assesses various sources of stress in the parent–child relationship and subscales help identify those areas that might benefit most from additional support. However, the PSI-SF is proprietary and costs are associated with its use. A free alternative is the Parental Stress Scale (PSS; Berry & Jones, 1995), which is briefer in duration than the PSI-SF but provides only a total score that may be used for interpretation.

Assessment Techniques to Avoid

Various assessment techniques have been suggested but either (a) lack empirical testing or (b) are not found to be reliable and/or valid for assessing PSB. Several projective techniques, such as human figure drawings and the Rorschach Inkblot Test, have been proposed to evaluate whether children are preoccupied with sexual thoughts, which might manifest in PSB. However, controlled research on these topics is lacking, and what research is available does not support the use of these methods, and the likelihood of a false positive is exceptionally high (e.g., Allen & Tussey, 2012). Some early studies seeking to evaluate CSA provided children with anatomically correct dolls and interpreted play that involved genitalia as indicative of a CSA history or PSB. However, studies suggest many children are drawn to the unique aspects of these dolls (i.e., genitalia) and exploration of or play with the genital areas may be a result of their novelty and not preexisting sexual preoccupation. They are not recommended for the purposes of clinical assessment (Aldridge, 1998). In short, indirect assessment methods that interpret a child's play or drawings as suggestive of PSB or underlying sexual fixation are not recommended.

OTHER IMPORTANT SOURCES OF INFORMATION

Much of the information most needed for conducting an effective assessment of PSB comes directly from the report of the caregiver. However, there are other sources of information that can provide important details and are worth exploring, if possible.

Reporters From Outside the Home

It is common to hear concerns about children exhibiting PSB in school or day care settings, as well as during other activities involving a social milieu of children (e.g., sports, music/art/dance programs). When PSB occurs in these settings, obtaining the input of reporters who observed the behavior is important, as it can corroborate the report of caregivers and provide additional information about the situation(s) in which the behavior occurred and how adults responded. Alternatively, when the behavior only occurs in these settings, the caregiver is inherently providing secondhand information and it may be more helpful to obtain a firsthand account.

Speaking with an observer outside of the home presents some challenges. First, caregivers may be unwilling to provide consent for the clinician to speak with someone outside of the family. For instance, even in situations where PSB occurs in schools, caregivers have been known to deny consent for speaking with the child's teacher. This is oftentimes related to fears about confidential information being shared with the teacher or that the child will be stigmatized within the school setting. Second, there are no assessment measures of PSB validated for use with secondary observers, such as teachers or day care providers. Although the clinician may provide the reporter with a measure, such as the ASB-C, the lack of norms prevents the use of such measures for classifying PSB. Nonetheless, the clinician may find benefit in asking the reporter to complete such a measure to obtain item-level data. Third, the willingness of the outside reporter to speak with the clinician is highly variable for a multitude of reasons. In short, it is preferable for the clinician to obtain the feedback of a reporter other than the caregiver; however, in the majority of cases, this is not possible, and the clinician must proceed with the best available information.

Caregiver-Child Interactions

Remembering the central role of caregivers in the etiology and maintenance of PSB, it should not be surprising that caregiver participation is critical for the effective treatment of PSB (see Chapter 3). As such, the quality of the relationship between the child and caregiver is an important assessment consideration. Various caregiver reporting measures are available, but they are inconsistently used across clinical settings and inherently provide only the perception of the caregiver. Although these measures may be helpful in some instances, it is recommended that the clinician attempt to observe live interactions between the child and caregiver in each case assessed. Such observations provide important information about the caregiver's communication and parenting style, the child's manner of responding to the caregiver, and the emotional qualities of the relationship. Such observations can be made in a more structured and formal way by following a specific protocol or merely by observing how the child and caregiver interact during unstructured play activities. Regardless of method, the clinician should be attuned to the presence of negativistic or disengaged caregiving responses, which may signal challenges with implementing many caregiver-focused treatment techniques, as discussed in later chapters.

SCREENING FOR PROBLEMATIC SEXUAL BEHAVIOR

Mental health and medical settings often assess a relatively long list of potential problems, risk and protective factors, and demographic variables. However, sexual behaviors are rarely on these lists, making it difficult to identify concerns until they have escalated to the point that clinical services are indicated. Unfortunately, little empirical work has examined potential screening tools that might be easily integrated into these settings. One exception, though, is a single-item measure that shows considerable promise (Allen & Ferrer Pistone, 2023). Using a simple paper-and-pencil method, caregivers are asked to answer the question, "Over the past month, my child performed sexual behaviors that are concerning to me." The caregiver responds by endorsing one of three options: not true, somewhat true, or certainly true. The inclusion of the "somewhat true" option allows unsure caregivers to answer in a way that accepts their uncertainty. However, for the purposes of screening, any response of "somewhat true" or "certainly true" is considered a positive screen and suggests the need for a further assessment. Using this single item, 78.9% of cases were correctly classified as displaying PSB or not. However, the false negative rate of 16.8% suggested that over 83% of PSB cases were successfully captured by the use of this screening tool. Given that completion of this item requires only seconds, its widespread use could lead to earlier identification of PSB.

CLINICAL DECISION MAKING

After identifying the presence of PSB and completing the assessment, clinicians must decide how to proceed with services. Oftentimes, PSB is the clinical priority because of clear issues of safety. Also, PSB may be the priority because of other negative consequences, such as suspensions from school or activities, caregivers who are scared to have visitors in the home, or disruptions to the caregiver's work schedule because of increased supervision of the child (see Clinical Tip 2.2: When a Diagnosis Is Needed). However, sometimes, the PSB is not a priority. This most commonly occurs when the

CLINICAL TIP 2.2. When a Diagnosis Is Needed

In many practice settings, a psychiatric diagnosis is necessary for the purposes of billing for assessment and treatment services. This can be challenging in cases of PSB because no current diagnostic system adequately classifies these behaviors. Examining the diagnostic criteria defined by the fifth edition of the *Diagnostic and Statistical Manual of Mental Disorders* (*DSM-5*; American Psychiatric Association, 2013), PSB certainly fits under the umbrella of disruptive behavior disorders. However, the only defined diagnosis within this group of concerns that mentions sexual behavior is conduct disorder, and very few children with PSB will meet the diagnostic criteria for conduct disorder. As such, it may be possible to employ the diagnosis of "disruptive behavior disorder not otherwise specified" in cases of PSB. An alternative solution is to diagnose "adjustment disorder with conduct disturbance" or "adjustment disorder with mixed disturbance of emotions and conduct," depending on the presentation. In these latter circumstances, the stressor or situation to which the child is adjusting may be difficult to discern, but many times, the discovery of the PSB results in significant changes in the child's life that requires adjustment. Lastly, if a child does qualify as experiencing another discernible diagnosis (e.g., PTSD, oppositional defiant disorder), then assigning a separate diagnosis solely for the purpose of identifying PSB may be unnecessary.

PSB does not create a safety issue and other issues are considered more pressing. Regardless, the first decision for a clinician is identifying the relative priority of the PSB and co-occurring concerns.

After determining that PSB is a priority for treatment services, the clinician must determine whether a PSB-focused treatment is the appropriate service. Given that PSB commonly co-occurs with significant behavioral and emotional dysregulation, in some instances, the child is not viewed as a suitable candidate for PSB-focused treatment. For instance, the child's broader behavioral concerns may require a more intensive service or present difficulties delivering aspects of a PSB-focused treatment (e.g., teaching rules, providing psychoeducation). Similarly, caregivers lacking even minimal parenting skills or the presence of a hostile caregiver–child relationship may indicate a poor prognosis for PSB-focused treatment, which stresses the role of caregivers in creating behavior change. In the majority of cases, concerns in these areas (e.g., child behavior problems, caregiver–child relationship) are not extreme and do not prevent the use of a PSB-focused treatment. In some instances, PSB treatment techniques may be integrated into another intervention, such as a behavioral parent-training model, which may allow for the treatment of PSB alongside other identified challenges (see Chapter 10).

Lastly, the clinician must identify the most appropriate caregiver(s) to participate in services. This is often a simple process as the caregiver attending the assessment sessions plans to also engage in treatment. However, this cannot be presumed, as some caregivers are unsure of the requirements for treatment. For instance, it is not uncommon for caregivers to believe that treatment will primarily occur between the clinician and the child and, as a result, they do not intend to transport the child to every treatment session. Alternatively, grandparents living in the home may be the child's primary caregivers, and they do not intend on participating in services. It is also fairly common for children to present with different caregivers from one session to the next based on the custody arrangement in place (see point 8 in Chapter 11). In other words, there are various forms of caregiving relationships and the intentions of caregivers vary regarding their participation in treatment. It is important for the clinician to emphasize the role of caregivers in treatment and identify whether a consistent caregiver is available. If a caregiver cannot be identified that will participate in regular outpatient sessions, then very little empirical research can be applied to the treatment of a child's PSB and the clinician is advised to examine other options. However, this is not a common situation.

If all of these conditions are met (i.e., PSB is a priority, the child is suitable for outpatient PSB-focused treatment, a consistent caregiver plans to participate), then PSB-focused treatment appears appropriate. The clinician should review the aspects of treatment with the caregiver, as discussed in the following chapters, to obtain informed consent prior to beginning treatment. Caregivers are often confused and upset about the child's PSB and may find treatment for PSB threatening in some way. Clinicians are encouraged to view the process of building and maintaining rapport with the caregiver as beginning in the assessment session and progressing throughout the course of treatment. As such, clinicians are advised to take extra care to reassure caregivers, fully answer their questions, and express respect and sensitivity to their concerns.

ASSESSING OTHER INVOLVED CHILDREN

In some instances, multiple children are involved in the occurrence of PSB as the initiating child's intrusive behavior directly engaged another child. In such situations, it is common for caregivers to have concerns about the well-being of the noninitiating child, particularly if that child lives in the same home (e.g., sibling). Similarly, concerns may also be present in situations where other children witnessed a child's PSB, even if direct contact did not occur. In these circumstances, it may be prudent for the clinician to assess the noninitiating child to determine the need for clinical services. For instance, the initiating child's behaviors may be akin to sexually abusive behavior and hold the potential for causing posttraumatic stress, anxiety, or any number of other concerns (Allen et al., 2014). The identification of significant emotional and behavioral concerns for the noninitiating child should be addressed through a referral for appropriate treatment services. Even if no significant concerns are identified, it is recommended that the child receive appropriate sexual psychoeducation and training in sexual abuse prevention skills (see Chapters 5 and 6). The clinician should be aware of potential conflicts of interest that may arise from treating both the initiating and noninitiating child. It is advisable for the clinician to refer the non-initiating child to a colleague for services, if possible.

CASE EXAMPLES

Throughout the upcoming chapters discussing the treatment model of PBT, three case examples will be highlighted to demonstrate the flexibility and applicability of the model. Each of these are real cases treated using PBT, but nonpertinent details are changed to protect the confidentiality of the children and their families. These cases were chosen because they represent the most common types of PSB, include children of different ages, and provide opportunities to discuss different clinical issues. The background information, assessment data (using the protocol depicted in Table 2.1), and conceptualization for each case is discussed.

Lydia E., 5 Years Old, Sexual Abuse Survivor

Background

Lydia presented to treatment with her foster parents, Mr. and Mrs. Thomas, who began caring for the girl 3 months earlier following allegations of sexual abuse against her biological mother and her mother's paramour. Lydia's 4-year-old sister, Jayla, also lived in the home. Mr. and Mrs. Thomas reported that on three separate occasions, they found Lydia and Jayla engaged in sexual behaviors, which included digital touching and oral contact. When the caregivers discussed it with the girls, both children said Lydia was the one who initiated the sexual contact. Lydia apologized after discovery of the behavior but did not appear particularly ashamed or concerned. The caregivers were very upset about the PSB and unsure whether they could continue to allow Lydia to live in their home.

Assessment Data

On the ASB-C, Mr. and Mrs. Thomas endorsed 13 separate behaviors as being observed in their home, for a total score of 23, which was well above the clinical cutoff of 12 (for children ages 3–5 years). In addition, they endorsed five critical items, which collectively included asking others to engage in sexual acts, rubbing her private parts on other people, touching the private parts of others, and continuing to perform the behaviors after being told to stop. In short, the caregivers reported a diversity of behaviors, including several that were intrusive in nature, and a high overall score. On the SDQ, the caregivers did not report any significant concerns with Lydia, although her score for impulsivity was in the "borderline" range. When interviewed using the CATS, Mr. and Mrs. Thomas noted they know relatively little about Lydia's previous trauma history, other than she was removed from her mother due to the sexual abuse allegations and they heard that substance use was an ongoing problem. However, on the symptom scale of the CATS, they provided a score suggesting significant posttraumatic stress symptomatology for Lydia. There were no significant findings on the ESS, the PHQ-9, or the PSI-SF.

Conceptualization

Lydia's presentation was representative of the "traumatic sexualization" framework (see Chapter 1). She experienced CSA in her biological mother's home and displayed both PTSD symptoms and PSB. Although unclear, it was possible that the "borderline" score for hyperactivity on the SDQ was related to the physiological hyperarousal symptoms of PTSD. Regardless, the concurrent PTSD symptoms alerted the clinician to the possibility that Lydia frequently thought about sexual behaviors as a result of posttraumatic intrusive thoughts of her sexual abuse experience. Also, CSA likely taught Lydia maladaptive lessons about sexual body parts, boundaries, and consent. What was uncertain from the assessment, however, was whether Lydia's PSB resulted from intrusive thoughts or other PTSD symptoms prompting her to act in sexually problematic ways or whether Lydia was initiating these sexually problematic behaviors at other moments (e.g., when not experiencing intrusive thoughts). To this last point, Mr. and Mrs. Thomas were unsure if these behaviors emerged spontaneously during moments when the girls were playing together or if Lydia was deliberately finding ways of isolating her sister for the purposes of engaging in the PSB.

Maria C., 8 Years Old, Self-Stimulating at School

Background

Maria C. was observed at school placing her hands between her legs and repeatedly rocking to the point she became flushed in the face and began making sounds that seemed sexual. Her teacher reported the behavior to CPS out of fear that the behavior indicated CSA. Maria did not disclose a history of sexual abuse when interviewed, and CPS referred her to treatment.

Her biological mother, Ms. Cortez, accompanied her to the assessment and planned to participate in treatment. Ms. Cortez noted she saw this self-stimulating behavior at home as well, typically when Maria was placed in time out for other forms of misbehavior. Ms. Cortez noted that she was a single mother also raising a 3-year-old son. Maria's father died approximately 7 years prior to the assessment. Ms. Cortez remarried, but divorced Maria's stepfather 4 years prior because of infidelity.

Assessment Data

On the ASB-C, Ms. Cortez endorsed only five behaviors, and three of them were related to self-stimulation. However, the frequency of these behaviors resulted in a total score of 17, above the clinical cutoff of 11 (for children ages 6–9 years). Only one of the five endorsed behaviors was a "critical item" and related to the behavior continuing despite correction. As such, Maria's sexualized behaviors appeared limited to only a few types, but those specific behaviors occurred with concerning frequency and were not responding to correction. On the SDQ, Ms. Cortez reported clinically significant concerns for emotional and conduct problems, as well as hyperactivity. She also noted problems with peer relationships. She reported no discernible exposure to sexual content on the ESS or trauma history on the CATS. However, Ms. Cortez was experiencing significant stress, as her score on the PHQ-9 suggested moderate depression and her total score on the PSI-SF was elevated.

Conceptualization

Maria displayed significant problems in the areas of emotion regulation, as evidenced by her high scores on the emotional and conduct problem subscales of the SDQ, and behavior regulation, as indicated by her elevated hyperactivity score on the SDQ. These types of concerns suggested the application of a developmental psychopathology framework (see Chapter 1). For unspecified reasons, Maria had begun engaging in repeated self-stimulating sexual behavior, and it appeared she lacked sufficient self-regulatory abilities to effectively inhibit this behavior. Ms. Cortez was a single parent of two children and was experiencing significant distress, which increased the probability that her responses to Maria's PSB were either ineffective or inconsistent. The clinician considered these findings when planning treatment, assuming Maria might have difficulty controlling her behavior in session and that Ms. Cortez may easily be overwhelmed or display difficulty implementing treatment directives at home. What remained unknown was how Maria learned this form of self-stimulatory behavior and why she performed the behavior so frequently.

Alex J., 10 Years Old, Coercing a Sibling

Background

Alex was discovered alone with his 6-year-old sister by his mother; both of them were naked, and the sister was performing oral sex on Alex. When the sister was interviewed by CPS, it was learned that Alex also performed oral sex on her. As far as can be discerned, this was the only incident that occurred. The sister disclosed that Alex said he would play games with her and give her a dollar if she engaged in the sexual behaviors. Alex presented to treatment with his father, Mr. James, and his mother was reportedly too upset to engage in services. Mr. James said they were referred to treatment by the police in lieu of pressing charges against Alex. The father was confused as to why Alex performed these behaviors on his sister. He attempted to talk with his son, but Alex started crying and only said that he was interested to know how oral sex felt. Alex attended the assessment session and appeared remorseful and sad when asked to describe the behaviors. He mentioned that other boys at school used the term "suck it" during recess and other activities and motioned toward their genital areas when doing so. He believed this was where he originally developed thoughts about oral sex.

Assessment Data

Mr. James completed the ASB-C and only endorsed four items, three of which appeared specifically related to the incident with his sister (the fourth referred to making sexual comments at inappropriate times). The total score across these items was only 5, which is below the clinical cutoff for a 10-year-old child. Nonetheless, two of the reported behaviors were "critical items" and suggested this one incident was sufficient to consider Alex's behavior as PSB and appropriate for treatment. No significant concerns or trauma history were reported on the SDQ or the CATS. Mr. James did not report any concerns for depression or parenting stress. However, on the ESS, Mr. James endorsed several examples of sexual behavior that occur in common areas of the home, including people touching the private areas of others, people discussing sexual topics, and people watching sexually explicit television programs or online videos.

Conceptualization

Alex's case demonstrated the rather significant influence that social learning can play on the development of PSB (see Chapter 1). Not only was Alex exposed to comments at school that led him to begin thinking about oral sex, but behavior by others in his home taught him rather loose personal boundaries between family members. Alex developed an interest in a sexual topic and coerced his younger sister into engaging in sexual behaviors to explore that interest. Although not discussed previously, it was quickly identified that Alex's parents had not taught either of their children any information about sexual body parts or behavior or the family's values around these topics. As such, Alex was exposed to unhealthy modeling of sexual behavior and was never provided corrective information. Prepared with this conceptualization, the clinician considered various reasons the caregivers did not teach information about sexual topics (e.g., never thought about it, found the issue objectionable) and how to approach this issue during treatment. Similarly, the clinician prepared to engage Mr. James in a discussion of how to reduce modeling of sexual behavior.

CONCLUSIONS

PSB may present in various forms. Similarly, prior experiences, family constellations, concurrent emotional and behavioral concerns, and parent-related factors widely differ among children presenting with PSB. As such, conducting a thorough and useful assessment is critically important to treatment planning. Ideally, a multimethod and multireporter approach is preferred, but the realities of clinical practice often result in information primarily being obtained from the caregiver and reliance on the clinical interview and assessment measures. Nonetheless, it is important to obtain accurate information that can be used to plan and implement treatment effectively. It should be remembered that the assessment protocol discussed in this chapter is strictly for the purposes of treatment planning and is not intended for use as a "risk assessment" or for investigatory purposes.

PART II PHASE-BASED TREATMENT FOR PROBLEMATIC SEXUAL BEHAVIOR

3 PHASE-BASED TREATMENT FOR PROBLEMATIC SEXUAL BEHAVIOR

An Overview

Phase-based treatment (PBT) for problematic sexual behavior (PSB) of preteen children was developed over the course of several years and informed by the available clinical and scientific literature. The developers aimed to specify an intervention that could be applicable to various forms of PSB (e.g., self-focused, looking and showing behaviors, intrusive behaviors), appropriate for children ages 3 to 12 years, and implemented with children and families from diverse backgrounds and histories. PBT is a flexible treatment approach designed for delivery by a trained mental health professional. This chapter provides a review of the development of PBT, its guiding principles, and the current research base for the intervention.

PREVIOUS APPROACHES TO PSB TREATMENT

Various approaches to the treatment of childhood PSB have been tried over the years. The limitations of these different interventions prompted the development of PBT and are briefly reviewed here for the purposes of distinguishing

https://doi.org/10.1037/0000516-004
Children With Problematic Sexual Behavior: Theory, Research, and Evidence-Based Practice, by B. Allen

PBT from other modalities. The first attempts to reduce PSB among children often utilized fairly unstructured, outpatient treatments that utilized a variety of individual, group, and family modalities, often including expressive arts techniques, supportive counseling, and/or communication enhancement strategies (Friedrich et al., 1992; Hall et al., 2002; Pithers et al., 1998). Although these techniques represented the standard form of treatment available within the community, they did not generally perform well for the treatment of PSB when evaluated.

Another line of research examined whether various treatment programs designed to treat children who experienced child sexual abuse (CSA) might reduce PSB. One study tested whether adding stress and anxiety management skills to a standard treatment focused on enhancing self-esteem, expressing feelings, and learning safety skills might be beneficial for post-CSA fear and anxiety, and included PSB as one of the outcomes (Berliner & Saunders, 1996). Results suggested that integrating these emotion regulation–focused components did not lead to greater reductions of PSB. Multiple examinations of interventions focused on treating posttraumatic stress symptoms subsequent to CSA have examined PSB as a secondary outcome. Several randomized controlled trials of trauma-focused cognitive behavior therapy (TF-CBT; Cohen et al., 2017) demonstrated greater improvements on a measure of PSB for children receiving TF-CBT than for children receiving nondirective play therapy (Cohen et al., 2004; Cohen & Mannarino, 1998; Deblinger et al., 2001). However, across these studies, no specific techniques directly targeted PSB as the primary focus was treating posttraumatic stress symptoms. Many of the children in these studies did not exhibit PSB at the beginning of treatment, and the extent to which TF-CBT may successfully treat PSB is unknown.

An alternative approach focused specifically on ameliorating intrusive forms of PSB by modifying principles from adult sex offender treatment programs for use with children. These interventions emphasized teaching relapse prevention strategies, which involved identifying potential triggers to sexual behavior and implementing responses designed to inhibit performing the behaviors (Hall et al., 2002; Pithers et al., 1998). Empirical evaluation of these PSB-specific relapse prevention programs with children did not support their efficacy as they typically performed on par with the less structured, less focused expressive arts therapy approaches.

One of the few attempts to define a protocol specifically for the treatment of childhood PSB, aside from relapse prevention programs, was undertaken by Barbara Bonner and her colleagues (1999). They designed a cognitive-behavioral group treatment program for children displaying intrusive PSB that focused on teaching rules about sexual behavior, providing psychoeducation about sexual topics, and training in impulse control and abuse prevention skills. Caregivers participated in a parallel group that taught behavior management skills, psychoeducation, and aspects of abuse prevention. Bonner and colleagues conducted a randomized controlled trial of this program which failed to demonstrate superiority over an expressive arts group program at the end of treatment. However, a later analysis showed that those who completed the cognitive-behavioral program were less likely to be charged with a sexual offense in the 10 years following the study than those who participated in the expressive arts treatment (Carpentier et al., 2006). Although initially tested with school-aged children, a pilot study with preschoolers suggested this program is also applicable to younger children (Silovsky et al., 2007).

To synthesize the disparate treatment literature, St. Amand et al. (2008) conducted a meta-analysis to identify the specific treatment techniques most correlated with improved PSB. They dissected the different protocols reviewed here, coded the treatment components included in each, and distilled five techniques that were statistically related to reductions in PSB. These techniques included: (a) teaching caregivers behavior management skills, (b) establishing rules related to sexual body parts and behavior, (c) psychoeducation for the caregiver, (d) caregiver-focused abuse prevention skills, and (e) teaching the child impulse control skills. Interestingly, only one of these techniques was focused on the child (impulse control skills) while the other four primarily involved the caregiver. Also, child-focused impulse control skills displayed the weakest relationship with PSB improvement of the five techniques identified. Clearly, effective treatment for PSB requires active caregiver involvement.

DEVELOPMENT OF PHASE-BASED TREATMENT FOR PSB

Looking across the treatment literature, a number of limitations were evident. First among these was that most attempts to treat PSB were either unsuccessful (e.g., expressive arts, relapse prevention) or the efficacy of the intervention was unclear (e.g., TF-CBT). This suggested a need to further develop and identify effective interventions. Second, with the exception of TF-CBT, attempts to treat PSB primarily relied on group-based programs. Although benefits to group modalities certainly exist, they raise concerns about feasibility, particularly in smaller clinical settings with a limited number of clinicians or when a sufficient number of children with PSB do not present in close succession. Two of the developers of PBT attempted to adapt a group-based PSB treatment to the individual treatment of a child (Allen & Berliner, 2015). While some aspects of this approach worked well, other group-based techniques were difficult to apply in an individual context, leading to the conclusion that a model designed specifically for individual administration was necessary. Third, those interventions that were specifically designed and tested for the treatment of PSB (i.e., relapse prevention, cognitive-behavioral program) commonly limited their consideration to intrusive forms of PSB. Given that the majority of PSB cases do not involve an interpersonal component, the extent to which these programs are applicable to other forms of PSB is unclear.

Recognizing these shortcomings, the developers of PBT (Brian Allen, PsyD; Lucy Berliner, MSW; Chad Shenk, PhD), each of whom was a practicing clinician and researcher, sought to define an intervention specifically focused on the treatment of PSB, in all its forms, that could be implemented in a standard individual therapy format. The team began the process by reviewing the extant empirical literature on the etiology and treatment of childhood PSB and the clinical literature describing various treatment approaches for this population. This led to the establishment of several principles that guided the development of the PBT protocol:

1. The intervention must be based on the available empirical research related to PSB.

2. The intervention must be trauma-sensitive given that a number of children with PSB exhibit a history of trauma. However, given the findings that many children with PSB did not experience trauma, the intervention should not be trauma focused.

3. Given the high comorbidity of PSB with other emotional and behavioral concerns, the intervention must be flexible enough that children experiencing comorbid emotional and/or behavioral concerns might still benefit. Specifically, a goal was set to develop a treatment that could be integrated into other interventions designed to treat posttraumatic stress (e.g., TF-CBT) or behavioral problems (e.g., parent–child interaction therapy).

4. The variety of behaviors subsumed under the broad umbrella of PSB (e.g., self-focused, looking behaviors, interpersonally intrusive behaviors) requires that the intervention be tailored to the unique presentation of each child. As such, the intervention must be assessment driven and the results of the assessment actively integrated into treatment delivery.

5. Given that most clinicians have little or no training in PSB, the intervention must not require a specialized skill set or expertise on the topic. Rather, the intervention must leverage the existing skills and knowledge of practicing clinicians, and be sensitive to the realities of community-based clinical practice (e.g., 45-minute sessions, high caseloads).
6. Recognizing the incredible diversity of cultural perspectives related to sex and sexual behavior, the intervention must be sensitive to varying viewpoints. It must be flexible enough to incorporate the beliefs and perspectives specific to a given child and family.

Having these guidelines in place, the developers met to define the initial protocol. It quickly became clear that the identified techniques generally grouped into three themes: (a) parent- or family-related factors, (b) psychoeducation and communication, and (c) applied skills. Each theme presented a unique goal for treatment, and the team set to work defining how to achieve the identified goal, resulting in the development of a step-by-step guide on the implementation of a coherent set of PSB-focused techniques. One of the unforeseen outcomes of this structure was the emergence of a distinctively phase-based approach to treatment.

Phase-based (or phase-oriented) protocols divide an intervention's techniques into smaller, coherent treatment packages that target a more circumscribed outcome than the overall treatment goal. For instance, phase-based protocols have become popular within the trauma field in recent years with a common structure of one phase targeting self-regulation skills, a separate phase aiming to provide imaginal exposure exercises, and a third phase designed to demonstrate the use of learned skills in one's social, emotional, and physical life, such as through in vivo exposure exercises or safety planning (e.g., Cohen et al., 2017; Darby et al., 2023). Often, there is a presumed ordering of the phases and the completion of a given phase is identified through the achievement of specific goals or benchmarks, as opposed to a specified number of sessions. However, this is not always the case, as some phase-based interventions are more flexible and allow for determining the sequence of administration based on clinical need.

The development team determined that addressing each of the three identified themes resulted in three distinct phases of treatment, each with its own set of techniques. The first phase, termed *family sexuality and response* (the caregiver- or family-related factors theme), emphasizes eliminating the social modeling of sexual behavior, defining rules of sexual behavior and teaching these rules to the child, and developing caregiver behavior management skills sufficient to effectively enforce the new rules. *Healthy sexuality* is the second phase and builds on the psychoeducation and communication theme by teaching the caregiver about normal childhood sexual development, fostering the parent's comfort and skill in discussing sexual topics with the child, and providing the child with age-appropriate sexual psychoeducation. The third phase, *skill development*, aims to teach the caregiver and child the applied skills associated with improved PSB, including impulse control and abuse prevention skills. These phases and their associated goals and techniques are summarized in Table 3.1.

After specifying the content and structure of treatment sessions across all three phases, the team consulted three practicing clinicians (two licensed clinical social workers, one licensed professional counselor) to ascertain their perspectives on the structure of the model and any potential concerns. Their feedback was integrated into the protocol, with the result being a 12-session treatment suitable for testing in research. Grant funding by the Children's Miracle Network allowed for the completion of a pilot trial to determine acceptability and feasibility of the protocol and to explore whether PSB improved by the end of the treatment (the results of this pilot are discussed in the Empirical Evidence for PBT section). The same three clinicians who provided initial feedback served as the clinicians for the pilot trial and

TABLE 3.1. Overview of the Structure of Phase-Based Treatment

Phase	Tasks of phase
1: Family sexuality & response	a. Establish a monitoring plan
	b. Reduce modeling of sexual behavior
	c. Develop rules for sexual behavior
	d. Teach rules of sexual behavior to the child
	e. Teach caregiver effective behavior management skills to enforce the rules
2: Healthy sexuality	a. Clarify caregiver values around sex and sexuality
	b. Provide sexual psychoeducation to the caregiver
	c. Facilitate the caregiver providing sexual psychoeducation to the child
	d. Open the line of communication between the caregiver and child as it relates to sexual topics
3: Applied skills	a. Teach the child and caregiver impulse control skills
	b. Teach the child and caregiver sexual abuse prevention skills
	c. Restructure any maladaptive thoughts related to sex and sexuality held by the child
	d. Teach the caregiver to monitor child peer groups

kept copious notes on their own experiences, feedback from caregivers, and responses of the child and caregiver during treatment administration. After the trial was completed, the development team met with the clinicians to review their comments and critiques, and the protocol underwent another round of revision in response. The result of this development process was a 10- to 12-session treatment protocol for PSB, based on the current empirical literature regarding the etiology and treatment of PSB, as well as diverse clinical experiences.

EMPIRICAL EVIDENCE FOR PBT

Initial evidence for the efficacy of PBT came from the aforementioned pilot trial (Allen et al., 2018; Dickmann et al., 2018). Caregiver–child dyads were assessed at pretreatment, as well as after every fourth treatment session (i.e., after completion of each individual phase), for a total of four assessments. Of the 11 dyads originally enrolled in the trial, one dropped out of treatment after two sessions, and no data were collected after the initial assessment. Of the remaining 10 dyads, six were female and the average age of the child was 8 years. The child attended sessions with a biological mother in nine of the cases, with the other case including a biological father. Six of the 10 cases completed all 12 treatment sessions and all four assessment sessions, three cases dropped out of treatment after the third assessment (i.e., did not complete phase 3), and one case dropped out after the second assessment (i.e., did not complete phases 2 and 3). In all cases, the last completed assessment was considered the posttreatment outcome.

Using the Child Sexual Behavior Inventory (CSBI; Friedrich, 1997), caregivers reported a significant reduction in child sexual behaviors from the beginning of treatment ($M = 28.8$, $SD = 17$) to the end of treatment ($M = 18.1$, $SD = 19.2$; $t = 2.87$, $p = 0.018$; Allen et al., 2018). Notably, the effect size observed was large in magnitude (Cohen's $d = 0.91$), and outside of the 95% confidence interval (0.27–0.78) observed for nondirective, rapport-focused treatment approaches established by St. Amand et al. (2008) in their meta-analysis. This offered preliminary support that PBT might outperform such conditions in a direct comparison. When the data were restricted to examine the number of interpersonally intrusive items endorsed by the caregiver, reductions were observed from a pretreatment mean score of 4.0 ($SD = 3$) to a posttreatment mean score of 2.1 ($SD = 2.3$). Again, this change was statistically significant ($t = 3.14$, $p = 0.012$) and the effect was large ($d = 0.99$). These last findings implied that PBT may be effective for both generalized forms of PSB, as well as the more specific form of intrusive behaviors.

The initial pilot revealed a number of other positive findings (Allen et al., 2018). First, caregivers completed an 11-item satisfaction questionnaire at the final assessment. Using a scale ranging from 1 (*very satisfied*) to 5 (*very dissatisfied*), caregivers reported a high degree of satisfaction with PBT (total scale $M = 1.25$, $SD = 0.35$, range = 1–1.73). Second, a qualitative element of the assessment occurred after the completion of the trial. The five caregivers who discontinued PBT prior to reaching the final session were asked to discuss the reasons for the early termination. Three of these caregivers said the child's problems were resolved, they felt more confident in how to address the child's behaviors, and they no longer desired services. Of the remaining two cases, both stated they dropped out for reasons unrelated to PBT (i.e., change in work schedule that could not be accommodated, began in-home treatment services). This qualitative feedback suggested potential efficacy of PBT in three of the discontinued cases, and no concerns were identified regarding acceptability of the intervention. Third, assessed secondary outcomes showed that PBT was effective for reducing sexual modeling in the home ($t = 3.12$, $p = 0.012$, $d = 0.99$) and general externalizing problems of the child ($t = 2.36$, $p = 0.046$, $d = 0.79$). As such, not only did PBT appear capable of improving PSB, but it also may have directly improved two correlates believed to underlie the display of PSB (see Chapter 1).

Despite the positive outcomes of the pilot, the sample size was small, and it was unclear how well PBT might function in typical community settings. In 2021, several state-level agencies began requesting training in PBT. Each of these agencies agreed to the inclusion of program evaluation metrics as part of the training and implementation of the protocol, thus allowing the opportunity to evaluate PBT on a larger scale. Trained clinicians treated PSB cases in their home agencies and administered the CSBI and the Strengths and Difficulties Questionnaire (SDQ) before and after treatment. These scores were then reported to the training team for evaluation (Allen, Berliner, & Ferrer Pistone, 2025). Results showed that 56.5% of cases ($n = 61$) that began PBT successfully completed the program, which is a higher completion rate than is documented for general community-based services (de Haan et al., 2013). Clinical outcomes also were impressive. Total scores on the CSBI decreased from a pretreatment mean score of 16.95 ($SD = 10.2$) to a posttreatment mean score of 5.93 ($SD = 6.08$), a statistically significant and very large change ($t = 10.81$, $p < 0.001$, $d = 1.39$; Allen, Berliner, & Ferrer Pistone, 2025). Similar effects were seen when the data were restricted to interpersonally intrusive items only ($t = 12.80$, $p < 0.001$, $d = 1.68$). Interestingly, significant improvements were also found for internalizing problems

($t = 3.04$, $p = 0.004$, $d = 0.41$), externalizing problems ($t = 4.05$, $p < 0.001$, $d = 0.55$), and hyperactivity ($t = 2.66$, $p = 0.01$, $d = 0.36$). These results suggested that PBT was effective and acceptable in community settings.

The only way to demonstrate the efficacy of PBT beyond nonspecific factors (e.g., passage of time, therapeutic rapport) is through the conduct of a randomized controlled trial (RCT). A small feasibility RCT is currently in progress comparing PBT to nondirective, rapport-focused play therapy. As of this writing, results are not yet available as the trial is in the early stages.

A NOTE ON PROGRESS MONITORING

A standard component of evidence-based treatment is ongoing progress monitoring throughout treatment to evaluate whether improvements are occurring as expected and to evaluate the effectiveness of the intervention at the end of services. It is similarly recommended that ongoing progress monitoring occur with PBT. Clinicians are advised to administer the Assessment of Sexual Behavior-Child version (ASB-C; Allen, Silovsky, Berliner, et al., 2026; see also Chapter 2, this volume) at the completion of each phase of treatment. Reviewing the measure on this basis can help clinicians determine those problems that appear to persist and allow for treatment directives to be tailored accordingly.

TRAINING AND SUPPORT

As mentioned previously, PBT was developed to leverage the existing skillset of practicing clinicians. As such, there are very few techniques within the PBT protocol that are unfamiliar to seasoned clinicians. The challenge for those first learning PBT is developing confidence in their ability to treat cases of PSB and avoiding common pitfalls. With this perspective in mind, the training program for PBT was developed to encourage clinician engagement, feedback, and immediate application of the protocol's techniques.

Training is a multistep process. First, clinicians watch a 90-minute video that reviews important aspects of working with children displaying PSB and their families, and highlights key aspects of the PBT intervention. Second, clinicians attend a 2-day training that focuses heavily on applying PBT to various types of cases. This training includes several exercises, including group work, one-on-one role plays, and demonstrations, as well as discussions designed to identify and respond to commonly encountered difficulties.

Third, clinicians participate in monthly consultation video calls with the trainer for 12 months with the goal of building confidence and experience as clinicians implement the model and troubleshoot challenges that arise. Lastly, clinicians are able to access several videos that demonstrate potential responses to common situations that occur during PBT sessions, such as a caregiver who is nervous about talking with their child about sexual topics or a caregiver who asserts a religious objection to the content of treatment. More information about training in PBT is available on the PBT website (see Appendix A).

CONCLUSIONS

PBT was developed in response to several limitations in the field of PSB-focused treatment. Defined based on the available clinical and research literature, PBT is accurately described as "evidence-informed." The current data for the protocol is very positive and suggests that PBT is more effective than treatment as usual; however, this can only be demonstrated with a randomized controlled trial. Nonetheless, the development of PBT offers hope for improving the quality of services provided to children with PSB and their families. The creation of a clinician-focused training program significantly increased the dissemination of PBT and will continue to do so for the foreseeable future.

4 PHASE 1

Family Sexuality and Response

Problematic sexual behavior (PSB) can often result in significant consequences for the child and family, such as exposing other children to sexual behavior, school suspension, and significant stress and emotional upheaval. It is important for the initial phase of treatment to acknowledge these concerns and focus specifically on trying to reduce, if not eliminate, the behavior as quickly as possible. In many instances, rules about sexual behavior were not clearly defined, resulting in the child being unaware they were violating rules in the first place. If caregivers delivered ineffective consequences and/or such behavior was modeled in some way, the child may be confused or have developed faulty assumptions about sexual behavior. It is critically important that expectations and consequences are clearly defined for the child. As such, the goal of the first phase of phased-based treatment for PSB (PBT) is to help the child understand and adhere to appropriate boundaries, including teaching them clearly defined rules, eliminating modeling of sexual behavior that may provide conflicting messages regarding those rules, and having the caregiver implement an appropriate monitoring plan and effective responses to the child's behavior. A session-by-session summary of the techniques used in this phase is provided in Table 4.1.

https://doi.org/10.1037/0000516-005
Children With Problematic Sexual Behavior: Theory, Research, and Evidence-Based Practice, by B. Allen

TABLE 4.1. Techniques of Phase 1, by Session

Session	Participants	Techniques
1	Caregiver	a. Orient caregiver to treatment and obtain buy-in
	Caregiver	b. Review family sexuality and gain a commitment to reduce child's exposure to content
	Caregiver	c. Develop ABC chains
	Caregiver	d. Develop a monitoring plan
2	Caregiver	a. Review progress since the last session; modify plans accordingly
	Caregiver	b. Define sexual behavior rules
	Caregiver	c. Identify appropriate consequences
	Caregiver	d. Review use of positive reinforcement skills
	Caregiver & Child	e. Teach the child the sexual behavior rules and consequences for breaking them
3	Caregiver	a. Review progress since the last session; modify plans accordingly
	Caregiver	b. Review the process of using scenarios to practice the sexual behavior rules
	Caregiver & Child	c. Practice the sexual behavior rules by having the child answer scenario-based questions
	Caregiver & Child	d. Discuss helpful and unhelpful responses to scenario-based questions
4	Caregiver	a. Review progress since the last session; modify plans accordingly
	Caregiver & Child	b. Continued practice with any skills the clinician believes need additional focus

SESSION 1

This session exclusively works with the caregiver and the attendance of the child is not required (see Clinical Tip 4.1). If the caregiver has already completed a measure of PSB (e.g., the Assessment of Sexual Behavior-Child version [ASB-C]), the clinician should bring it into session; if such a measure was not completed during the assessment, the caregiver should complete the measure prior to beginning this discussion.

Objective

This first session begins by orienting the caregiver to the treatment and providing a rationale for their active involvement. By the end of this session, ideally, the caregiver will commit to reducing any modeling of sexual behavior

CLINICAL TIP 4.1. Developing Rapport With the Child

Clinicians in the pilot of PBT noted that later sessions may benefit from developing rapport with the child. However, PBT does not include child-focused rapport-building activities. The point is well taken that children may be more engaged in later sessions if they are comfortable with the clinician. If the clinician wishes to implement rapport-building activities with the child, a few points require consideration. First, for safety reasons, the initial session must focus on developing a monitoring plan, which necessitates the development of the ABC chains and the specification of the plan itself. The clinician is advised to complete these tasks with the caregiver first. Second, many clinicians are prone to focusing on child-centered aspects of treatment at the cost of time spent with the caregiver. This is not an option in PBT, as the literature suggests relatively little progress may be expected working primarily with the child. If a clinician chooses to include rapport-building activities with the child, these activities cannot dominate the sessions. Lastly, given the considerations just mentioned, it is recommended that rapport-building techniques with the child either (a) be delayed until after the completion of Phase 1 or (b) occur during extended sessions. This last option requires the use of 60- or 75-minute sessions as opposed to the standard 45-minute clinical hour.

that is occurring, identify situations where PSB is most likely to occur, and agree to implement a suitable monitoring plan designed to eliminate the opportunity for the child to perform PSB.

Techniques

Orient the Caregiver to Treatment

Given that PBT is primarily caregiver focused, the development and maintenance of rapport with the caregiver is of critical importance and begins with the clinician's first contact with the family. Caregivers present to treatment with varying degrees of commitment. Some are extremely upset about the child's behavior and are willing to implement whatever recommendations the clinician provides. Others may be anxious about the topic or view any discussion about sexual topics related to a child as inappropriate, which may result in a degree of hesitancy that can appear standoffish or dismissive. In rarer cases, a caregiver may be overtly hostile to the idea of being involved in treatment, as they believe the clinician is blaming them for the child's behavior or resent being ordered to treatment by a judge or Child Protective Services (CPS). Regardless of the caregiver's presentation, it is usually helpful for the clinician to try putting the caregiver at ease.

An empathic response is often effective. For instance, when a caregiver describes feeling confused or shocked by the child's behavior, a clinician might say, "Yes, I'm sure it is confusing. This isn't something a parent typically thinks about." For a caregiver who expresses self-blame, the clinician might respond by saying, "Sometimes, it is very difficult to know why this happens. There are a lot of possible explanations." It is helpful for clinicians to remember that caregivers often experience personal distress as a result of a child displaying PSB and validating a caregiver's feelings can be an effective tool for building rapport.

One of the first tasks of PBT is explaining the importance of caregiver participation. Even though it is advisable to minimize any feelings of self-blame on the part of the caregiver, the clinician should foster a sense of caregiver efficacy. While the PSB may not be the caregiver's fault, it will be the caregiver's responsibility to implement techniques in the home and community to change the child's behavior (e.g., monitoring plans, consequences for breaking rules). A primary goal of this first session is to obtain caregiver commitment to active participation. Caregivers often respond well to a discussion that emphasizes the amount of time spent with the child—for instance, "We will only spend 45 minutes together per week, but you spend over 45 hours in a week with the child. You will have more of an impact than I will." When a caregiver remains unsure, it is often helpful to employ active listening skills to understand and empathically respond to the caregiver's concern. If hesitancy persists, motivational enhancement (also known as motivational interviewing) techniques may be considered.

Once the caregiver understands the importance of their participation, the clinician can more effectively review the different components of the treatment. The clinician can summarize these activities for the caregiver (see Chapter 3, Table 3.1). It is important to remember that the caregiver does not need a detailed list of all activities but rather should understand that they will be asked to (a) monitor the child, (b) implement consequences for the child's behavior, and (c) discuss sexual topics with the child during sessions. These three general topics typically suffice for the caregiver to accurately understand what will occur in treatment going forward.

Reduce Modeling of Sexual Behavior

Discussing modeling of sexual behavior with caregivers can be a difficult conversation. In some instances, it necessitates caregivers disclosing information about their own behavior that might be embarrassing or uncomfortable. This process can be aided by the use of a questionnaire that allows the caregiver to answer questions on paper as opposed to in a conversation with the clinician. Two options are the Exposure to Sexuality Scale (ESS; see Appendix C) and the Family Sexuality Index (FSI), discussed in Chapter 2. If one of these measures was not completed during the pretreatment assessment, it is appropriate to ask the caregiver to complete it during this first session. However, the questions may be discomforting to some caregivers and it is best for the clinician to preface the measure before handing it to the caregiver. A good introduction prepares the caregiver for the questions while also placing them at ease regarding their potential responses. For example, a clinician might show the measure to the caregiver and say, "We are going to be teaching the child rules around sexual behavior and we want to make sure they don't get mixed messages. This measure lists several different ways children are commonly exposed to sexual topics at home or elsewhere. Please fill it out and we can discuss anything that might concern you afterward." A disclaimer such as this normalizes the fact that exposure to sexual behavior does happen in many families while not placing the blame for the child's behavior on the caregiver.

Review the endorsed items on the ESS or FSI with the caregiver. Some of the items are regularly endorsed, such as those dealing with bathroom privacy, bathing young children together, or exposure to sexual comments. It is fairly easy to normalize these behaviors as occurring in typical home settings before shifting the discussion to the importance of trying to minimize their occurrence. In effect, if the caregiver is going to teach the child that it is inappropriate to display their private parts to others, for example, people within the home should similarly follow this rule to avoid sending the child conflicting messages. Some of the less frequently endorsed items (e.g., performing sexual behaviors in front of the child) often are the result of inadvertent exposure, such as the caregivers believing the child was asleep only to be interrupted during sex because of a nightmare. Similarly, these behaviors are easily normalized in that they were consenting adults who attempted to avoid exposing the child to their sexual behavior. The clinician can then transition into a discussion of how to prevent a recurrence. Some items on these measures may be endorsed, and the caregiver did not realize they were potentially problematic. For instance, some homes have teenagers that discuss or display sexualized behaviors and the caregiver views such behaviors as developmentally typical. However, the caregiver may not have given much thought to the impact of this exposure on younger children. Regardless of the items endorsed, caregivers typically respond well when the clinician helps them consider the perspective of the child and how this might influence the child's perception of sexual behavior. At that point, the clinician can help the caregiver develop a feasible plan to reduce exposure to sexual modeling. For special considerations on how to handle sensitive topics that might arise during these discussions, such as questions about same-sex relationships, see Clinical Tips 5.1 and 5.2 in Chapter 5.

Three special circumstances deserve mention. The first is when the caregiver denies any form of sexual modeling on the ESS or FSI. This is not uncommon, and many caregivers take great strides to ensure children are not exposed to sexual material as their standard approach to parenting. Alternatively, caregivers may deny any such exposure in their own home but stress that they cannot vouch for the behavior in another home (e.g., an ex-spouse) or whether exposure occurred in a previous caregiving placement (e.g., foster home). In this instance, it is advised that the clinician still spend a few minutes reviewing the items of the measure with the caregiver to reinforce the importance of preventing the child's exposure.

The second situation presents when a caregiver minimizes the impact of or blatantly resists reducing the display of sexual content in the home. This most commonly occurs because of a caregiver's desire to foster a positive self-image for the child. For instance, a caregiver does not want the child to be ashamed of their body and/or wants the child to be aware of the sexual aspects of life. Clinicians can empathize with this goal and redirect the caregiver to a consideration of what is learned in active discussion as opposed to what is learned through passive exposure. Future sessions of PBT will teach the child the values and information a caregiver wishes to impart and they can include a discussion of what the child might see and hear in the home or elsewhere. But, for the time being, the goal is to provide a consistent message between the rules that will be implemented and the behavior that is displayed in the home.

The last special circumstance occurs when there is concern that a caregiver may be intentionally sexualizing the child. Although this is highly unusual, this type of behavior may be considered sexually abusive or exploitative and clinicians should be aware of the mandated reporting laws for the jurisdiction in which they practice. PBT is not typically implemented with a caregiver who commits sexual abuse and it is not advised to continue treatment with a caregiver whose aim is to encourage sexual behavior on the part of the child.

Construct ABC Chains

An ABC chain is a simple tool that clearly identifies what occurred before and after the display of PSB. "ABC" is an acronym for antecedent–behavior–consequence, and is a very basic form of behavior analysis. The ABC chain is constructed with the caregiver and will form the basis for the development of a monitoring plan and identify any potential reinforcers of the behavior.

To begin this conversation with the caregiver, it is often helpful to focus on the behavior and to reference a measure such as the ASB-C (see Chapter 2). The clinician reviews the measure with the caregiver to gain a better understanding of the child's behavior. Several of the behaviors may have occurred during a single incident and should be treated as such. In effect, only one

ABC chain may be needed. However, in other cases, the behaviors may represent several distinct incidents and the clinician is best served developing multiple ABC chains (see case of Alyssa P., Chapter 7). Once the behaviors to be targeted are accurately specified, it is helpful to write them down on a piece of paper leaving space to the left and right for recording the antecedents and consequences. This will yield a visual model for the caregiver.

After specifying the behavior(s), the clinician can then prompt the caregiver to identify the situation(s) where the behavior(s) occur. These antecedents may include locations, people present, times of the day, and specific emotional states, among others. In short, the goal is to identify the situations when the PSB is most likely to present, which will be helpful in developing an effective monitoring plan. Some caregivers are able to quickly identify these antecedents while others have more difficulty. When caregivers struggle to identify specific situations where the PSB occurs, it is usually because the behavior has repeated several times and it is challenging to identify the commonalities across the occurrences. Clinicians can help caregivers by suggesting a potential shared characteristic and ask whether it is accurate given the caregiver's knowledge (e.g., the children are left alone in each situation, the behavior only occurs when the child is angry or sad). Once the antecedents are identified, include them on the piece of paper where the behavior was written to add to the visual model.

Lastly, help the caregiver consider different consequences that happen as a result of the behavior. When considering this portion of the ABC chain, it is important to remember that the word "consequences" refers to the immediate result of the behavior itself and not necessarily the punishments delivered by the caregiver after learning of the behavior. Again, sometimes these are easy to identify, while other times, it is more difficult. The PSB may serve several different functions, including self-soothing, attention seeking, satisfying curiosity, and social acceptance. For instance, negative attention seeking is common among children, and sexualized behavior often elicits a significant response from shocked caregivers. In some cases, the PSB may be reinforced by obtaining the caregiver's attention. In such instances, caregiver attention is the consequence that immediately followed the behavior. A difficult situation arises when there does not seem to be an apparent consequence for the behavior. This commonly happens when a child performs a given behavior in private as they are not seeking attention and likely are not satisfying curiosity if the behavior is repetitive. In such situations, it is important to consider that the child may be deriving a pleasurable sensation from the behavior, a topic that must be addressed delicately

CLINICAL TIP 4.2. When a Pleasurable Sensation Is a Possibility

For some children, it is possible that the PSB is motivated by the fact that the behavior creates a pleasurable sensation. This is often difficult for caregivers to hear and may result in negative emotions (e.g., anger, disgust) and maladaptive thoughts (e.g., a belief the child has lost their innocence). It is important to remember that caregivers often approach sexualized behavior through an adult lens and interpret the behavior in the same way they would if it was displayed by an adult. Clinicians can manage this discussion by placing the concept in biological terms. For instance, various body parts respond to stimulation by sending a message to the brain that allows one to know they are being stimulated. For example, when something sweet is placed on the tongue, the taste buds send a message to the brain that allows the person to understand its taste. This is the same process that occurs with the genitals. When they are stimulated, the message sent to the brain is often one that indicates a pleasurable sensation. On this note, it is beneficial to anticipate and preemptively address the topics of sexual arousal and orgasm. These are not typically relevant concepts for children (although they become more pertinent as the child approaches adolescence). Most children receiving PBT have not experienced an orgasm, and their PSB is not motivated by a desire to experience sexual arousal or engage in mature sexual activity. Rather, the child may have learned that the behavior creates a pleasurable sensation, which results in the behavior being used as a coping skill when upset or bored, for instance. Presenting the topic in this manner often allows the caregiver to think about the behavior and the child in a different light and to discuss responses to the behavior in a more effective way. How this issue might be addressed with psychoeducation is discussed in Chapter 5.

(see Clinical Tip 4.2). Add the consequences of the behavior to the visual model to complete the ABC chain.

Throughout this process of developing ABC chains, it is important to place the caregiver in the role of expert on the child's behavior. A goal of PBT is to develop parenting efficacy and to support the caregiver's values around sexual topics. If the clinician is overly directive and the caregiver perceives treatment as dictating what should be believed and taught to the child, some caregivers may become irritated and disengage. The clinician is encouraged to review the chain in its entirety with the caregiver to verify the caregiver's agreement with the sequence of events. It may be helpful to praise the caregiver's responses and note their ability to identify troubling situations. While reviewing the completed chains, the clinician can highlight the antecedents and use this as a bridge to transition into the development of a monitoring plan.

Develop a Monitoring Plan

Before the end of the first session, it is imperative that the clinician and caregiver develop a monitoring plan. The goal of this plan is to remove the opportunity for the child to perform the behavior, or at least to increase the likelihood it is identified quickly and addressed. As such, it requires enhanced supervision of the child by the caregiver or another responsible adult who is familiar with the child's behavioral concerns. The antecedents identified in the ABC chain(s) provide the context for developing the plan. For example, interpersonally intrusive behaviors most frequently occur when the child is left alone around other children. In this situation, the monitoring plan must include an emphasis on the child not being allowed around other children unsupervised. As another example, children with problematic self-focused behavior commonly perform this behavior at moments when they are already unclothed, such as during a bath or when using the restroom. This situation argues for identifying ways to minimize the amount of time the child is alone. In brief, if PSB occurs when the child is unsupervised, then reduce unsupervised moments.

Oftentimes, identifying the context in which the behavior occurs will provide clear directives on how to proceed with developing the plan. However, in some situations, it may be unclear what the antecedents are and, thus, how to increase monitoring. This is a common challenge in situations where the presence of a caregiver may itself be the antecedent, such as when the child's PSB is motivated by attention seeking. In this situation, the child's PSB may increase in frequency because the caregiver spends increased time monitoring the child. Situations such as this will be handled in Sessions 2 and 3, when discussing parenting techniques.

In developing the monitoring plan, it is critically important that the clinician work with the caregiver to devise a feasible strategy. It is the role of the clinician to help the caregiver think through the various situations where the PSB may occur and how to ensure that an adult is monitoring those situations. Given that families present with widely varying resources, living situations, and schedules, a plan that works for one family cannot be presumed to work for another. The clinician must help the caregiver brainstorm how to construct a plan that works within their own limitations or restrictions and will effectively monitor the child. Similarly, caregivers may suggest ideas that the clinician believes will not be effective at supervising the child; the clinician should discuss these concerns with the caregiver with the aim of revising appropriately. For an example of a common situation when this occurs, see Clinical Tip 4.3.

There are a few additional points to consider regarding the monitoring plan. First, some clinicians recommend constructing a detailed, multistep plan that can go on for several written pages. Although this may be helpful in some cases, for most situations and families this is unnecessary. If the caregiver acknowledges the concern and is committing to increased supervision of the child, writing out a more simplistic plan that identifies troubling situations

CLINICAL TIP 4.3. The Use of Video Cameras and Audio Alarms

In recent years, caregivers increasingly have used video cameras for an assortment of reasons, sometimes at the recommendation of clinicians. As it relates to PBT, it is most often discussed as a method of monitoring the child. However, its use is typically described in a passive way. For instance, caregivers might place video cameras around the home, so, if an allegation is made against the child, they can check the video and know what happened. This makes the video camera a poor tool for monitoring, as the behavior is allowed to occur and only discovered later. The goal of a monitoring plan is to prevent the behavior from occurring. Unless someone is actively monitoring the live feed from the video camera and can respond if needed, it should not be used for monitoring purposes. An electronic device that might be helpful is a motion-activated audio alarm. These devices are typically cost effective and have a variety of uses. For most families, there are natural moments of the day when it is not possible to actively monitor the child, such as during the night. However, placing a motion-activated alarm on the door of the child's room will notify the caregivers that the child is awake and moving in the home. This allows the caregiver to attend to and monitor the child. It should be stressed that the child is not to be disciplined because they left their room, as the reason may be legitimate (e.g., needing to use the bathroom, had a nightmare). Rather, the motion-activated alarm is merely a tool to awaken the caregiver and ensure monitoring is quickly in place.

and how the family intends to respond is typically sufficient. How detailed the plan should be for a given child and family is a decision best left to the clinician. Second, whatever plan is devised must be written down in clear language and with the active participation of the caregiver, and provided for the caregiver to take home after the session. This provides the caregiver with a reminder of what is to occur moving forward. Lastly, it is recommended that the clinician discuss with the caregiver the long-term nature of this plan. After discovery of the PSB or upon implementation of the monitoring plan, children often refrain from displaying PSB. Caregivers may believe the behavior was eliminated and begin to loosen the monitoring plan within a few weeks of beginning treatment. When the PSB recurs during an unsupervised moment, they then take this as evidence that treatment is ineffective. Clinicians can prevent this occurrence by stressing with the caregiver that treatment continues over several weeks and that the monitoring plan should remain in place throughout treatment. Near the end of treatment, plans can be made for slowly stepping down from the intensive nature of the monitoring plan.

SESSION 2

This second session includes both the child and caregiver, but the clinician meets first with the caregiver alone. If there is no available option for monitoring the child while the clinician and caregiver meet, it may be possible to provide the child with an activity while remaining in the room. The clinician comes into this session with the ABC chains completed in the previous session and sexual behavior rules printed out.

Objective

By the end of this session, the clinician and caregiver will define rules related to sexual behavior and implementable consequences for breaking these rules, and the caregiver will teach these rules and consequences to the child.

Techniques

Review Reduction of Sexual Modeling and Monitoring Plan

This session begins with a basic review of the past week and the success (or failure) of the caregiver to eliminate modeling of sexual behavior and to effectively monitor the child. If problems occurred with either of these efforts, the clinician and caregiver problem solve these barriers and revise the plans accordingly. A caution is warranted. Some caregivers become fixated on discussing challenges and unexpected issues that occurred, and it is tempting for a clinician to linger for an extended period of time in reviewing these topics. While it is necessary to examine how well the plans worked and to make needed revisions, this session includes other important techniques and should not be dominated by a focus on revising the previously defined plans.

Define Sexual Behavior Rules

For many children, rules regarding private areas and sexual behavior were never clearly defined. Indeed, it is fairly common for younger children, in particular, to report not understanding why they were in trouble after the discovery of PSB. By clearly defining rules, ambiguity is removed, boundaries are clearly specified, and consequences can be effectively implemented when a rule is broken. To prepare for establishing the rules, it is best practice for the clinician to come into this session with rules already defined and printed on a sheet of paper. The behaviors defined in the ABC chains guide the clinician in selecting the rules as each of the behaviors must be addressed.

Given that the rules will be taught to children, who will be asked to memorize and apply them, it is generally best to limit this list to no more than four rules. Clinicians are encouraged to use their judgment in writing the rules but bear in mind certain considerations. First, the rules cannot be lengthy as children may forget important pieces. Second, the rules must be specific to the behaviors targeted but not overly specific to the point that similar behaviors are not covered adequately. For instance, if the rule states, "It is not OK to touch the private parts of my sister," the option is left open to touch the private parts of another sibling or a friend. However, if the rule states, "It is not OK to touch other people's private parts," then this directive is applicable to all individuals. By the same token, the clinician must take care not to make the rules overly broad, which may result in losing the focus on the sexual aspects of the child's behavior. For instance, a rule that reads, "It is not OK to touch people" does not teach the child about appropriate sexual behavior and prevents acceptable forms of touch, such as hugging a caregiver. Third, it is important that the rules focus on teaching appropriate behavior and not be used as a tool to improve caregiver monitoring. For example, a rule such as "It is not OK to be alone with your brother" is counterproductive, as the goal of treatment is to eventually return to a point where the child is trusted to be alone with a brother. Although clinicians may find it helpful to write their own rules for a given case, several potential rules are provided in Appendix D.

Some clinicians may note that the rules violate a basic assumption of teaching behavior management skills: They are not positively stated. As a general rule, it is advisable for rules to clearly specify the behavior one wishes to see (e.g., "Please walk"), as opposed to the behaviors one wishes to eliminate (e.g., "Please don't run"). However, a problem arises when trying to teach appropriate sexual behavior rules. It is often difficult to clearly specify a rule related to sexual body parts that is stated in the positive sense. Take, for example, touching other people's private areas. If the rule is left broad and the child is taught to "keep your hands to yourself," there are many exceptions that need to be addressed (e.g., hugging caregiver, shaking hands, dancing, playing certain sports). This form of rule also neglects to mention anything specific to the sexual body parts that are the focus of the rule being taught. Some rules may be successfully stated in positive terms, but repeated efforts to make all applicable rules positively stated have failed. As such, some rules are left written in the form where the child is taught that certain behaviors are not allowable and their performance will result in consequences.

When discussing the rules with the caregiver, it is helpful to begin the conversation by providing a rationale for teaching children explicit sexual behavior rules. Next, clinicians present the rules to the caregiver and seek their feedback. Caregivers may have their own thoughts on how best to frame the rules, including the wording to use, and clinicians can revise the rules through this process. One common consideration relates to the name of the rules. In pilot work on the PBT protocol, clinicians noted that some caregivers were uncomfortable with the term "sexual behavior rules" and preferred terms such as "house rules" or "body safety rules" (Allen et al., 2018). Again, it is a goal of PBT to build parenting efficacy and to tailor the intervention to the specific child and family. Feedback from the caregiver should be respected and integrated. Another consideration is that it is preferable for all members of the family to adhere to these rules in public areas of the house. This decreases stigma directed toward the child and provides examples of individuals following the rules (i.e., social modeling). Ultimately, the final form of the rules is the result of a collaborative effort between the caregiver and clinician. With an adequate introduction to the rules and tying them specifically to the completed ABC chains, this process is usually completed relatively quickly.

Identify Appropriate Consequences

After defining the sexual behavior rules, the next step is helping the caregiver identify appropriate consequences to implement if the child breaks one of them. It is often helpful to have the caregiver describe or model how they typically respond to the child's misbehavior. Building on existing approaches will be easier for the caregiver as long as the procedures are considered effective. However, only nonviolent consequences are endorsed given the considerable evidence against the use of physical discipline (Gershoff & Grogan-Kaylor, 2016).

For the purposes of PBT, the primary methods of correction are logical consequences and the removal of privileges. Logical consequences are those that naturally extend from the child's PSB. For instance, if a child exposed their private areas to people earlier in the day, they may not be allowed to join the family on a fun outing later in the day. In this case, the child's inappropriate behavior around others precluded them from enjoying a public setting. The removal of privileges involves the caregiver restricting the child's access to an object or activity that is ordinarily available. Common responses here involve the loss of preferred toys, screens and devices, and desserts. It is advised that clinicians review with the caregiver the timing and length of any removal of privileges. Sometimes, caregivers hold the mistaken belief that a longer period of removal (e.g., 2 weeks) equates to a more effective consequence. However, children are amazingly resilient and often move on to another activity. After a few days, the consequence may have no further effect, but the caregiver loses the ability to use the consequence for any future violations of the rules. It is recommended that removal of privileges be limited to no more than 48 hours and occur as close in time to the display of the PSB as possible. Also, the clinician can help the caregiver identify multiple privileges that may be removed and recognize any inappropriate penalties the caregiver suggests (e.g., isolated in their room for 48 hours, not eating dinner).

A note is warranted about the use of time out procedures. Although they are well validated in the literature, teaching caregivers to implement them in accordance with contemporary standards, as found in various evidence-based treatments, is not practical in PBT. Instructing caregivers in time out procedures often necessitates several sessions and would significantly lengthen the time required in treatment. Also, most evidence-based treatments utilizing time out emphasize teaching caregivers the use of praise, and other positive parenting skills, prior to instruction in the timeout procedure. Again, this would significantly lengthen the time required in treatment. If the caregiver previously learned how to effectively implement timeout, the clinician may discuss integrating that technique into the consequences defined for breaking the sexual behavior rules, but clinical experience teaches that the use of timeout is not typically required.

Before ending the discussion of consequences, it is essential to review the use of positive reinforcement with the caregiver. Whatever sexual behavior rules are specified, the child will spend most waking hours adhering to those rules. As such, there is no shortage of opportunities throughout the day for the caregiver to call attention to the child's appropriate behavior and deliver positive feedback. Praise is the most commonly and easily utilized form of positive reinforcement, but some caregivers struggle to provide it. If this is the case, it may be worth the time and effort to explore the reasons for the caregiver's reluctance. Other forms of positive feedback, such as rewards and extra privileges, can be discussed with the caregiver and plans for their delivery developed. It is often the case that praise works better when it identifies and reinforces the opposite of the undesired behavior. For instance, consider a child who frequently touches their private areas in the presence of others. It may be awkward and potentially embarrassing to praise the child by saying, "Thank you for not touching your private parts." Instead, the caregiver may say, "Thank you for keeping your hands where I can see them. You're doing a great job following our body safety rules."

Teach Rules and Consequences to the Child

Once the clinician and caregiver agree on the rules and consequences, the clinician prepares the caregiver for the next step, which is teaching the rules to the child. It is a goal of PBT to increase caregiver efficacy by increasing their confidence and ability to discuss sexual topics with the child. Having the caregiver teach the rules to the child, as opposed to the clinician, is the beginning of this process. Clinicians may model for the caregiver how to approach this task or provide brief suggestions. Even though teaching the behaviors is rather straightforward, it is important for the caregiver to feel prepared and supported throughout the treatment. For this reason, the clinician reviews with the caregiver how they wish to teach the rules and consequences to the child.

Once the caregiver is ready, the child joins the session. The clinician facilitates a conversation between the caregiver and child, remembering that the objective is for the caregiver to remain in the lead throughout the conversation. The caregiver reviews each individual rule with the child, providing examples of behaviors that violate that rule. This may involve revisiting the PSB that occurred, but care must be taken that the session does not devolve into blaming or shaming the child. Rather, the rules are presented as a learning opportunity for the child, and the caregiver is helping the child learn more appropriate behavior. For younger children, it may be beneficial to review "swimsuit space" (e.g., body parts covered by a swimsuit) prior to discussing private areas as this may help the child better understand the rules. After reviewing the rules, the caregiver then describes for the child the consequences for breaking the rules.

Following the conjoint portion of this session, the caregiver is provided a copy of the rules to take home and asked to review them with the child daily. In addition to helping the child learn and remember the rules, this rehearsal provides an opportunity for the caregiver to praise the child for following the rules. This review is not meant to take a considerable amount of time or turn into a test of the child's memory. Such an approach could foster shame and frustration for the child and caregiver. Rather, it is another learning experience designed to increase the likelihood that the child acts in appropriate ways.

SESSION 3

Beginning with the caregiver only, the clinician reviews the child's behavior since the previous session, as well as the caregiver's ability to implement the various plans developed to this point. The child joins the session later. Prior to this session, the clinician drafts 10 to 12 brief scenarios, discussed in detail in this section, that are designed to aid in helping the child to better understand the rules. These scenarios, and the rules defined during the previous session, should be printed and brought into session.

Objective

The aim of the third session is to continue to strengthen the child's understanding of the sexual behavior rules, including how to apply them in various situations.

Techniques

Review Progress

By this point in treatment, the caregiver has been asked by the clinician to do several things: reduce modeling of sexual behavior in the home, implement an effective monitoring plan, review sexual behavior rules with the child at home, and deliver consequences if the child breaks one of the rules. Most caregivers report minimal problems with these tasks; however, some do struggle with one or multiple responsibilities. For the reduction of modeling in the home and the monitoring plan, this session represents a second attempt to solve any barriers interfering with these efforts. Depending on the concerns or challenges voiced by the caregiver, it may be necessary to restructure the plan or discuss alternatives not previously considered, as occurred in the case of Maria A. (discussed later in this chapter). As for reviewing the rules at home, it is fairly common that caregivers report not practicing the rules. This session will provide an opportunity to determine whether the child effectively remembers the rules, which can provide a demonstration to the caregiver of the need to practice them during the week.

One of the more challenging situations for some parents is effectively delivering consequences when a child breaks the rules. Many caregivers report no opportunities since the prior session to deliver consequences, as the child did not break the rules (which is excellent progress), while other caregivers are comfortable implementing the consequences as designed. However, some caregivers struggle because the child responds to logical consequences or the removal of privileges with a temper tantrum, angry outbursts, or other behavioral problems that annoy or scare the caregiver. In these instances, the clinician must help the caregiver develop a plan of how to respond in such moments, as demonstrated by the case of Maria A. Another situation that happens occasionally is when a caregiver executes the plan accordingly, but it appears unsuccessful. In these situations, it is commonly found that the consequences designed were ineffective and need to be changed. Depending on the age and cognitive level of the child, it may be helpful to ask the child why the consequences did not work. For instance, in one case, the caregiver removed the child's gaming system for 48 hours as a consequence for breaking a sexual behavior rule. When the child was asked about this situation, he disclosed that he merely played games on his tablet until the gaming system was returned. Clearly, an effective consequence required removing all devices that might be used for gaming.

Use Scenarios to Practice Applying the Rules

Before having the child join the session, review with the caregiver the next part of the session. The clinician will ask the child to recite the sexual behavior rules. If the child struggles, the rules will be reviewed and a printed copy will be used to provide a visual reminder for the rest of the session. The clinician then will present the child with several different brief scenarios. At the end of each scenario, the child will be asked whether a sexual behavior rule was broken. The purpose of this exercise is to challenge the child to apply the rules to real or potential situations in the child's life. The caregiver should wait for the child to respond and then either (a) praise the child for an accurate response or (b) help the child think through the situation if they are unsure of the answer or respond incorrectly. The clinician should stress to the caregiver that this is a learning exercise and the child should not be shamed, ridiculed, or punished for incorrect answers. When the caregiver understands the task, the child joins the session.

The clinician begins this conjoint part of the session by asking the child to state the sexual behavior rules. If the child does so successfully, the clinician and caregiver praise the child and the clinician lays a printed copy of the rules on the table. If the child is unable to recite the rules or misremembers some aspects, the clinician presents the printed copy of the rules and reviews them with the child, including asking the child to say each rule out loud. In this latter instance, the clinician suggests to the child and caregiver that practicing the rules at home will be helpful.

The scenarios developed by the clinician are typically no more than two or three sentences and are designed to be relevant to the child's life. Several example scenarios are provided in Appendix E, but clinicians are encouraged to write their own to make them specific to the circumstances of the child and family. The majority of the scenarios should be directly related to the types of problematic behaviors displayed by the child, and all of the scenarios should relate in some way to the rules defined for the child. When writing these scenarios, the clinician should aim to include some that yield clear "Yes" answers (i.e., a rule is being broken) and clear "No" answers (i.e., a rule is not being broken), as well as a few "gray area" scenarios where the child may struggle to respond. For example, if one of the child's rules stressed not showing their private parts to other people, then a clear "Yes" scenario might end with the child deliberately exposing private parts, such as walking out of a school bathroom without first pulling up underwear and pants, while a clear "No" scenario might end with a doctor wanting to look at the child's private parts to determine whether there is a medical problem. However, a "gray area" scenario might end with the child using the bathroom, with the door closed, when a younger sibling opens the door and sees the child's private areas. Children often believe they have violated a sexual behavior rule in this last case because their private areas were exposed to a sibling. A discussion is required to help the child understand issues such as intentionality. Even if the child was previously instructed to lock the door and forgot, it remains an honest mistake as there was no foreknowledge that the sibling would open the door and, thus, the child did not intend to break a rule.

After the presentation of each scenario and the child's response, spend time processing the situation and the child's rationale. It may be helpful to ask the child to explain their thought process and to invite the caregiver to provide their perspective to the situation described. The "gray area" scenarios are meant to challenge and engage the child with the goal of prompting a conversation with the caregiver. Again, it is important for the clinician to allow the caregiver time to speak and, preferably, take the leading role in this conversation. Some caregivers are quite adept at discussing these topics, while others are not and clinicians must be ready to engage a hesitant caregiver. Many times, caregivers are surprised when children struggle with "gray area" scenarios, and it is a moment the clinician can use to help the caregiver better understand the perspective and cognitive understanding of the child.

Children also present varying abilities with this task. Some struggle to accurately answer the questions, while others freely discuss and provide appropriate responses, even to the "gray area" scenarios. Regardless of how well the child performs, the caregiver's responses are important as it represents another step toward improving caregiver–child communication related to sexual topics. The number of scenarios delivered during this session fluctuates widely based on the length and depth of the discussions and the age of the child. Although the clinician should enter the session with 10 to 12 scenarios ready to use, it is not uncommon that younger children successfully complete no more than three or four scenarios during the session. Older children often complete more, but this may depend on the child's performance, the engagement of the caregiver, and how the conversation unfolds. Ideally, at least two scenarios will be discussed for each of the sexual behavior rules; if four rules were defined for the child, a minimum of eight scenarios should be completed. However, it may be prudent to discuss more than the requisite number. If time does not permit the presentation of a sufficient number of scenarios, this activity can be revisited during the next session.

SESSION 4

In some cases, the caregiver reports the successful implementation of all caregiver-focused skills and the child sufficiently responded to scenarios during the prior session. In these instances, the clinician may decide this extra session is unnecessary. However, in the majority of cases, the child and/or caregiver will benefit from additional time focused on achieving the goals of this first phase.

Objective

This final session of the first phase is designed to provide additional practice and review for any skills or plans that might benefit from additional time and focus. In other words, the objective of this session is to ensure that the activities of this first phase are sufficiently mastered.

Techniques

The specific techniques of this session are dependent on the needs of the child and caregiver. The most common situations are when the caregiver reports continued struggles with reducing modeling of sexuality, monitoring of the child, or implementing consequences for a child breaking the rules. In these circumstances, the clinician may find it most helpful to reevaluate the causes of the caregiver's difficulties. Often, it is the result of unsupportive partners in the home, caregiver mental illness, or a core regulatory deficit for the child (e.g., behavior regulation). The most appropriate response, however, is case specific and requires an honest and supportive conversation with the caregiver. Depending on the situation, clinicians may be best served by referring caregivers for their own mental health treatment, identifying appropriate case management or psychosocial services, referring the child for more intensive behavior management treatment, and/or seeking a psychopharmacological consultation.

Another common situation is the child who could benefit from additional practice applying the sexual behavior rules. The previous session focused on using scenarios to examine situations common in the child's life where the rules might be applied. However, sometimes, relatively few scenarios are reviewed because of time constraints. This session may be used to deliver additional scenarios that provide practice with a more diverse set of situations. Again, the scenarios should include a variety of appropriate answers and challenge the child with the use of "gray area" scenarios. This exercise can also provide caregivers with more practice discussing such topics with the child, including providing praise for their engagement and responses.

CASE EXAMPLES

The examples in this section discuss the implementation of Phase 1 with the three cases first introduced in Chapter 2.

Lydia E., 5 Years Old, Sexual Abuse Survivor

Session 1

The caregivers appeared skeptical of treatment and began the session by continuing to question whether it was appropriate for Lydia to remain in their home. The clinician empathized with their concern and acknowledged their desire to protect Lydia's sister from ongoing exposure to sexual behavior. The clinician transitioned into a discussion of the boundaries and behaviors Lydia learned while living in her previous home environment, and the caregivers recognized her previous experiences are likely to blame for her current behaviors. This allowed the clinician to highlight the importance of teaching new, more appropriate limits and behaviors to Lydia. This discussion emphasized the role that Mr. and Mrs. Thomas (foster parents) could play in helping Lydia act in more acceptable ways, which then sets her on a better course of development and improves future outcomes. The foster parents remained skeptical but understood the possibility that they could "undo what's been done to her."

Following the orientation to the treatment and gaining the caregivers' agreement to participate, the clinician reviewed the results of the ESS with the caregivers. This was a rather straightforward process, as the caregivers denied any exposure to sexuality occurred in their current home. However, Mr. and Mrs. Thomas repeatedly noted that they cannot speak to what occurred in the biological mother's home. The clinician recognized this fact and redirected the conversation to a discussion of preventing Lydia's exposure moving forward. The caregivers were asked to continue monitoring the home for any potential exposure to overt sexual behavior or nudity and to reduce or eliminate such exposures if they occur.

The completed ASB-C was presented to the caregivers and the clinician summarized their report. Several of the behaviors endorsed were intrusive in nature and included exposing private parts to others, asking others to engage in sexual behaviors, rubbing private parts on others, and touching and putting her mouth on the private parts of others. The clinician asked whether all of these behaviors were related to the incidents with her sister or if they occurred during other contexts. The caregivers noted these behaviors described various aspects of her intrusive behavior with her sister; Lydia had not behaved in such ways with other individuals. This information allowed the clinician to describe one overarching behavior for the caregivers: "Sexual acts with sister." The caregivers agreed that this was an accurate description and the clinician wrote it down on a piece of paper. The remaining endorsed items appeared either developmentally typical (e.g., stands or sits too close to others) or occurred only once or twice in the past month (e.g., talks about private parts or sexual topics at inappropriate times). Given the significance of the intrusive behavior, the clinician decided to focus specifically on that concern.

Having defined the behavior (B) for the caregivers, the clinician asked when these behaviors tend to occur. The caregivers appeared unsure and said they happen without warning and may be at any time of the day. This prompted the clinician to respond, "If they happen without warning, then I assume Lydia attempts these behaviors in front of you?" That question puzzled the caregivers, who looked at each other for a moment. Mr. Thomas then responded, "Well, no, we usually walk in to the room and find this." The clinician easily rephrased this response by stating, "So, these behaviors only occur when the girls are alone?" Both caregivers agreed and held their own brief conversation, asking each other whether they ever observed the beginning of an incident. Neither remembered doing so. The clinician then wrote "The girls are left alone" on the same piece of paper, placing it before the behavior in sequence.

Next, the clinician asked the caregivers to consider what comes immediately after the behavior occurs. Mr. Thomas quickly snapped that the girls are in trouble, separated, and sternly talked to, including being told that such behavior is "disgusting and not okay." After reflecting the foster father's response, the clinician noted that this consequence can only occur during those instances when the behavior is discovered and asked whether any other events or effects may be happening as a result of the behavior, including during those times that went undiscovered. Mr. Thomas looked uncertain of how to answer the question. Mrs. Thomas asked, "You mean what are they getting out of it?" The clinician agreed with the phrasing of her question but restated it by saying, "Why would they be doing this?" The caregivers again looked at each other, appearing unsure of a suitable answer. Mr. Thomas stated he did not know why they performed these behaviors, and Mrs. Thomas suggested that maybe they learned this in the past and it became "something they like to do together, for some reason." The clinician reinforced Mrs. Thomas's idea while reframing it to focus on the behavior of Lydia, given that she seemed to be the initiator of the behavior: "Lydia gets something out of it." Both caregivers appeared unsettled by the answer but agreed and the clinician wrote this down on the piece of paper after the behavior, in sequence. This resulted in the paper now containing the following sequence:

The girls are left alone (A)

↓

Sexual acts with sister (B)

↓

Lydia gets something out of it (C)

The clinician presented the ABC chain to the caregivers, who agreed that it appeared to accurately reflect incidents between Lydia and her sister.

At this point, the clinician asked the caregivers how this might help to prevent the behavior from occurring. Mrs. Thomas quickly stated, "We probably shouldn't leave the girls alone anymore." Mr. Thomas nodded his head in agreement. The parents then engaged in a larger discussion about how they were surprised each time the behavior was discovered and were unclear why their admonishments had not resolved the problem. The clinician revisited the earlier discussion that the girls, especially Lydia, likely learned a different perspective in their previous placement and the brief discussions by the caregivers were probably not able to sufficiently counter these prior influences. The caregivers were reassured that treatment would focus on teaching Lydia more adaptive and helpful information. But, as it will take some time, the best course of action at that moment was to institute an acceptable monitoring plan to prevent the girls being alone together.

The development of the monitoring plan was relatively simple with the family. Mrs. Thomas stayed at home during the day caring for the girls. She felt confident in her ability to prevent the girls from being alone together in a room. Nonetheless, the clinician reviewed situations where this possibility was more likely to occur. For instance, when Mrs. Thomas uses the restroom, is preparing meals in the kitchen, or steps outside to retrieve the mail. It was clear that Mrs. Thomas had not considered these situations and the clinician helped the caregivers develop a plan for such instances. In moments when Ms. Thomas uses the restroom, she determined she could separate the girls into different rooms and then video call her own smart phone by using the family's tablet, which could then be set up to monitor the hallway between rooms. When preparing meals or retrieving the mail, she could involve at least one of the girls in the process. Before ending the session, the clinician reviewed how the caregivers can review this monitoring plan with babysitters or family members who might be in a caregiving role.

Session 2

The session began by reviewing the monitoring plan developed in the first session. Mrs. Thomas noted success with preventing the girls from being unsupervised. She reported one instance, which happened the day after the prior session, when she walked out of the room and left Lydia and her sister alone. However, she realized the situation in less than a minute and returned to the room; no concerning behavior was observed. The clinician praised the caregivers and encouraged their continued monitoring of the girls, before presenting them with the list of four rules, described as the "body safety rules":

1. It's not OK to touch other people's private parts.
2. It's not OK to look at other people's private parts.
3. It's not OK to show other people my private parts.
4. If someone touches my private parts, I tell mom and dad.

The caregivers reviewed the rules and agreed that they included all relevant behaviors being targeted by treatment. Neither caregiver recommended any modifications.

As the clinician started to transition into discussing potential consequences for breaking the rules, Mrs. Thomas interjected and expressed concern that Lydia could memorize the rules. She suggested that the rules were too long and too much for a 5-year-old to accurately recall. The clinician reflected Mrs. Thomas's concern and pointed out the common ending of the first three rules allowed for simplification. More specifically, the clinician suggested combining them into the following: "It's not OK to touch or look at people's private parts, or show my private parts." Mrs. Thomas felt more comfortable with this combination being presented as one rule, with the fourth rule remaining as its own. She further clarified that she could teach her "It's not OK to touch, look at, or show private parts." The clinician agreed but added the stipulation that "touch" and "look at" must be clearly understood as relating to the private parts of other people, as certainly there are situations where a person must touch or look at their own private areas.

The caregivers were then asked to consider consequences that might be implemented for Lydia in the event she breaks one of the rules. Both caregivers noted that removal of screens (i.e., tablet, television) would be a good consequence. The clinician helped the caregivers think through the details of removing screens, including the length of time they would be removed. The caregivers decided the remainder of the day was an appropriate consequence for the behavior. The clinician asked the caregivers to consider another consequence that might be implemented, particularly if Lydia was not interested in using a digital device or her time for the day had already expired, such as the behavior occurring near bedtime. Removing the screens for the totality of the next day was viewed as possible, as well as removing her dolls or instituting an early bedtime (depending on the time of day).

After specifying the rules and consequences, the clinician discussed with the caregivers the importance of positive feedback. Both caregivers easily identified several situations throughout the day where Lydia does not violate the now established rules, and those moments were reframed as opportunities to provide positive feedback. The example was given of times the girls played together while being supervised and the play was appropriate. In this situation, the caregiver might comment, "You are both doing such a great job following our body safety rules. Thank you so much." Mr. Thomas seemed unconvinced and asked, "We're supposed to just tell them they are doing a good job not touching each other?" Before the clinician had a chance to respond, Mrs. Thomas quickly interjected, "No. It's a learning opportunity, right? If we give them punishments for breaking the rules, then we give them positive things for not breaking the rules." The clinician agreed with Mrs. Thomas and suggested that other forms of positive feedback are also possible, such as stickers, treats, extra screen time, or a later bedtime. Mrs. Thomas looked excited and said, "I get it. So, if they've gone a week without breaking the rules, we can make that a big deal and, maybe, make ice cream sundaes." The clinician smiled and encouraged Mrs. Thomas to do exactly that. The clinician briefly discussed how the caregivers can teach these rules and consequences to Lydia, and they decided that Mrs. Thomas would take the lead and Mr. Thomas would acknowledge and support her during the process.

Lydia joined the session and the clinician made several complimentary statements about her shirt and hair to try and place her at ease. She chose to sit on Mr. Thomas's lap but often kept her head down. Mrs. Thomas rubbed her arm and said in a neutral tone of voice, "Lydia, we are going to have some new rules in the home to keep everyone safe. These rules go for everybody, me and dad, and you and your sister." Mrs. Thomas then reviewed each of the four rules in their entirety, before summarizing them with her shortened "touch, look, show" phrase. At each step, she did an excellent job referring to the private areas as "those body parts covered by underwear." Mr. Thomas occasionally made supportive comments, such as, "These rules will keep us all safe" and "You can do this." Lydia said very little, other than "Okay" and "Uh huh" in response to Mrs. Thomas asking if she understood the rules. Similarly, Lydia only nodded in the affirmative when Mrs. Thomas reviewed the consequences of breaking the rules. The clinician ended session by praising both Lydia and her caregivers and gave them the list of rules to take home. (Note: After this conjoint session, Mr. and Mrs. Thomas repeated the process by reviewing the rules and consequences with Lydia's sister. See Chapter 11 for recommendations on working with siblings.)

Session 3

Mr. Thomas was called away unexpectedly for work and only Mrs. Thomas attended this session with Lydia. The clinician began by reviewing progress the past few weeks with her, and she again noted no significant concerns regarding monitoring or incidental exposure to sexual modeling. She was pleased to report that no incidents of PSB had been observed since beginning treatment. Mrs. Thomas reviewed the body safety rules with Lydia regularly throughout the prior week, and she believed Lydia could repeat them sufficiently.

Lydia joined the session after only a few minutes and the clinician again attempted to create a friendly space for Lydia. This included bringing a few simple games into the session and playing them with Lydia and Mrs. Thomas. As Lydia began to feel more comfortable, the clinician mentioned that Mrs. Thomas had just said some wonderful things about her, including that she had done an excellent job following the body safety rules. Lydia nodded her head in agreement but said nothing. The clinician then said they were going to play a different type of game and presented several stickers that Lydia could earn if she was able to answer some questions correctly. Lydia appeared interested and agreed.

The first question was if she could name just one of the body safety rules. Lydia gave the clinician a shy look and then whispered in Mrs. Thomas's ear, who announced, "She said we don't touch, look, or show private areas." The clinician praised Lydia's answer and gave her a sticker of her choice. The clinician then asked what the other rule was, and the situation repeated itself, with Lydia correctly whispering in Mrs. Thomas's ear and receiving a sticker. The clinician used this game approach to present the scenarios to Lydia. Given her age, the scenarios were presented in simplistic form that did not involve much detail. For example, the first scenario simply stated, "If you knew mom was in the shower, is it okay to go look at her there?" Lydia shook her head in disagreement, and the clinician rewarded her with a sticker. To test whether Lydia accurately discriminated between self and others as it related to the "touch" and "look" topics (as the clinician cautioned Mrs. Thomas in the prior session), the clinician asked, "You go to the restroom and see your own private parts. Did you break a rule?" Again, Lydia answered correctly and received a sticker. Several other scenarios were presented, all of which Lydia answered correctly with head nods and shakes.

The clinician then presented a "gray area" scenario by asking, "If you fell and hurt yourself in the private area, could you ask mom to look at it?" Lydia's face showed a degree of concern and uncertainty, and then she shook her head, indicating she believed it was unacceptable to ask such a thing. Mrs. Thomas's eyebrows raised as she was surprised by Lydia's response. The clinician acknowledged Lydia's concern, "That's a tough one. The rule says not to show other people your private areas, but in this case, you need help. Hmm . . . What do you think, mom?" Mrs. Thomas smiled at the opportunity to teach Lydia and told the girl, "If you are hurt and need help, you can ask me or dad. We can make it okay to ask for help from me and dad. It's okay for a doctor to help, too." At the end of the scenarios, the clinician praised both Lydia and Mrs. Thomas and recommended continuing with the positive work in the week ahead.

Session 4

Only Mr. Thomas attended the session with Lydia, as Mrs. Thomas was sick. The clinician reviewed the events of the previous session with Mr. Thomas, though his wife updated him following his return from the work trip. He noted no significant concerns regarding PSB from Lydia and continued use of the monitoring plan. He transitioned this discussion into asking about when the monitoring plan might be discontinued, as he believed the problems were resolved and the plan placed some strain on his wife. The clinician cautioned against removing the monitoring plan, as it had still only been a few weeks since the last occurrence of the behavior and there was more in the treatment ahead that might be helpful to prevent a recurrence. The clinician assured Mr. Thomas that weaning off of the monitoring plan would be discussed closer to the end of treatment (see Chapter 11). Mr. Thomas agreed. The clinician then brought Lydia into the room and allowed her to pick a game to play. The clinician, Lydia, and Mr. Thomas then played for the final part of session as a form of rapport building with the child.

Maria C., 8 Years Old, Self-Stimulating at School

Session 1

Ms. Cortez appeared distressed from the first moment of beginning treatment. Given Maria's significant emotional and behavioral concerns, as well as the stress Ms. Cortez reported, two treatment options were offered. The first was PBT. The second was a behavioral parent training intervention designed to improve behavioral problems and parenting skills, with the qualification that PSB could be targeted during that intervention but would not be the exclusive focus of treatment. Ms. Cortez opted for PBT because of a desire to eliminate the self-stimulating behavior as quickly as possible, given the disruption to the school environment was significant and created the most concern. The clinician proceeded with PBT. Since the ESS suggested no significant exposure to sexual modeling, the clinician provided a brief review of the importance of minimizing such influences and continued to the next step.

Constructing the ABC chains proved difficult. The behavior was clearly defined (i.e., self-stimulation), but the antecedents and consequences were more challenging. Maria performed the behavior in a public setting at school, suggesting it was not something she attempted to hide. Similarly, she performed the behavior at home in front of Ms. Cortez, meaning the behavior was not confined to the school setting. Given that the PSB most frequently occurred at home when Maria was placed in time out, the clinician decided to press Ms. Cortez on whether it occurred at other times as well. Only a few scattered incidents were recalled, but each of these times appeared to be when Maria was upset and prior to being placed in timeout. In other words, Maria's self-stimulating behavior occurred only at moments when she was in a negative emotional state (e.g., in timeout for misbehavior, angry and on the verge of being in trouble). The clinician asked about the timing of the behavior in the school setting. Ms. Cortez was unsure but noted that Maria's teachers typically report that she is frequently inattentive and appears to be "in her own world." Maria also struggled in school, and her grades were below average. The combination of this information from home and school suggested that the antecedent for Maria's self-stimulating behavior may have been negative emotional experiences, such as anger, boredom, or frustration.

Having potentially identified the situation in which the PSB was more likely to occur, the consequences of the behavior appeared understandable. Given her significant self-dysregulation, it was likely the case that the PSB served as a form of coping skill. When Maria experienced significant negative emotion, the self-stimulation served to provide at least a distraction but potentially a pleasurable experience that elevated her mood. With this understanding, the following ABC chain was constructed and presented to Ms. Cortez, who agreed it seemed plausible:

Maria experiences a negative emotional state (A)

↓

Self-stimulation (B)

↓

Improved emotional state (C)

The clinician used this diagram to brainstorm ways to help Maria improve her behavior. A monitoring plan in the traditional sense was not indicated, as Maria frequently performed the behavior in the presence of others. Instead, the monitoring plan in this case called for observing Maria's emotional state and attempting to implement responses that dissuaded her from self-stimulation. Ms. Cortez suggested teaching Maria different ways to feel better and the clinician agreed. However, the clinician pointed out that Maria might not have the motivation to use those new skills and may not perceive the need to change. Instead, the clinician recommended using distraction as a primary skill. By being observant for indications that Maria was beginning to move toward negative emotion, Ms. Cortez could implement any number of activities that would shift Maria's attention in a more positive direction. For instance, Ms. Cortez identified several games that Maria enjoys and stated that she likes cooking and drawing. The clinician helped Ms. Cortez develop a plan that included signs Maria was becoming irritated, angry, or bored and how to engage her in a more positive activity in those moments.

While Ms. Cortez believed she was capable of implementing the monitoring plan at home, the challenge remained of how to take such steps in the school. Understandably, Ms. Cortez was concerned about the clinician talking with Maria's teacher. Sexual behavior is often stigmatizing and she was concerned that the teachers would look at Maria differently knowing she was in therapy and that her behavior was being conceptualized as "pleasurable." The clinician reframed Ms. Cortez's concerns, asserting that it was more helpful to think of Maria's behavior as a distraction from whatever negative emotion she was feeling. The clinician also reminded her that Maria was already performing the behavior in school and, as such, if stigmatizing was to happen, it likely had already occurred. Her teacher was concerned about Maria and contacted authorities to seek help for the girl. It seemed reasonable to conclude that the teacher would like for the behavior to cease and might be willing to help in the process. Ms. Cortez still did not want the clinician to contact Maria's teacher but agreed to talk with the teacher herself to identify any distracting behaviors or activities that might be possible in the classroom. The clinician suggested writing down a specific plan to reduce confusion and encouraged developing a form of ongoing communication with the teacher (e.g., email).

Session 2

Ms. Cortez returned for the second session, again appearing stressed. The clinician inquired about progress the past week and she said that the behavior continued with little change. The clinician asked how many times Ms. Cortez utilized the distracting activities, and she replied that she only used them once. When asked what barriers prevented implementing the plan with greater frequency, Ms. Cortez said that Maria only performed the behaviors after she was placed in time out. This led to a larger discussion of the reasons Maria ends up in time out and the frequency with which Ms. Cortez uses this as a consequence for misbehavior. It was learned that Ms. Cortez placed Maria in time out three or four times per day, but, often, it was because of relatively minor infractions, such as yelling at her brother or "dawdling." This led the clinician to discuss with Ms. Cortez other potential responses, such as ignoring certain behaviors that may be motivated by attention seeking (e.g., yelling, whining) and removing privileges (e.g., dessert at dinner, screen time) instead of immediately placing Maria in time out. It was helpful to reframe the discussion for Ms. Cortez as one of preventing the opportunity for Maria to perform the behavior as a first step in teaching her more adaptive ways of regulating emotions. Ms. Cortez agreed to try reducing the number of instances where time out was utilized.

The discussion of consequences and the types of behavior that warrant them led naturally into a discussion of the rules that the clinician defined prior to the start of session. There were only three rules specified and were labeled by Ms. Cortez as "safety rules":

1. It's not OK to touch my private parts around other people.
2. It's not OK to make inappropriate sounds around other people.
3. If someone touches my private parts, I tell mom.

Ms. Cortez did not ask to revise any of the rules but did ask if Maria would understand what was meant by the rules, including the "inappropriate sounds." The clinician helped Ms. Cortez think through how to teach these rules to Maria, including defining inappropriate sounds as those noises she makes while touching her own private parts. Ms. Cortez was noticeably uncomfortable with the topic, but the clinician reassured her that the discussion would occur together in a conjoint session.

In thinking about the consequences, the clinician emphasized Ms. Cortez's responses discussed just minutes before in relation to other behavior concerns. This was done by having her think through several different types of behavioral problems and how she might respond. Negative attention-seeking behaviors may be responded to by ignoring them, as providing attention may serve a reinforcing function. However, behaviors such as hitting her brother and breaking one of the "safety rules" should elicit the removal of a privilege, which she identified as losing screen time, not allowing dessert after dinner, and an earlier bedtime. Given Ms. Cortez's described use of time out, the clinician encouraged her not to employ this technique for the time being and to utilize the other skills discussed. Ms. Cortez agreed.

Before Maria joined the session, the clinician reviewed with Ms. Cortez the concepts of praise and positive reinforcement. Ms. Cortez admitted that she did not provide many instances of positive feedback during the course of the day. She mentioned taking care of Maria's younger brother and the stress she experienced as a single mother as the prime causes. The clinician empathized with her statement before refocusing the conversation on "searching for the positives." More specifically, the clinician noted that Maria does adhere to the safety rules throughout most of the day, given that the self-stimulating behavior only occurs when she is in time out. As such, there are nearly unlimited opportunities to note Maria refraining from such behavior and to provide words of positivity and encouragement. Ms. Cortez understood and agreed to attempt to increase the positive feedback in the coming week.

When Maria joined the session, she quickly sat down in a chair and asked, "What are we going to talk about?" Her mother, following the clinician's recommendations, calmly stated, "We're going to discuss how to keep you safe and help you not get in trouble so much." Maria seemed interested in the last point. Ms. Cortez cautiously read the rules to Maria, who listened intently. Although she did not ask any questions, Maria simply stated afterward, "That's easy. I can do that." Ms. Cortez was encouraging of her daughter and then proceeded to discuss the consequences that would follow breaking the rules. At that point, Maria looked noticeably irritated and said it was not fair for her to receive consequences, although she did not elaborate. Maria's mother began desperately pleading with Maria, telling her that it was important to follow the safety rules for her own good. Maria continued to appear annoyed and crossed her arms. The clinician motioned to Ms. Cortez to cease the pleading and then said, "It's okay, mom. A lot of children don't like consequences. You know it's for her own good, so you can just ignore the attitude and deliver the consequences if she breaks one of the safety rules." Afterward, while Maria was picking out a sticker at the end of session, the clinician noted that the attitude just displayed by Maria could also be ignored. The mother understood and agreed to try.

Session 3

When Maria and her mother returned to session the following week, Ms. Cortez asked to speak with the clinician alone. She told the clinician that she had been trying to ignore some of Maria's attention-seeking behaviors, but one day, Maria became more irritated and started shouting for her mother to look at her. When she did, Maria had her hand in her pants as if simulating the self-stimulating behavior and then started making exaggerated and highly sexualized sounds. Ms. Cortez said she was shocked to see this, yelled at Maria to stop, and then Maria started laughing. She worried that the treatment was not working and appeared frustrated. The clinician had Ms. Cortez construct an ABC chain focused specifically on this event. Ms. Cortez provided the following sequence: she asked for my attention (antecedent) → began self-stimulating behavior (behavior) → started laughing (consequence). The clinician pointed out that her laughing did indeed follow the behavior, but it seemed from the story Ms. Cortez told that the laughing was not because of the self-stimulation. Ms. Cortez quickly deduced that it was her yelling and attending to Maria that most immediately followed the behavior, which appeared to be the motivation considering Maria asked her mother to look at her. The clinician emphasized that Maria's behavior in this context was attention seeking and not a form of self-regulation, and that Ms. Cortez's attention may have inadvertently reinforced the behavior. However, Ms. Cortez said if she just ignored the behavior or walked away that Maria may have escalated the behavior and then she would not have known how to respond. The clinician agreed that ignoring the negative attention seeking is the more effective approach but reminded the mother that the consequences can still be implemented. The mother seemingly forgot about this response in the moment and did not deliver consequences.

After Ms. Cortez felt more confident in her approach, Maria joined the session. She marched into the room, gave the clinician a displeased look, and collapsed into a chair. Her annoyance was clearly etched on her face. The clinician began presenting the previously defined scenarios, but Maria was not cooperative. When the clinician provided a scenario that ended by asking whether it would break a safety rule to touch her own private areas in her bedroom, Maria replied, "I don't know. Do you touch your private areas in the bedroom? Probably. Ask my mom, I'll bet she does." Ms. Cortez looked shocked and the clinician quickly began speaking to the mother to prevent her from giving attention to the rude comment: "It appears Maria is not in the mood to have a conversation today. That's okay. You and I can speak alone." Maria was allowed to select coloring supplies and placed in an adjoining room.

The clinician emphasized the need for Ms. Cortez to ignore these types of behaviors from Maria, as they are designed to elicit shock as a form of negative attention seeking. Ms. Cortez agreed. However, the clinician continued, it is critical that consequences be consistently applied when she breaks the rules. Ms. Cortez noted that the self-stimulating behavior did seem to decrease over the previous week, even with the upsetting incident of her deliberately mimicking the behavior. She also noted more frequent pleasant interactions with Maria as a result of an increased number of activities together, as defined in the monitoring plan. The clinician encouraged Ms. Cortez to continue with both approaches and noted that sometimes the change in behavioral contingencies requires a few weeks to see their full effect.

The clinician asked Ms. Cortez to discuss the conversations she had with Maria's teacher. She relayed that the teacher was very positive in their interactions and gave Maria greater access to coloring materials during class in the event she was bored. The teacher also agreed to send a brief email at the end of each day to Ms. Cortez to notify her of whether the self-stimulatory behavior was observed that day. The behavior occurred three times between the first two treatment sessions. Following the second session and the clinician's encouragement to use consequences, Ms. Cortez began implementing the removal of privileges at home when the rule was violated at school. It happened once more at school, and Maria lost access to screens for that evening. Although Maria was very upset, the behavior had yet to occur again at school. The teacher noted that she was coloring more at her desk, potentially using this as a replacement behavior for the self-stimulation.

Session 4

Ms. Cortez again asked to speak alone with the clinician at the start of session. She said that Maria's behavior is much improved over the last week, but she becomes very upset when her behavior is ignored. This anger usually results in her yelling and stomping around the house but not in PSB or aggression. The clinician reassured the mother that this is a normal response when attention-seeking behavior is no longer effective. The teacher continued to send positive reports and no incidents were observed at school over the prior week. Ms. Cortez did state that she walked into Maria's room to put clothes away one day and discovered her self-stimulating, but such behavior had not occurred in front of her or her brother. The clinician encouraged Ms. Cortez to view this as a significant improvement, but the mother was very concerned about the self-stimulating behavior in private, as she believed this suggested masturbatory behavior aimed at pleasure seeking. The clinician reflected the mother's thoughts and empathized with the clearly concerned nature of Ms. Cortez's comment. The clinician asked Ms. Cortez if it would be permissible to discuss that topic more in the next session, when it would be just the two of them, to maximize the amount of time spent with Maria during the current session. Ms. Cortez agreed.

When Maria joined the session, the clinician began by asking her about the past week, her experiences, and any concerns she might have. Maria took the opportunity to suggest that the clinician was convincing her mother to act mean toward her. The clinician nodded to indicate understanding and then pivoted by saying, "I'm helping your mother figure out ways to encourage more positive behavior for you. That should keep you safe and help you do better at school." Maria rolled her eyes and crossed her arms. Using a tactic previously arranged with Ms. Cortez, the clinician told Maria, "I'll tell you what. I have 10 questions to ask you. If you get eight of them right, you can pick out a candy bar at the end of session." Maria sighed but then nodded her head to indicate acceptance of the terms.

The clinician then proceeded to provide the scenarios originally intended for delivery during the previous session. Maria performed well, answering most of them with little hesitation. Even the "gray area" questions were answered quickly. For instance, one question, which coincidently corresponded with Ms. Cortez's concern, asked Maria whether it would violate a rule if she was touching her private areas in her bedroom and someone walked in. She did not believe it violated a rule as she abruptly stated, "They shouldn't have walked into my room. Maybe I was changing my underwear or something." Although Ms. Cortez provided excellent positive feedback throughout the questions, this answer caused her to shift her look from Maria to the clinician as if unsure how to respond. The clinician then commented, "You're right. There are certainly reasons that people need to touch their private areas sometimes and that should be done in a private place." Ms. Cortez's eyebrows raised and she began nodding her head in agreement, seemingly relieved to have dodged a more detailed discussion of the behavior. As the session ended, Maria selected her candy and the clinician reassured Ms. Cortez that the behavior of concern would be revisited the next session.

Alex J., 10 Years Old, Coercing a Sibling

Session 1

Mr. James was quiet when he entered session, appearing somewhat confused about why he was attending without his son. The clinician explained that the intervention will focus on restructuring the home environment to maximize the impact of treatment and on helping open the line of communication regarding sexual topics between him and his son. Mr. James asked several follow-up questions and was noticeably defensive, alternating between blaming himself for Alex's behavior and believing there was an internal problem with Alex that required intensive treatment. The clinician empathized with Mr. James's confusion and discussed that there are several reasons a child may display PSB and, sometimes, the reason is never identified. The clinician used this as an opportunity to transition into a discussion of the previously noted social learning experiences.

First, the clinician mentioned the comment Alex made regarding friends motioning to their private areas while saying "suck it," which apparently happened multiple times. Mr. James quickly declared that hearing about it from friends does not give Alex the right to perform the behaviors with his sister. The clinician agreed but reframed the issue as one of exposure to sexual suggestions that may create questions for Alex. Next, the clinician reviewed the results of Mr. James's ESS, which showed various forms of sexual modeling occur in the home. The father immediately began defending himself, as if he interpreted the clinician's comments as blaming him. This was followed by a justification, "I'm a grown man and married. I'm free to do as I please with my wife in our own home. That doesn't mean Alex can be sexual with his sister." The clinician clarified for Mr. James that the intent of reviewing the ESS was not to suggest that he was at fault for Alex's behaviors. Rather, these behaviors within the home, combined with the modeling provided by peers, resulted in Alex observing a significant amount of sexual content. As such, Alex may have developed several questions about sexual behavior.

After Mr. James appeared more at ease, the clinician brought the conversation to a discussion of what the parents have taught Alex about sexual behavior. The father again appeared incredulous, "What are you supposed to teach a kid? He's only 10 for crying out loud. Ten-year-olds don't need to know about this stuff." The clinician reflected Mr. James's comment and attempted to normalize it by assuring him that many other caregivers hold the same perspective and certainly he is not alone in his hands-off approach. Mr. James followed this exchange by discussing that his parents never taught him about sexual behavior, but he learned it at some point and never performed sexual behaviors on his sister. Again, the clinician attempted to allay the father's fears and assure him that no one was casting blame on him or his parenting style. The goal of the discussion was to suggest that, perhaps, Alex developed questions about sex through his various experiences and never received instruction on the rules that govern such behavior. Mr. James appeared confused by this approach, "What do you mean, 'learn the rules?' It seems pretty clear to me that people know you don't touch other people's junk." The clinician agreed that this is a common understanding but reminded the father that the focus of this conversation was a child, leading the clinician to ask how Alex might have learned this information. After thinking for a moment, Mr. James responded, "I don't know."

Seeing Mr. James concede the apparent reality that Alex not only may have been curious about sexual topics as a result of the social modeling experienced, but also lacked knowledge of sexual topics and behavior, the clinician sought to gain buy-in from the father. "This is all stuff we can fix. That's what we'll do here in treatment: Teach Alex rules, answer his questions, and take steps to prevent this behavior from occurring again." Mr. James nodded his head in agreement. The clinician then emphasized that, at least until those goals are accomplished, it would be best to not give Alex conflicting messages. For example, if rules were to be established governing sexual behavior, it is best for Alex to see all individuals within his environment adhering to those rules. In other words, it was necessary to eliminate, to the extent possible, modeling of sexual behavior in the home. The clinician reviewed the ESS with Mr. James and obtained his commitment to remove such modeling from the home.

The next step involved developing the ABC chain that described Alex's behavior, which was a relatively straightforward task. Mr. James quickly identified that the behavior (i.e., oral sexual contact) was preceded by Alex being alone with his sister (antecedent). When discussing what immediately followed the PSB, Mr. James almost immediately volunteered, "It probably felt good. It's oral sex, right?" Although many caregivers have difficulty with the proposition that their child derived a pleasurable sensation from some form of sexual behavior, this was not the case with Mr. James. However, he quickly added that Alex was immediately disciplined, which included yelling at him, removing his video games, and grounding him. In this instance, because the behavior was immediately followed by two different consequences, they were each written down and integrated into the following diagram:

Alex left alone with sister (A)

↓

Oral sexual contact (B)

↓

Pleasurable feeling (C)/Being in trouble (C)

The clinician reviewed the diagram with Mr. James, who agreed to its structure. To build the father's confidence and reinforce his parenting efficacy, the clinician identified that this sequence suggests that Alex and his sister should not be left alone, which Mr. James previously reported was immediately implemented by him and his wife. The clinician encouraged them to continue that monitoring plan until the end of treatment and talked with him through several practical issues regarding babysitters, dividing responsibilities between him and his wife, and the requirement that the clinician notify the juvenile probation department in the event the family was noncompliant with treatment (this last aspect was due to the unique circumstances of the referral, and Mr. James signed an appropriate release of information form).

Before leaving the session, Mr. James's face dropped and he appeared unusually solemn. The clinician noticed the concerning look and asked Mr. James if he had questions. The father softly asked, "Is my son gonna be a sex offender?" The clinician empathized with Mr. James by noting that it must be difficult to have that concern. This led to a brief discussion of the longitudinal data that showed this is unlikely to be the case but that the chances are probably reduced with effective treatment. The clinician also highlighted that Alex displayed significant negative emotion when discussing the PSB, as well as remorse for having potentially hurt his sister. These aspects of Alex's presentation were cast as positive prognostic signs and the clinician encouraged the father to view Alex's behavior as an isolated incident unless repeated, though an incident that should be taken seriously. And Mr. James was praised for doing the right thing for his son by bringing him to treatment.

Session 2

The second session proved less tense than the first. Mr. James was much less defensive and reported that he and his wife effectively restricted the display of sexual modeling within the home. They waited to watch the television shows that include sexually explicit material until after Alex was in bed, and they refrained from touching each other in sexualized ways within the common areas of the home. At least twice during the week, one of the caregivers made a sexual comment toward the other, but it was quickly recognized and the conversation did not continue. The father reported that his wife was very receptive when he shared with her the contents of the previous session, but he found making such changes aggravating. Although he understood the reason for changing his behavior in front of his son, he still did not like it. The clinician reflected his comments and praised Mr. James's efforts.

The clinician came into session with the list of four rules below to review with Mr. James:

1. It's not OK to touch other people's private parts.
2. It's not OK for other people to touch my private parts.
3. It's not OK to look at other people's private parts.
4. It's not OK to show other people my private parts.

These four rules were identified given the nature of Alex's behaviors, which included both touching and exposure of private areas. When presented to Mr. James, he looked over the rules and simply replied, "You think he doesn't know these?" The clinician reframed the conversation not necessarily as teaching him new information but of explicitly stating expectations and boundaries. Indeed, it is likely the case he knew these rules or at least had some sense of expectations around private areas. However, discussing the rules in clearly stated terms allows for a conversation around them. It also permits the delivery of consequences in the event a rule is broken; it is difficult to provide consequences if expectations were never established. Mr. James acknowledged this rationale and approved of the rules as written, declining to make changes.

The clinician then asked Mr. James to identify what might be used as consequences if Alex were to break a rule in the future. Mr. James replied, "All he cares about are his video games. He's lost those since this happened, so I don't know what else to use." The clinician then asked Mr. James the conditions under which Alex's video games might be returned. The question confused him for a moment, and it became clear he had not considered returning them. The father asked the clinician what amount of time would be the most effective. Given that it had already been several weeks since the PSB, the clinician asked Mr. James whether Alex asks about the video games or complains about not having access to them. His answer suggested that Alex likely had moved on and found other activities to fill his time, and Mr. James concluded that their removal no longer had an effect on Alex. The clinician agreed but noted that returning the video games allowed the opportunity to remove them again as a consequence if an undesired behavior occurred. Mr. James nodded his head and said, "I guess we can give them back." The clinician recommended making their return a part of the upcoming conversation, in the sense that they may be removed again for breaking any of the rules. Two other consequences were identified: additional chores and an earlier bedtime.

When Alex joined the session, Mr. James looked unsure how to begin the conversation with his son. This prompted the clinician to provide a brief introduction to the topic for Alex in the hopes of providing a prompt to the father: "We're just going to talk about some different rules, Alex, that we want to make sure you know. You're not in trouble right now and are welcome to ask any questions you have." Alex looked on warily, but Mr. James understood the comment: "That's right, Alex. I just want to make sure we are clear on expectations. So, we're going to talk about some rules." With that, the father presented the rules and placed them in front of Alex. Upon seeing them, Alex immediately put his head down and started to weep. The father looked concerningly at the clinician, who made a head motion to comfort the child. Mr. James responded by rubbing his son's back while saying, "It's okay, son. I probably should've have taught these to you before. You're not in trouble. We're doing this so we can move on to better things." The father appeared sincere in his statement and the clinician nodded approvingly.

Alex looked up just enough to demonstrate engagement. Mr. James then hurriedly read through the rules, which caused the clinician to interject after the second rule was read: "Alex, these rules really just clarify that touching private areas is not acceptable for a person your age. It doesn't matter who is doing the touching. Does that make sense?" Alex gave a brief statement confirming that he understood. The father appreciated the clinician's clarification and received the implicit message to slow down the presentation. Mr. James then read the third rule and provided some examples, including looking at people in the shower or when using the restroom. He then read the fourth rule and continued his examples by encouraging his son to close bathroom doors to prevent others from seeing his private areas. Alex was tracking the presentation of the rules with his eyes, clearly reading them along with his father. As planned, Mr. James then clarified that it is expected that all members of the family will adhere to these rules. Alex's eyebrows raised as if surprised and then asked his father, "Is that why you and Mom aren't watching TV anymore?" Mr. James agreed that it was and used the opportunity to demonstrate for Alex that all family members are joined together to improve the situation.

Mr. James then transitioned the discussion to state that Alex's video games will be returned, which elicited a smile from the boy. The father then stipulated that any violation of the rules just specified will result in the video games being removed once again. Alex uttered, "I understand, but I won't do that again." The father nodded his head and said that he believed his son. Nonetheless, Mr. James briefly reviewed the other consequences that may be used if removal of the video games is not possible for some reason. At the conclusion of the session, Mr. James thanked his son for listening to the rules and for engaging in the conversation. Given the father's initial hesitancy, the clinician was pleasantly surprised at how well Mr. James performed throughout the session and praised him for his ability to effectively discuss the rules.

Session 3

Mr. James and Alex both entered the session in good spirits and reported no significant concerns over the past week. The clinician began by asking Alex to recite the sexual behavior rules, which he did with little effort. The clinician then transitioned into reviewing scenarios. Alex performed well applying the rules to the clear "yes" and "no" situations but struggled when it came to "gray area" cases. One scenario stimulated a significant discussion among Alex and his father: "You and a friend are hanging out and watching videos on a tablet. Your friend then shows you a video that included naked people. Did this break a rule?" Alex answered quickly, "Uh, no." This surprised Mr. James who then told his son that it would, indeed, break a rule. Alex replied that a video "isn't really like looking at people." Mr. James sought to explain that such behavior was still not acceptable for a 10-year-old and Alex responded by defending the action, including suggesting that it was not specified whether the content of the video was known before watching it and, thus, the behavior may have been unintentional. Mr. James conceded that it is important to consider intent when evaluating whether someone broke a rule but continued to stress the unacceptable nature of viewing sexually explicit content.

Alex also struggled with a scenario that depicted sexually suggestive material. Given his previous exposure to peers making hand gestures that included sexual commentary, another scenario presented a situation where Alex mimicked a friend performing a sexually inappropriate motion. Alex struggled to understand why this action would break a rule, as the defined rules only involved touching and looking at private areas. In addition, Alex did not see the harm in the behavior if others were performing similar motions and they found the behaviors humorous. Mr. James appeared stuck at this moment as Alex's point was valid; these behaviors did not explicitly violate a rule. The clinician validated Alex's response, acknowledging that the scenario did not specifically identify breaking a rule, but "these types of behaviors do encourage looking at or touching of private areas." The father quickly joined in: "That's right. The whole goal of these behaviors is to make jokes of sexual things, which can lead to other sexual things." Alex nodded his head and stated that when he heard his friends using the term "suck it," he knew it referred to oral sex.

The conversation progressed well, and the clinician praised the father's ability to engage in these discussions with his son. As the session drew to a close, Mr. James asked to speak alone with the clinician for a few minutes. Once Alex left the room, the father asked, "Is it normal for kids to give those answers? I mean, why did he think it was alright to watch porn?" The clinician reviewed some basic information about typical child development, including that Alex's preadolescent age likely resulted in him having more questions about sex than when he was younger. This increases the risk that he might seek out answers from peers or online. The clinician also discussed the possible role of peer pressure or a desire for acceptance as influencing his response to a friend offering a video. The fact that Alex provided a thoughtful answer and reviewed his justification was presented as a positive sign. He was willing to engage in these discussions with his father, which means future sessions focused on psychoeducation may be more interactive. The father sighed, as if nervous for those conversations. The clinician reassured Mr. James and praised his efforts.

Session 4

Given Alex's difficulty interpreting boundaries within "gray area" scenarios during the previous session, the clinician decided to implement a few additional scenarios. All situations presented to Alex represented "gray area" dilemmas, which allowed Alex and his father to quickly reengage in the conversation that characterized the previous session. Alex was more adept at answering the questions during this session and often talked through options before arriving at a specific conclusion, which allowed Mr. James and the clinician to observe his thought process. Mr. James appropriately praised Alex's efforts and the clinician, in turn, applauded the father's participation and support of his son.

The father again asked to speak with the clinician at the conclusion of session. Once alone, Mr. James noted that he remained surprised by Alex's seeming lack of understanding of sexual behavior expectations but that he was convinced by Alex's responses that his son really was unaware of boundary limitations. He thanked the clinician for helping in this respect, as he believed he gained a better understanding of his son's needs. The clinician continued to emphasize that the father was responsible for the son's change, as Mr. James freely engaged in the discussions in a nonshaming manner. It was becoming apparent that Alex was more comfortable discussing these issues with him. The father acknowledged the clinician's statements but quickly reiterated that he was "nervous about the next sessions." Again, the clinician reflected the father's statement and reminded him that the clinician would provide support throughout the process.

SUMMARY

The first phase of PBT utilizes the two techniques most strongly associated with improvement of PSB: caregiver behavior management skills and establishing rules related to sexual behavior (St. Amand et al., 2008). Combining these techniques with the elimination of modeling of sexual behavior provides the most focused and immediate approach to address PSB by targeting both social learning and self-regulation mechanisms. It also begins the process of building caregiver efficacy, both in terms of managing the child's behaviors and in discussing sexual topics with the child. The establishment and maintenance of effective rapport with the caregiver is a vital part of this phase, as it is critically important for the entire course of PBT.

5 PHASE 2

Healthy Sexuality

Children are naturally curious about sexual topics, whether it be anatomical differences, the functions of genitals, or how babies are conceived. Unfortunately, many caregivers are uncomfortable talking about typical sexual development and children may develop the belief that such topics are not to be discussed within the family. As a result, some children seek out information on sexual topics from other sources, such as friends or the internet, and what they learn may be inaccurate or too developmentally advanced. In many cases, this exposure can lead to the child acting in problematic ways. The goal of this phase is to define "healthy sexuality" for the child and caregiver, provide sexual psychoeducation to the child and caregiver, and build communication skills between the child and caregiver related to sex and sexuality. A session-by-session summary of the techniques used in this phase is provided in Table 5.1.

https://doi.org/10.1037/0000516-006
Children With Problematic Sexual Behavior: Theory, Research, and Evidence-Based Practice, by B. Allen

TABLE 5.1. Techniques of Phase 2, by Session

Session	Participants	Techniques
1	Caregiver	a. Orient caregiver to the purpose of Phase 2 and its activities
	Caregiver	b. Identify family beliefs regarding sex and sexuality in a nonjudgmental manner
	Caregiver	c. Construct the caregiver's perspective of "healthy sexuality"
2	Caregiver	a. Prepare psychoeducational materials prior to beginning session
	Caregiver	b. Deliver psychoeducation to the caregiver
	Caregiver	c. Revise the caregiver's perspective of healthy sexuality, as indicated
	Caregiver	d. Prepare the caregiver for a conjoint session with the child
3	Child	a. Orient the child to the purpose of Phase 2 and its activities
	Child	b. Ascertain any questions or mistaken beliefs the child seems to hold
	Caregiver	c. Review with the caregiver the results of the session with the child
	Caregiver	d. Revise the plan for the conjoint session, if indicated
4	Caregiver & Child	a. Facilitate a conversation between the caregiver and child
	Caregiver & Child	b. Assist the caregiver as needed; ensure the caregiver remains in the lead
	Caregiver & Child	c. Model helpful responses for the caregiver

SESSION 1

Most clinicians are experienced providing psychoeducation, as it is a common technique in several interventions. However, delivering psychoeducation about sexual topics without knowing the caregiver's beliefs or values can lead to caregiver discomfort and potentially cause disengagement. Again, developing and maintaining rapport with the caregiver is critically important in phase-based treatment for problematic sexual behavior (PBT). The clinician approaches this first session of Phase 2 with an open mind and a desire to learn about the caregiver's or family's perspective on these issues. Only the caregiver is needed for this session.

Objective

Through an empathic and supportive discussion, the clinician encourages the caregiver to identify their own values related to sex and sexuality, define acceptable and unacceptable child sexual behavior, and determine the information the child should learn. In effect, this session is meant to be an open discussion to learn about the family's values and/or clarify them, particularly in cases where the caregiver is unsure of the family's values.

Techniques

Orienting the Caregiver to Phase 2

Sometimes, caregivers display significant uneasiness discussing sexual topics. It may present as nervous laughter, confusion, or even anger. But providing the caregiver with a rationale for discussing these issues with the child typically eases the process, even if they continue to hold reservations. Given that the child has displayed problematic sexual behavior (PSB) in the past, the clinician can use this behavior to demonstrate that the child has some knowledge, or potential questions, about sex and sexuality. This leads to a logical conversation of what the caregiver has already taught the child or what discussions were had around these topics. Although some caregivers have done an excellent job providing age-appropriate sexual psychoeducation to their children, it is far more common that caregivers report having few, if any, discussions with their child about these issues. If this is the case, clinicians should ask the caregiver, in a supportive manner, why such topics have not been broached with the child. The most common answers involve a lack of consideration (e.g., "They're only 8 years old. Why would they need to know about this?"), uncertainty or fear of making incorrect statements (e.g., "I'm not sure I even know what an 8-year-old should know. I'll probably mess it up."), or disagreement with teaching such content (e.g., "Nine-year-olds don't need to know this stuff. Let them be kids."). Regardless of the caregiver's perspective, the answers provided can help the clinician plan future approaches to the material. For instance, the caregiver who expresses active disagreement with the topic may require more empathic reflecting or normalizing of their dissent, while the caregiver showing a fear of making mistakes will require reassurance and preparedness.

After ascertaining whether the caregiver has discussed sexual behavior with the child, and potentially the information provided, the clinician is ready to provide the caregiver with a suitable rationale for the remainder of the phase, including the upcoming conjoint caregiver–child discussion on sexual topics (see Session 4). There are many potential avenues through which a clinician can build the case for having this discussion. Some of the most frequently used include counteracting misinformation the child has already received (e.g., friends, internet, sexual abuse incident), opening the line of communication so the child feels comfortable coming to the caregiver in the future, sufficiently answering the child's questions to prevent information seeking from other sources, and teaching the family's values. Once the caregiver understands the reason for having this conversation with the child, the clinician may wish to reassure the caregiver that it will be a collaborative effort and the clinician will be available to help throughout the process.

Identify Family Beliefs

It is important to gather information about the beliefs the family holds regarding sex and sexuality. Often, caregivers present to treatment afraid that the clinician will attempt to define for them what is acceptable, which can create hesitation to discuss the topic. Asking the caregiver to discuss their views reduces anxiety and places the caregiver in the role of the expert. In some cases, it may be helpful to explicitly state that the caregiver is the expert on their own family and the clinician wants to learn about the family's values and perspectives. Regardless of the caregiver's level of comfort, it is advisable to begin this conversation by simply stating, "I don't want to assume I know you and your family's beliefs, so could you just tell me a little about your and your family's views on sex?" This starting point can go in many ways, but it allows the caregiver to dictate the direction. It is helpful for the clinician to write down information provided by the caregiver as this discussion largely informs the techniques for the remainder of this session and the rest of Phase 2.

It is fairly common that caregivers have not given much thought to their values regarding sexuality, particularly as it pertains to what they wish to teach their child. In this situation, the clinician can take a posture of curious questioning of some potential areas for discussion. For instance, the caregiver may be asked the names the family uses for private areas, whether the child has asked questions about how babies are conceived and the family's responses, or the conditions under which sex is considered permissible (e.g., age, marital status). The caregiver's initial answers to these questions may spur a more detailed conversation that begins to provide a clearer picture of the types of information the caregiver believes is appropriate or helpful for the child. As the discussion unfolds, the clinician should look for opportunities to discuss material directly related to the child's PSB. For instance, in the case of a child whose behavior is primarily self-stimulating, it is useful to know the caregiver's view on whether masturbation is morally acceptable and, if so, the age at which such behavior is permitted. As another example, for the child looking at internet pornography, it is informative to know whether the caregiver believes pornography viewing is acceptable at any age.

Some caregivers display significant rigidity and believe the topic is inappropriate. Sometimes, this is justified by the caregiver on the basis of the child's age and a belief the child is too young to learn such information (i.e., "lost innocence"). In these situations, the caregivers may hold on to the perspective that children should not know anything about the topic. A useful tactic is to encourage the caregiver to think of the child from a developmental perspective. This is usually accomplished by having the caregiver consider the kinds of information the child already knows about sexual topics as a due course of typical development. For instance, even children as young as 3 years of age typically know that males and females possess different genitals, and most caregivers will recognize this fact. Similarly, by the age of 7 years, children generally know that both a man and a woman are needed to produce a baby, even if they are unsure of the reproductive process. Providing these types of examples creates a level of flexibility on the part of many caregivers as they realize the discussion is primarily biologically based. Once these more basic elements are agreed to and the caregiver begins discussing the issue, the questions can then shift to the more subjective values the caregiver wishes to place on these types of knowledge and behavior.

It is also common that caregivers object to this discussion because of a sense of moral properness. In these situations, caregivers might reference a religious belief that children should not know about sex or a concern that teaching about sexual topics will sanction the child engaging in immoral behavior (see Clinical Tip 5.1). Trying to create flexibility by appealing to a sense of typical childhood behavior is unlikely to be successful. A helpful approach in these situations is to ask the caregiver to consider the age at which they believe a child should learn about these behaviors. Almost as a reflexive response, many caregivers will respond by referencing the child's wedding night. The clinician must reframe the discussion as not being about when such behavior is permissible by the caregiver's moral standards but rather about when knowledge about sexual topics is learned. Most caregivers will concede that youth learn about sexual relations long before their wedding night and then begin searching for a more suitable answer. Whatever answer is provided next, the clinician can help the caregiver think through the implication of that answer in practical terms. For instance, a caregiver who suggests youth should not know about sexuality until the age of 16

CLINICAL TIP 5.1. Working With Cultural Differences

There are few topics more laden with cultural dictates than sexual behavior. Culture is a complex and multifaceted term, and these intricacies are critically important for clinicians to recognize when addressing childhood sexual behavior. Religious beliefs often receive the majority of attention as it relates to the topic of sexual behavior. However, clinicians should not presume to know a family's view on sex and sexuality because of a stated religious perspective. For instance, some caregivers object to teaching their children anything about sexual behavior by invoking their Christian faith, arguing that such discussions violate their religious principles. However, other caregivers reference their Christian beliefs only in the context of teaching the child the bounds of acceptable sexual behavior and see no concerns with discussing sexual topics. The same can be said for various other cultural values, including those commonly associated with specific races and ethnicities, geographical locations, and socioeconomic levels; how those values are interpreted by the family and caregiver, and how closely they identify with those values, vary widely. The clinician is best served by directly eliciting beliefs and perspectives from the caregiver and not making presumptions based on cultural factors.

(a common response), can be reminded that this is the equivalent of 10th grade and then asked whether it is realistic to expect that youth will not come to learn about sexual behavior until they are in high school. This discussion often winds its way to the point the caregiver concedes that certain types of information should be conveyed to the child at their current age.

Construct the Caregiver's View of Healthy Sexuality

Following delineation of the caregiver's beliefs about sex and sexuality, this information is used to construct a definable picture of healthy sexuality for the child. The adjective "healthy" was chosen because of its value-neutral status; it is generally a safe assumption that caregivers desire for their children to be healthy and the definition of the term is relative to the caregiver defining it. This process is designed to clarify the caregiver's beliefs about what is developmentally acceptable and identify what types of psychoeducation might be helpful to provide to the caregiver during the next session.

An easy way to create the picture of healthy sexuality is to ask the caregiver, "What should [child's name] know and not know about sex?" The clinician writes two columns on a piece of paper, one labeled "Should Know" and the other labeled "Should Not Know." The caregiver then attempts to populate both columns. Sometimes, this information flows rather easily from the caregiver and this exercise takes only minutes. However, other times, caregivers may struggle to complete one side of the table or the other. Even after the previous discussion about family values, many caregivers continue to believe the child should not know anything about the topic and will develop a long list under that heading. The clinician may need to revisit the earlier conversation with the caregiver and reference those specific elements identified as suitable for the child to know. Again, the clinician can reference the child's PSB as evidence that the child does know certain pieces of information and this knowledge must be addressed and misunderstandings corrected. It is also helpful in this situation to reiterate the values the caregiver previously described and encourage viewing this exercise as an opportunity to teach those values to the child.

Although less frequent, some caregivers are quite open with their children and do not identify anything under the Should Not Know category. This is also unhelpful, as there are some elements of sexual behavior and sexuality that are likely difficult for even a 12-year-old child to comprehend. For instance, fetishes are not typically relevant for children and may be beyond their cognitive ability to understand. The goal of developing these lists is to define the boundaries around the information that might be shared with the child during a conjoint session, and there should be at least a few topics under each category.

By the end of this process, a clear picture of healthy sexuality should emerge for the caregiver. It is best to view this initial definition as a working concept or a starting point that is open to revision during the next session when psychoeducation will be provided. Nonetheless, clinicians should be aware that some value-laden topics will emerge and must be handled with care (see Clinical Tip 5.2). The clinician may wish to conduct a final review with the caregiver to obtain their concurrence that the lists accurately reflect their view of healthy sexuality for the child before ending the session.

SESSION 2

Clinicians should bring the previously constructed Should Know/Should Not Know lists into session as the concept of healthy sexuality may be revised by the caregiver in response to the psychoeducation provided. Only the caregiver is needed for this session.

Objective

Having clarified the caregiver's values and understanding of childhood sexual behavior in the previous session, this session aims to provide helpful sexual psychoeducation to the caregiver. The final step of this session is discussing the specific forms of sexual psychoeducation to be provided to

CLINICAL TIP 5.2. Addressing Sensitive Topics

When helping caregivers identify acceptable bounds of sexual behavior, several sensitive topics commonly emerge for discussion and can create uneasiness for clinicians. One prominent issue relates to sexual orientation. A minority of caregivers will clearly and strongly assert that the child should be taught that only heterosexual relationships are permissible. Indeed, some caregivers can be quite forceful on this point. It is understandable that some clinicians may view this as an opportunity to create attitude change, but attempting to change the caregiver's perspective is rarely effective. These views probably formed over the course of many years, if not decades, and it is highly unlikely the clinician can change the caregiver's opinion in the course of a 45-minute session. However, a clinician rejecting the caregiver's desire to teach this perspective to the child may result in premature termination of treatment, refusal to engage in a conjoint session with the child, and/or significantly prolonged treatment, all of which undermines the clinical goal of reducing PSB. Although objectionable to many clinicians, the best course of action may be to recognize the caregiver's values and proceed with treatment.

Another common sensitive topic involves self-stimulatory behavior the caregiver finds disgusting or offensive. The fact of the matter is that the child probably learned that such stimulation creates a pleasurable sensation, and there is no way to force the child into forgetting or "unlearning" that fact. For some caregivers, it can be helpful to discuss the behavior in biological terms and emphasize that the sensation derived from the stimulation does not necessarily translate into more adult-oriented goals, such as achieving orgasm. Many caregivers are also amenable to placing limits on the behavior (e.g., behind closed doors) that, if adhered to, reduces the problem to their satisfaction. The critically important aspect for clinicians is to recognize and validate the caregiver's concern and not dismiss it by asserting the child's behavior is "normal." This allows the clinician to engage with the caregiver to develop a solution that respects their views.

the child and preparing the caregiver for teaching this information in a conjoint discussion.

Techniques

Prepare Psychoeducation Materials

Prior to the start of this session, the clinician must consider the discussion with the caregiver that occurred in Session 1 and determine the most helpful psychoeducational material. The definition of healthy sexuality developed in the previous session may or may not contain unrealistic or unhelpful beliefs about childhood sexual behavior. For example, some caregivers initially believe it is inappropriate for a 12-year-old child to touch their own genitals in private or for a 6-year-old child to ask where babies come from. If unrealistic expectations are present, the clinician selects psychoeducational materials that address those beliefs. At a minimum, psychoeducation with the caregiver should include a discussion of commonly observed behavior for the child's age, as well as typical developmental progression, regardless of the accuracy of the caregiver's views. However, a caution is warranted. The goal of psychoeducation is not to change core values the family holds around sexual topics (e.g., when sexual behavior is permissible), and attempting any such effort is likely to be unsuccessful and damage rapport with the caregiver. Commonly utilized psychoeducation materials for discussing these issues with caregivers include fact sheets, tables, and other handouts (see Appendix A for a list of potential resources).

In addition, by the end of this session the clinician will prepare the caregiver for teaching the child appropriate sexual psychoeducation. As such, any materials that might be helpful for that process should be identified and brought into session by the clinician. It is important that the clinician review these materials with the caregiver, gain their consent to use the materials, and rehearse how the caregiver will present the information to the child (discussed in the Session 4 section in this chapter). The exact materials selected and presented to the caregiver is a clinical decision best made by the clinician working with a given case. Nonetheless, the clinician must have previously reviewed the materials and understand the content they contain (see Clinical Tip 5.3).

Provide Psychoeducation to the Caregiver

It is helpful to frame the discussion with the caregiver in the vein of presenting developmental milestones or expected behavior at different ages. In this manner, the clinician can discuss what is "typical" or "common" of

CLINICAL TIP 5.3. Selecting Psychoeducation Materials

There are numerous materials a clinician might use when providing psychoeducation to the caregiver. Similarly, there are several options available for helping the caregiver teach the information to the child. These resources include discussions of typical sexual behavior and development, reproduction, body safety skills, interpersonal relationships and boundaries, and other topics the clinician may find applicable. PBT does not require a clinician to use any specific books or handouts, as the needs of children and families differ and the clinician must remain flexible in this respect. However, it is critically important that the clinician is aware of the information presented in different materials. For instance, some books are available from Christian publishers that include religious content. This may be appropriate for some caregivers and objectionable to others. Similarly, some books contain content that the caregiver may previously have identified as not something they want to teach the child and, as such, are books the clinician should avoid. It is often helpful to receive recommendations from other clinicians, but it is the responsibility of the clinician to know what is being presented in session.

children at a given age. It is advised that clinicians avoid using the word "normal." Caregivers often view the word "normal" in a value-laden manner that differs significantly from the statistical use of the term. For instance, a caregiver may take exception to describing self-stimulatory behavior as "normal" for a 12-year-old child but are much less likely to be offended by referring to such behavior as "common." As discussed before, caregivers generally recognize that certain behaviors regularly occur at a given age but may disagree as to whether they are appropriate.

A helpful tactic is to present the psychoeducation materials to the caregiver in the context of further developing and refining their idea of healthy sexuality. It is often a challenge for the caregiver to integrate the material presented with the values they already hold around these topics. The clinician can help the caregiver in this task by reviewing the Should Know and Should Not Know lists and moving topics from one to the other as appropriate. It usually becomes clear that the content being moved is the more biological, cognitive, and/or developmental pieces and not the values the caregiver holds. This places many caregivers at ease and the lists then provide an updated concept of healthy sexuality. Although the topics on the lists will differ based on the age of the child, the caregiver's values, and the specific form of PSB, there are minimum recommendations for the Should Know side of the table. These include (a) anatomically correct names of genitalia, (b) the reason(s) for people having genitals, (c) boundaries governing sexual behavior, (d) the importance of consent, and (e) any case-specific issues relevant to the child (e.g., why self-stimulation creates a pleasurable sensation, definition of oral sex). This last point regarding case-specific issues will be demonstrated in the case examples at the end of this chapter.

Some caregivers may not hold any notable unrealistic and/or maladaptive beliefs within their definition of "healthy sexuality" and few, if any, changes are required. In these instances, clinicians should still review appropriate psychoeducation with the caregiver but place the information in the context of preparing for a discussion of sexuality with the child. In those situations where caregivers demonstrate unrealistic or unhelpful expectations, simply providing psychoeducation may be sufficient to prompt a change in the caregiver's perspective in many cases. However, some caregivers may be reluctant to change their perceptions regarding what is age appropriate and cling to perceptions that are unrealistic. In these instances, clinicians may find it helpful to implement cognitive change techniques. For instance, a commonly employed tactic is to ask caregivers when the objected-to behavior or knowledge is appropriate for the child. Whatever the answer, the clinician can then ask who will teach the child at that age and the likelihood the child will reach the identified age without learning of it beforehand. The point of this exercise is to demonstrate that a longer period of time increases the likelihood that (a) the caregiver loses control of the message, (b) the child learns the information from elsewhere, and (c) the information is unhelpful or inaccurate. Similarly, the clinician can ask the caregiver to reconcile positions that cannot be reconciled. For instance, some caregivers rigidly adhere to a belief that the child should not know anything about sexual topics, which is used as an excuse to not teach the child sexual content. However, given that the child displays PSB, the clinician can point out the child clearly has learned some things about sexual behavior and then ask the caregiver how that information can be countered if discussing sexual topics is not allowed. These types of cognitive change techniques place the caregiver in an untenable situation that can only be resolved by acknowledging the need to discuss these issues with the child.

Prepare the Caregiver for the Conjoint Session

It is not uncommon for caregivers to display anxiety or uncertainty when the clinician begins the discussion of directly teaching sexual information to the child. Clinicians can explore this hesitancy by asking caregivers to describe their thoughts or emotions and empathizing with their responses. Indeed, discussing sexual topics is a challenging task for many caregivers, regardless of whether the child displays PSB. As part of this process, the clinician can refocus the caregiver's concerns by underlining their desire to promote the well-being of the child, both in the short and long term. This includes not just reducing or eliminating PSB but also opening the line of communication related to sexual topics so the child is more willing to approach the caregiver in the future with questions.

This process is aided by relying on the caregiver's concept of healthy sexuality, focusing on the Should Know list. The items placed on the Should Know list form the basis for the psychoeducation that will be provided to the child. For younger children, topics typically include more factual information regarding names of body parts, where babies come from, and how to keep private areas healthy (e.g., they are delicate, safe and unsafe behavior). For older children, these topics may include more abstract and value-laden issues, such as dating, when sex is permissible, and sexual acts or topics not designed for procreation (e.g., oral sex, sexual messaging in media). The clinician presents to the caregiver the materials selected to teach the desired information to the child. It is helpful to link the content within the psychoeducation tools directly to the Should Know list. This allows the caregiver to see that the materials are keeping to their concept of healthy sexuality and not attempting to change or subvert their values. It may be helpful to present several options to the caregiver and allow them to review and select their preferred materials.

The clinician advises the caregiver how best to present the material to the child with the goal of promoting a conversation and avoiding the appearance of a lecture. Several suggestions are available. First, the caregiver is best served by presenting the material in small segments as opposed to reading or talking for a long period of time. Many caregivers prefer written materials they can read (e.g., books), as this medium frees the caregiver from developing their own script. However, caregivers may attempt to finish the book as quickly as possible to alleviate their anxiety, but this prevents discussion and the ability to ensure the child understands the content. By pausing at prespecified moments, the caregiver can encourage discussion, allow the child to ask questions, and promote opportunities to praise the child for their participation.

Second, it is vital for the caregiver to maintain a positive and accepting tone throughout the conjoint session. Children also may be nervous during this session, particularly in families where these topics were historically unwelcome and discussing them resulted in punishment. Praise and positivity can place the child at ease while irritability or negativity on the part of the caregiver may discourage the child's engagement. Similarly, it is important for the caregiver to understand that no question from the child is off limits. If the child asks a specific question, it implies (a) that the question is in the child's mind and (b) they feel comfortable enough to ask it. Responding with an answer such as "I'll tell you when you're older" or "You don't need to worry about that" serves to reinforce the child's belief that such topics are not allowed, inhibits communication, and may prompt the child to seek the answer elsewhere. The question can be answered in a developmentally appropriate way that considers the caregiver's values. Examples of this situation are described in the cases of Maria C. and Alex J.

Third, the caregiver and clinician can prepare several questions to directly ask the child. For instance, when reviewing the proper names of private areas, the child might be asked about other names they heard at school, home, or elsewhere. Similarly, the child may be asked to describe their understanding of how babies are made. Questions such as these asked directly to the child can help ease the conversation as they implicitly provide approval for the child to discuss the topics.

To the extent possible, the clinician strives to develop in the caregiver a sense of confidence to discuss these topics with the child. It may be helpful to role play the discussion, including reviewing different ways the child may respond. The clinician can review their role in the conjoint session with the caregiver, including monitoring the pace at which content is provided, observing the responses of both the caregiver and child, and interjecting when needed to help the caregiver. Of course, the responses of the child cannot be predicted and children are known to ask questions that sometimes demonstrate greater knowledge than the caregiver realized. It is useful for the caregiver and clinician to devise a signal that communicates the need for help in the event the child provides a question or statement for which the caregiver is unprepared. These situations will be discussed in more depth during Session 4.

SESSION 3

To the extent possible, it is an aim of the clinician to make the upcoming conjoint caregiver-child discussion as surprise-free as possible. At this point in treatment, what the child understands about sexual behavior and their questions on the topic are unknown. In this session, the clinician will meet with the child to ascertain this information. As such, this session requires the participation of both the caregiver and child. However, the age and cognitive sophistication of the child will dictate whether this session is necessary. Experience teaches that children under the age of 7 years are unlikely to provide any substantive questions not already prepared for during the previous session. Correspondingly, this session may be unnecessary for these children, but this is a decision best left to the clinician. It is recommended that this session occur for all children aged 7 years and older.

Objective

The goal of this session is to identify any questions or issues from the child's perspective that may need to be addressed during the conjoint session that were not already prepared for in Session 2. This involves the clinician meeting with the child and probing for any potentially relevant questions or inaccurate beliefs that may need addressing during the conjoint session and then preparing the caregiver accordingly.

Techniques

Meeting With the Child

The clinician begins this session by meeting alone with the child, as it may be uncomfortable for children to discuss sexual topics in front of a caregiver. Given that the child may have a negative association with any discussion related to sexual topics, the clinician should open the discussion in a cautious manner. A good starting point may be to ask the child if they know anything about "private parts." Practically all families refer in some way to genital areas, even if they use slang terms and discourage conversations around them. As such, this starting point generally elicits little, if any, negative emotion from the child, although they may be fully aware of the reasons they are attending treatment (i.e., PSB) and may be hesitant to engage in any discussion on the topic. The purpose of this question is merely orientation to the topic and, if needed, the clinician may review "swimsuit space" with the child. It is important for the clinician to remember that the job of psychoeducation will fall to the caregiver and occur in the next session; the clinician only provides the information necessary to facilitate identifying questions relevant to the upcoming conjoint session.

Once it is clear to the child that the discussion at hand relates to sexual body parts, the clinician may shift the focus by asking the child whether they have ever heard the word "sex" and what the word means. The child's response to the question is typically telling and the clinician should be prepared for a variety of responses. It is helpful to write down anything the child says related to the topic, accurate or inaccurate, to aid in sharing the information with the caregiver. Developing an effective therapeutic rapport with the child can facilitate this discussion (see Clinical Tip 5.4). If the child displays significant emotional reactions to this conversation, the clinician can provide empathic and encouraging responses. Reassure the child that

CLINICAL TIP 5.4. Developing Rapport With the Child, Revisited

As the reader may recall from Chapter 4, developing rapport with the child in the early sessions of PBT is discouraged, as it may prolong Phase 1 or inhibit the more immediate implementation of Phase 1 techniques (e.g., monitoring plan, development of rules). However, greater flexibility is available in Phase 2. The first few sessions of this phase generally involve less sense of urgency and, provided the monitoring plan and implementation of rules are effective, the PSB may have been absent for several weeks. Given that discussions in Phase 2 may be anxiety provoking for the child, it is often helpful for the clinician to develop an effective rapport. A common approach involves reducing the amount of time spent with the caregivers in the first two sessions of this phase in order to implement rapport-building activities with the child. For instance, the clinician may spend 25 minutes in Session 1 discussing the caregiver's view of sexuality and use the final 20 minutes to develop rapport with the child. This often increases the number of sessions required in Phase 2 from four to five or six, but this is not typically concerning. However, the clinician must not allow treatment to stall because of a desire to better develop rapport with the child. Prolonging treatment by three or more sessions for this purpose risks reducing the caregiver's ability to remember the plan for the conjoint session and increases the possibility that treatment loses its focus on the PSB.

they are not in trouble and will not be punished for discussing these topics. Regardless of the clinician's efforts, there is a minority of children who will remain silent or otherwise refuse to engage in the conversation.

Once the child is sufficiently engaged in the discussion, ask open ended questions designed to identify the child's thoughts on and exposure to the topic. For instance, the child might be asked if they have heard about sex at school, on television, or in music. The clinician might also ask the child to discuss the PSB. If the child is known to make sexual comments to others, it is often helpful to ask them what they believe the comments mean (see the case of Alex J.). It is also advised that the clinician directly ask the child whether they believe the behavior involved in the PSB qualifies as "sex" or "sexual." The child's responses to these questions often provide insight into the child's understandings or reveal a prior experience where the child was exposed to the behavior. It is recognized that some clinicians may be uncomfortable directly asking the child about the PSB for fear that it may result in withdrawal, shame, or sadness. However, referring to the PSB in vague terms (e.g., "that thing that happened," "what you got in trouble for") sends the message that the behavior is shameful and should not be discussed directly. Stating the behavior in accurate terms and in a straightforward manner reduces stigma and allows for greater understanding on the part of the child.

Before ending this conversation, it is important to elicit questions from the child. However, they may not provide answers to bluntly stated questions, such as "What do you want to know about sex?" Rather, the clinician is better served by fostering an inquisitive nature to the conversation. One approach to creating this type of interaction is to acknowledge a potential lack of understanding in the child's comments. For example, if the child uses a slang term to refer to a sexual act, the clinician might ask the child to define what is meant by the term. It is not uncommon that the child struggles to do so; they know it relates to something sexual, but they do not know what the term describes. Another approach is to ask the child pointed questions when they appear confused or unsure. For instance, if the child states, "Sex is when two people love each other and a baby comes out," the clinician can respond by pointing out exceptions. In this situation, the clinician might respond by asking the child, "You love your mom and dad, right? But you don't have a baby with them. So, it seems something else needs to happen. What might that be?" It may also be useful to ask clarifying questions that prompt children to think about issues in a deeper manner. Consider an older child who asserts, "Sex is something fun for a boyfriend and girlfriend to do together." The clinician might ask the child for other reasons people have sex and if sex might have any negative consequences. Again, the clinician should refrain from correcting inaccurate beliefs as these topics and questions will be answered by the caregiver in the conjoint session. The clinician ends this discussion by thanking the child for their openness and willingness to discuss the topic and reassures them that future sessions will provide answers to their questions.

Meeting With the Caregiver

The clinician meets with the caregiver to review the child's questions and knowledge on the topic. It is advisable to start by informing the caregiver of what the child seems to accurately know about sex, if any such information was obtained. Some caregivers underestimate their child's knowledge on the topic, and it is often surprising to them to hear of their child's prior exposure and familiarity. This basic understanding can be disarming and smooth the remainder of the discussion by demonstrating the need to teach the child healthy information. Next, the clinician can review the seeming misperceptions displayed by the child and emphasize that these mistaken beliefs need correction. Lastly, the questions posed by the child can be presented to the caregiver, and the clinician can help in formulating an accurate and developmentally appropriate response.

After reviewing the child's responses with the caregiver, a plan is developed on how best to address the child's questions and dispel any mistaken beliefs. Again, the clinician can rely on the previously developed Should Know and Should Not Know lists, as the clinician's conversation with the child may alter the caregiver's responses. Correspondingly, it may be necessary to develop new approaches to psychoeducation, including identifying different materials. Depending on the number of topics identified, it may be necessary to prioritize the topics and not all issues may be discussed in the conjoint session. In this case, it can be emphasized for the caregiver that the conjoint session is conceived as the beginning of the discussion and not the whole of the discussion. Opening the line of communication implies that future conversations will occur and some topics may be reserved for a later discussion after the conjoint session. The caregiver may identify those topics they wish to discuss with the help of the clinician, and those topics are placed near the top of the list.

One word of caution is warranted. In rare situations, caregivers are shocked to learn of their child's knowledge or questions on the topic of sex and display significant emotional responses, such as anger or disgust. It is understandable that the caregiver may wish to know more about where the child learned the information or want to address the issue immediately.

Regardless of the caregiver's responses, it is best practice for the clinician to stress the importance of not confronting the child or otherwise discussing the issues raised until the next session. The clinician will be present during that session and the child and caregiver can discuss the issues in a more effective manner, as both parties will feel supported and be given sufficient time to discuss their perspective.

SESSION 4

The last session of Phase 2 is a conjoint discussion that involves the child, caregiver, and clinician. The caregiver presents the psychoeducation materials to the child and teaches the values they wish to impart regarding sexual behavior. The child is provided the opportunity to ask questions and the caregiver remains encouraging and open throughout the session.

Objective

The objective of this session is to provide healthy and adaptive information to the child and open the line of communication between the child and caregiver as it pertains to sexual topics.

Techniques

Facilitate a Discussion of Sexual Topics

With the child and caregiver in the room, the clinician orients both to the structure of the session. This brief discussion includes stating that the session will talk about sex, provide information to the child, and answer the child's questions. It is recommended that the clinician explicitly state that the child may ask any questions they have and they will not be punished or otherwise in trouble as a result. The caregiver should acknowledge and reinforce this statement to demonstrate its accuracy for the child.

How to start the conversation is a clinical decision that may be influenced by several factors (e.g., caregiver comfort, child's engagement). It is most common for the caregiver to begin the discussion by reviewing the psychoeducation materials; however, in some cases, the child may have pressing questions that represent a more appropriate starting point. It is also important to pay attention to the flow of the session. Consider a case where the child responds to the opening introduction from the clinician by asking whether it is acceptable to discuss a particular sexual topic (e.g., what people look like naked, a scene from a television show). In this case, dismissing the child's question in the interest of adhering to a preconceived plan might result in child withdrawal. It may be more effective to begin the conversation by having the caregiver respond to the child's question and eventually transition into the psychoeducation materials.

The format the conversation takes often fluctuates as a result of the age and cognitive sophistication of the child. Younger children, in general, are less talkative and the material presented is more factually based, resulting in less interaction and more caregiver teaching. Older children may be expected to engage more readily in a conventional form of discussion and to provide their own ideas and experiences. Ideally, the session involves a sustained child–caregiver conversation that allows for bidirectional communication and, hopefully, understanding of each other's perspectives.

Remembering that a primary goal of this session is to build caregiver efficacy in their ability to discuss sexual topics and to open the line of communication, it is important for the clinician to remain in a facilitative role throughout the session. The clinician can model for the caregiver positive feedback to the child's verbalizations and prompt the caregiver to address a particular question from the child, but the caregiver should be the one responding to the child. The most preferred sessions are the ones where the caregiver and child engage in a conversation with little need for the clinician to interject or provide direction. Before finishing the session, the clinician reasserts for the child and caregiver that this discussion is viewed as the beginning of the conversation and not the entirety of the conversation. Future discussions of sexual topics are allowed, encouraged, and expected, particularly as the child develops new questions.

Clinician Guidance

Experience provides a number of helpful recommendations for how clinicians can maximize the impact of their facilitative role. First, be an active observer. As the session unfolds, watch for any signs that indicate a potential need for clinician feedback. This includes signs of negative caregiver emotion (e.g., anxiety, irritation), negative child emotion (e.g., anxiety, embarrassment), a caregiver rushing through the material, or a child disengaging from the conversation. These moments may signal a need for the clinician to recognize the moment, label it for the child and caregiver, and take corrective action. Examples of these moments are provided in the case vignettes at the end of this chapter.

Second, help the caregiver respond in difficult moments. One of the most common situations of caregiver anxiety occurs when a child asks a question the caregiver is unsure how to answer. Even though the clinician prepares caregivers for the fact that there is no way to predict what a child might say, it may still be shocking when a caregiver hears certain questions come from their child. The clinician can respond in this moment by first stalling for time to give the caregiver a moment to collect themselves and then providing a comment that suggests a helpful response. Consider the following example where a child asks a question after the caregiver describes sexual intercourse:

CHILD: Do you and Dad do sex like that?

MOTHER: (shocked and unsure how to respond, gives clinician a look that was previously designated as a signal for assistance)

CLINICIAN: That's an excellent question. Given that mom just described how babies are born, I think it makes sense that you would wonder about that. After all, you were a baby and you have a mom and dad. Well, mom, maybe we should talk about when sex is OK between two people.

This response by the clinician is validating, normalizing, and allows the mother a moment for the shock to wear off. It also points the mother in a helpful direction: Discussing the values the mother wants to teach her child about when sex is permitted. On occasion, a child will continue to press the issue and ask more specific questions about the sexual activities of the caregiver, or even the clinician. In these moments, answers can reinforce the idea that consenting adults, within the bounds of the values taught by the caregiver, are free to engage in sexual activity. The answer can also reinforce interpersonal boundaries by pointing out that it is generally not acceptable for people to discuss their sexual activities outside of that relationship.

Third, only correct the caregiver in a nonconfrontational manner that does not undermine their authority with the child. Some caregivers may respond to questions impulsively or forget the previously developed response and provide an inaccurate or undesirable response as a result. However, it is counter to the goal of building parenting efficacy and encouraging conversation to correct the caregiver. A more helpful response is one that prompts the caregiver to reconsider and restate their answer. This example describes one situation where this occurred:

CHILD: What does it mean to 'go down on someone'? I heard that at school.

FATHER: It's something gross. You don't need to worry about it.

CLINICIAN: Yeah, dad, I think a lot of people think it is gross. But it seems like he knows it has something to do with sexual behavior and it is really great he felt comfortable asking that question. Maybe there's a way we can describe it for him so he doesn't ask somebody else.

This response by the clinician not only validates the father's reaction but also reminds the father that it is better to answer the child's question than to have the child seek out the information elsewhere. It also demonstrates the progress being made in that the child felt comfortable enough to ask a question about sexual behavior. The father is prompted in a supportive way to formulate a sufficient answer to the question, and the clinician may help in this process if needed.

Lastly, be prepared with questions and comments designed to elicit interaction. The aim is for the conversation to fill the 45-minute session and, if the child rarely speaks, there may be a significant amount of unused time. Caregivers often are pleased when the child does not ask questions, as it alleviates anxiety and speeds up the conversation. However, it can be unclear in these moments if the child understands the material. As such, the clinician may be in a position of needing to find ways to stimulate engagement and conversation. For example, the clinician might ask the caregiver to provide their perception of the child's participation in session or ask the child to discuss how easy the topic is to talk about with the caregiver. The clinician might encourage both parties to describe times when they have encountered unexpected sexual topics in their lives. It is important that the clinician not ask the caregiver or child embarrassing, personal, or otherwise difficult questions, remembering that these moments are designed to encourage conversation.

CASE EXAMPLES

The cases of Lydia E., Maria C., and Alex J. are continued here to demonstrate how Phase 2 was used to address their diverse presenting concerns.

Lydia E., 5 Years Old, Sexual Abuse Survivor

Session 1

The clinician began session by discussing the need to teach Lydia more helpful information about sexual topics to counter the previous information she learned through her sexual abuse experiences. Mr. and Mrs. Thomas understood that Lydia's previous experiences taught her unhelpful information and wanted to discuss the topic with her to clarify misperceptions. However, the caregivers were not sure what information was appropriate to teach a 5-year-old child. Given this lack of direction, the clinician asked them to step back from considering specific topics and to think of the values they wished to teach both Lydia and her sister. Given that Mr. and Mrs. Thomas intended to adopt the girls following termination of the biological mother's parental rights, the clinician encouraged them to consider this as the beginning of instilling in them the family's moral beliefs.

Mr. and Mrs. Thomas were initially confused by the phrasing of the clinician's question and it was clear they had not previously discussed the issue from a moral perspective. Mr. Thomas volunteered that perhaps they should teach Lydia only the basics, such as the anatomical names for body parts and the possibility of harming private areas if they are not treated properly. Mrs. Thomas responded that this approach neglected the touching that occurred between the sisters and, clearly, Lydia knew there were reasons people touch the private areas of others. The clinician concurred with Mrs. Thomas and emphasized that this is an excellent place to build in the values of the family. In other words, the caregivers were asked to consider when they believe sexual contact was permitted.

Identifying the family's values regarding when sexual behavior was allowed resulted in an impromptu conversation and brief disagreement between the couple. Mr. Thomas quickly responded that sex is only acceptable within marriage, to which Mrs. Thomas responded that the two of them were engaged in a sexual relationship prior to their wedding and teaching this would make them hypocrites. Mr. Thomas then questioned his wife, "What are we supposed to tell them then? Have sex whenever you feel ready? They're doing sexual stuff now!" The clinician reframed the discussion as pointing out the two extremes of the issue: either having no rules around sexual contact or restricting sexual contact only to the context of a lifelong commitment. This prompted Mrs. Thomas to suggest that a middle ground may be possible. The conversation continued for several minutes until the couple eventually settled on several points they wished to teach Lydia: Sexual behavior is only allowed (a) when she is an adult, (b) with a person who is not a relative, (c) within the confines of a committed relationship, and (d) when both people want to participate.

Having specified the larger context of the family's beliefs about sex, the clinician asked the caregivers to consider the information Lydia needs in order to understand the values they described. Mr. Thomas asked the clinician whether this included details about the act of sexual intercourse. The clinician rephrased the question by asking the caregivers if there is any indication that Lydia is already aware of sexual intercourse. Both caregivers denied any such signals, but Mrs. Thomas stated that they know Lydia is aware of sexual touching and oral sex, as she displayed these toward her sister and they were perpetrated on her during previous sexual abuse incidents. The clinician suggested that psychoeducation to Lydia may be more effective if restricted to these topics.

At that point, the clinician crafted two columns on a piece of paper, labeling one "Should Know" and the other "Should Not Know." Under the first column, the clinician wrote the previously defined information regarding when sexual contact is permitted, as well as the broad statement of "touching and oral sex." Under the second column, the clinician wrote the word "intercourse." The clinician then asked the caregivers to continue populating the two lists. Mrs. Thomas suggested adding the "doctor's names" of private parts to the first column. She stated they already used the correct terms in the home, but it may be helpful to review them. The clinician suggested giving some sense of why bodies have private areas and why male and female anatomy differs. This comment elicited a cautious look from Mr. Thomas, which the clinician addressed: "I know that sounds strange. It looks like you might be concerned. What are your thoughts?" Mr. Thomas responded, "I thought you just said we don't need to teach about intercourse. It sounds like you are saying to teach her about babies." The clinician reflected this concern and asked Mr. Thomas if he would find it acceptable to discuss reproduction if there was a way to do it without discussing intercourse. He agreed to consider the possibility.

The caregivers continued to develop their lists, which ultimately included a handful of topics on each side. Under the Should Know heading were the topics of (a) the "doctor's names" for private areas, (b) the role of private areas in reproduction, maybe, (c) private areas are delicate and can be easily injured, (d) touching another person's private areas is allowed only under the specified conditions, and (e) using mouths and hands to touch private areas is not allowed because the conditions specified in point (d) are not met. As for the Should Not Know column, the couple included the topics of (a) intercourse, (b) reproduction, maybe, (c) "one-night stands," (d) anal sex, and (e) pornography. The clinician presented these lists to the caregivers to ensure accuracy and they both concurred. The clinician then labeled the paper as the caregivers' idea of healthy sexuality, writing this term at the top.

Session 2

The clinician brought into session the healthy sexuality lists, a fact sheet on sexual behaviors of children, and two psychoeducational books written for young children on the topic of sex and sexual behavior. The clinician reviewed the fact sheets with the caregivers to provide a helpful overview of the types of behaviors typical for children Lydia's age and to prepare the caregivers for the types of behavior that may emerge in the near future. The goal of this was to place some of Lydia's behavior in developmental context and to encourage Mr. and Mrs. Thomas to consider how future types of behaviors might be addressed. This process unfolded without significant difficulty as both caregivers were open to the information. Only one topic yielded a focused conversation, and this occurred after the caregivers saw that children commonly begin asking questions about "where babies come from" around the age of 5 to 7 years. The clinician attempted to provide some context by suggesting that it is fairly common to see pregnant individuals in public, if not in the home, and children understand that pregnancy is a precursor to the birth of babies. This naturally creates the question for children of how and why babies grow within the human body. Mr. Thomas in particular was surprised to learn that such questions were common at Lydia's age, but appreciated the rationale.

The clinician used the discussion of pregnancy and children asking such questions to pivot to the previous uncertainty around teaching Lydia about reproduction. Two psychoeducational books were then presented to the caregivers, both of which provided a basic review of genital names before describing their associations with eggs and sperm. The books mentioned how the joining of sperm and egg results in the conception of a baby, but neither book discussed intercourse or how the two microscopic gametes join. The clinician urged the caregivers to consider the discussion as one of a basic biological process. For instance, noses are used to smell, ears are used to hear, legs are used for running, and genitals are used to reproduce. The clinician also emphasized that there were no discussions in the books about concepts such as orgasm or sexual arousal or physical attraction. These disclaimers put Mr. Thomas at ease and, after flipping through the books, he agreed to move reproduction to the Should Know side of the paper. However, Mrs. Thomas raised a question, "Didn't we say before that it seemed like Lydia was getting something out of performing these behaviors with her sister? How do we discuss that if we don't talk about sexual arousal?"

Mrs. Thomas's question referenced the earlier ABC chain (see Chapter 4) that suggested Lydia derived some sort of positive outcome from engaging her sister in these behaviors. This is a topic that must be handled delicately given the discomfort of many caregivers. The clinician acknowledged Mrs. Thomas's concern and discussed options of how to present that possibility in an acceptable way. Specifically, the clinician suggested talking of private areas as creating a strange physical sensation and relying on the idea that it is just a message sent to the brain. The analogy of taste buds was used to demonstrate the concept. When something salty is placed on the tongue, the taste buds send a message to the brain to notify it that the taste bud is being stimulated. Private areas work much the same way; there is a unique sensation that might be felt because it is the message sent to the brain to notify you that they are being touched. Mrs. Thomas appreciated this description and had the idea of linking it back to the idea of private areas being delicate. In brief, the genitals being stimulated may signal to a person that private areas are being touched in an inappropriate way that could be harmful. The clinician praised Mrs. Thomas's thoughts and highlighted that this can be a useful message later when Lydia processes her sexual abuse experiences (see Chapter 10). The topic of "a feeling that sends a message to the brain" was added to the Should Know list. The caregivers then consented to the concept of healthy sexuality as updated in this session.

The clinician transitioned the session into discussing the mechanics of presenting the information to Lydia. Given the assumption that Lydia would say relatively little during the conjoint session, the clinician focused the preparation on how to present one of the books in as engaging a way as possible. The caregivers picked the book they preferred and the clinician began reviewing it with them. A focus was on pausing at various points to offer Lydia the opportunity to ask questions. In the event she did not, the caregivers were instructed to link the different parts of the book to the rules previously established in Phase 1. This emphasis was designed to connect knowledge development with the boundaries previously established, while not shaming Lydia for previous behaviors or presenting the topic as "gross" or "wrong."

The clinician spent the last few minutes of the session cautioning the caregivers that there is no way to predict what Lydia might say when the opportunity is presented to her. It was suggested that if the caregivers find themselves struggling with how to respond to a question, they look to the clinician and say, "That's a good question." At that point, the clinician would join the conversation and provide direction. Also, the clinician notified the caregivers that it is not uncommon for some caregivers to inadvertently go through the material too quickly while failing to pause to engage with the child, and if that situation arises the clinician would interject.

Session 3

Given Lydia's young age and her reserved nature around the clinician, Session 3 of the PBT protocol was omitted from treatment.

Session 4

Lydia and her caregivers attended session with Lydia choosing to sit on the lap of Mrs. Thomas. The clinician provided a brief introduction thanking everyone for coming and told Lydia that the focus today was on talking about a few different things that might help her better understand her body. At that point, the clinician looked at the caregivers and asked them to review the parameters previously established in session, which included Lydia being free to ask questions without fear of being in trouble. Lydia did not speak but provided a brief head nod as if in agreement.

Mrs. Thomas presented the psychoeducational book selected by the caregivers and read the title, followed by the first few pages. By that point, it appeared Lydia understood the topic clearly enough and had turned more into the body of Mrs. Thomas as if trying to hide. The clinician paused the reading and stated, "It looks like Lydia is a little uncertain about the topic. That's okay. These types of things aren't talked about a lot." The clinician then gave a look at Mr. Thomas, who appeared to receive the signal. He rubbed Lydia's back and was reassuring, telling her, "I know this might seem strange, but Mom and I want you to be safe and so we're talking about these things to help with that. That's all. No one's in trouble right now." Mrs. Thomas seconded Mr. Thomas's comment and gave Lydia a tight hug. The girl appeared more at ease as she turned back toward the book, while still leaning in toward Mrs. Thomas.

Mrs. Thomas continued reading the book, which included defining "doctor's names" for body parts, including vagina and penis. Mrs. Thomas then paused reading the book to discuss with Lydia the fact that private areas can be very sensitive and need to be treated with care. This allowed for a transition into the rules previously established, and Mrs. Thomas did an excellent job presenting the rules in the context of enhancing safety and health. Lydia then whispered in Mrs. Thomas's ear. The foster mother stated for the room, "Lydia wants to know why birth mommy's friend touched her vagina if it is not safe. I think that's a good question." (Note the family used the term "birth mommy" to distinguish the biological mother from Mrs. Thomas.) The second sentence from Mrs. Thomas invoked the previously defined signal for help from the clinician and was accompanied by a discomforting look from Mrs. Thomas. The clinician responded, "Yes, that is a good question. Hmm . . . I think there are probably a lot of rules that we have, like not stealing, that people break sometimes." Mr. Thomas quickly picked up on the prompt and, turning to Lydia, said, "We have rules to keep people safe, like not touching other people's private areas, but sometimes, people break those rules. And, when people break the rules, they get in trouble. Birth mommy's friend made a bad choice and hurt you in the process. Now, he's in trouble." Lydia nodded her head as if understanding. The clinician then added, "I think it is really wonderful though that Lydia is strong enough to ask that question." Mr. Thomas again received the message and responded, "It is. I'm really proud of you, sweetie, for asking that question."

Mrs. Thomas then continued to parts of the book that discussed reproduction, which often elicited surprised looks from Lydia. Although Mrs. Thomas occasionally stopped to ask whether Lydia had questions, the girl repeatedly shook her head. The values the family wished to teach were integrated into the end of this discussion and presented as attempts to increase safety. The foster mother also made the point of mentioning that this was the reason why Lydia was in trouble for the PSB that occurred with her sister. Lydia put her head down as if ashamed. The clinician interjected, "I think that last point made Lydia a little upset. Maybe we can discuss how we learn to behave in certain ways and that we can change these behaviors when we learn new things." Referencing a conversation from earlier sessions, Mr. Thomas noted to Lydia, "Mom and I think that the behavior with your sister was because of the things you learned from birth mommy's friend. You weren't taught very helpful things about private areas. But now that you've learned better things, you can behave in different ways and won't be in trouble anymore." Mr. Thomas delivered these statements in a positive and hopeful manner, which elicited a brief smile from Lydia.

Although Lydia remained silent for most of the session, Mr. and Mrs. Thomas praised her participation. They both hugged her as the session ended and expressed their belief that she would continue to behave in safe and healthy ways. Lydia jumped down from Mrs. Thomas's lap and walked toward the door. Mr. Thomas stood up, looked at the clinician, and said, "That was great. I'll be honest, I thought it was going to be a train wreck." Mrs. Thomas smiled, let out a deep breath, and nodded her head in agreement.

Maria C., 8 Years Old, Self-Stimulating at School

Session 1

In the session prior to beginning Phase 2, the clinician deferred a conversation regarding Ms. Cortez's discovery of Maria self-stimulating in private. The mother entered this session noticeably uncomfortable and the clinician opened the discussion by reminding Ms. Cortez, "When you were here last week, you had some concerns about behavior you witnessed Maria performing in her room. I was hoping we could discuss that." The mother's discomfort became more pronounced and she shook her head as if unsure of what to say. After fumbling over her words, she managed to explain that she found the behavior gross and immoral. The clinician empathized and normalized Ms. Cortez's statement, assuring her that many other caregivers hold the same views. This provided the clinician an opening to orient Ms. Cortez to the phase and the purpose of the current session. In particular, the clinician emphasized that this phase provided Ms. Cortez the opportunity to teach her values to Maria and to help her daughter better understand the topic. Ms. Cortez appeared somewhat relieved and asked, "But what if I don't agree with what you think she should know?" The clinician responded, "We're here to teach Maria your beliefs, not mine. So, I would like to spend today learning about your beliefs."

Ms. Cortez, seemingly more at ease, relayed that she was a Christian, and her religious beliefs informed her views on sexual morality. The clinician reflected her statement and then asked the mother to specify what those views were in greater detail, so as to make them clear for the clinician and Maria. Ms. Cortez stumbled and was unsure how to respond: "I don't understand. I'm Christian. I believe what the Bible says about sex. That's what she [Maria] needs to know." The clinician again reflected and normalized the mother's comment, "You want to teach her the biblical view of sexual behavior. We hear that a lot, but people still tend to have different views of what the Bible says on this topic. So, I'm just curious about your view."

Ms. Cortez continued to struggle with clearly stating her beliefs on sexuality, leading the clinician to ask a more direct question: "When is it acceptable, do you believe, to have a sexual relationship with someone?" Ms. Cortez quickly exclaimed, "When you're married!" The clinician reflected this statement, wrote it down, and clarified for Ms. Cortez that this is the level of specification requested. The mother understood, but continued to struggle, leading the clinician to ask more direct questions. Ms. Cortez brought the conversation back to the topic of self-stimulatory behavior and stressed that she believed this behavior was immoral. The clinician asked if this was also based in her biblical understanding, and Ms. Cortez hesitated. She stated that it was, but said she was not certain whether it was in the Bible or not. Rather, she discussed that her 8-year-old daughter was too young to be "pleasuring herself." Again, the clinician reflected her statement but pointed out that Ms. Cortez's answer emphasized the age of her child, which led to the question of whether the behavior is more acceptable at an older age. Ms. Cortez appeared deep in thought and stated that she did not know how to answer the question.

The mother's inability to clearly define beliefs regarding sexual behavior and, instead, relying on a poorly specified religious explanation continued to complicate the construction of a healthy sexuality concept. However, the clinician was able to create flexibility within Ms. Cortez's perceptions by encouraging the mother to shift her focus from identifying what was inappropriate for an 8-year-old to when certain behaviors and knowledge were appropriate. For example, consider the following conversation:

CLINICIAN: When do you believe children should know where babies come from?

MS. CORTEZ: Not when they're 8. They don't need to know that.

CLINICIAN: I understand you think 8 years is too young for that information. When do you think they should know that information?

MS. CORTEZ: Maybe when they're 16. It can wait until then.

CLINICIAN: When she's 16. Okay, so that's roughly 10th grade, sophomore year. Do you think teenagers, attending school, won't know about reproduction until they're in their second year of high school?

MS. CORTEZ: Well, uh, no. I mean . . . I guess they learn it before that. So, I guess, maybe 13 years.

By the end of the session, the clinician was only able to write down a few aspects of Ms. Cortez's concept of healthy sexuality, as much of the time was spent with Ms. Cortez displaying significant uncertainty about her beliefs. Although she began the session with a default response that her beliefs regarding sexuality were encapsulated by a religious system, it became clear that she had given relatively little thought to her beliefs on this topic. Nonetheless, the clinician normalized the mother's answers, empathized with her concerns, and created significant flexibility in her perceptions. Several times Ms. Cortez asked a question of the clinician regarding what was developmentally typical, providing a guidepost for selecting psychoeducational materials to use in the next session.

Session 2

Prior to the second session, the clinician identified several fact sheets that described typical sexual development of children, including when knowledge of reproduction and self-exploration commonly emerges. The clinician also anticipated that Ms. Cortez might object to books for children that show drawings of genitalia and took care to select materials with fewer pictures depicting private areas. The goal of the second session was to help Ms. Cortez better understand her child's behaviors and clarify her thoughts and perceptions regarding the values she wanted to teach her daughter.

When the clinician presented the handouts to the mother, her look was one of engagement and hesitation. She asked questions and seemed willing to discuss the material but continued to question the appropriateness of the material for an 8-year-old child. The clinician quickly reframed Ms. Cortez's comments by stressing that the material made no conclusions about what was appropriate or inappropriate but rather emphasized that data suggested the types of behaviors described are common and, thus, not "problematic." Ms. Cortez understood the distinction but still appeared uncomfortable and repeatedly asked why children would display such behaviors. The clinician decided to more directly place the discussed behaviors into developmental context. In relation to asking questions about reproduction, the clinician noted that "Children know that eyes allow them to see, ears allow them to hear, and legs help them to walk. So, it seems only natural that they would wonder what job a vagina serves." This explanation resonated with Ms. Cortez as she responded, "Yeah, I guess that's never talked about." The clinician quickly agreed and followed up the comment by discussing how children commonly explore different parts of their body: "In the same way, children stick their fingers in their ears or nose, look into a mirror to look at their eye, etc. They are exploring their body. So, it's not uncommon that children also might touch their vagina to see how it works. This can lead to various feelings that they don't understand." Ms. Cortez again agreed and acknowledged that children may display interest in private areas as a course of typical development.

Having gained some appreciation for the sexual development of children, Ms. Cortez asked, "So, how can we make her stop touching herself?" The clinician suggested that the only way to guarantee that such behavior does not occur is to continuously monitor her, but that seems unreasonable, as it is certainly common for an 8-year-old to be left alone at times (e.g., using the restroom, at bedtime). The mother agreed, but asked about implementing consequences in response to observing the behavior. The clinician redirected the conversation back to the safety rules established in previous sessions. The developed rule stated that Maria is not allowed to touch her private areas around other people. If she adheres to this rule, then the behavior should not appear in her mother's presence, and, thus, the mother would not be able to implement consequences for her breaking the rule. Similarly, trying to catch her self-stimulating when she is alone creates a situation where the mother is attempting to observe her child engaged in a form of sexualized behavior, which carries a number of concerning implications. The clinician suggested the best course of action was to make this a point of discussion during the conjoint session. Ms. Cortez agreed.

However, Ms. Cortez agreeing to discuss the issue of self-stimulation with Maria created an additional concern. The mother's perspective was that Maria should not engage in such behavior because it is immoral. As such, a significant potential existed for shaming the girl or otherwise inducing negative emotions, especially if she found herself having difficulty refraining from such behavior. The clinician discussed this issue with Ms. Cortez, who acknowledged the concern but also felt it was important to teach Maria that such behavior is not acceptable. The clinician reframed Ms. Cortez's concerns as being in the best interests of her daughter, in a desire to see her healthy and developing into an upstanding individual. Ms. Cortez smiled and nodded in agreement. The clinician suggested using that as the message and discussing how to treat her private areas in ways that are positive and promote health. Teaching Maria the purpose of a vagina (i.e., reproduction) allows for explaining the difference between "healthy" and "unhealthy" touches without criticizing the girl for self-stimulatory behavior. The mother agreed to this approach.

The clinician then presented Ms. Cortez with the child-focused psychoeducation materials. The mother was surprised to see such books were available for children and curiously flipped through the pages. On several occasions her eyes grew large and she asked the clinician, "You say this to children?" The clinician typically nodded in agreement and mentioned that such books are used with preschool children. The mother was surprised to hear that, but admitted that perhaps her daughter was capable of hearing such things. The clinician then summarized the Should Know and Should Not Know lists being developed through the conversations of the past two sessions and helped Ms. Cortez reference those elements within the two psychoeducational books she was considering. Ultimately, the mother decided which book she preferred and identified two elements within that book she did not want to teach to Maria (i.e., the physical act of intercourse, an element of interpersonal relationships). The clinician then discussed with Ms. Cortez the points in the book at which she could insert the values she wanted to teach Maria (e.g., having a baby is only permissible after marriage).

The clinician ended the session by role playing with Ms. Cortez the conjoint session with Maria, including inserting different questions that Maria might ask. Ms. Cortez frequently looked surprised and unsure how to answer the difficult questions. The clinician reassured Ms. Cortez that help can be provided if needed, and the two agreed on a signal: Ms. Cortez would look at the clinician and repeat Maria's question. The clinician encouraged the mother to give some thought to how she would respond if Maria asked questions about certain aspects that Ms. Cortez intended not to discuss, such as, "How does the sperm get to the egg?" Ms. Cortez agreed to think about an answer to that question.

Session 3

This session was an opportunity for the clinician to talk with Maria to ascertain what she already knew about sex and elicit questions that might be answered by Ms. Cortez. Maria agreed to meet with the clinician and the two played a game together. As before, Maria provided dismissive comments and mentioned several times that attending treatment was "lame." When the clinician asked what Maria knew about private parts, she responded by saying, "None of your business. Why you wanna talk about that with a kid?" The clinician reminded Maria that the focus of treatment was her prior behavior at home and school and this made it relevant whether anyone ever taught her anything about those body parts. Maria remained uncooperative, and the conversation was unable to identify any of her thoughts or experiences related to sexual behavior. They finished playing the game and the clinician returned Maria to the waiting room.

Ms. Cortez joined session and the clinician reviewed the rather unproductive conversation with Maria, which did not surprise the mother. The clinician used the remaining time in session to prepare Ms. Cortez for the upcoming conjoint session. This included reading the selected book one more time with the inclusions and exclusions, role playing potential questions Maria may ask, and reviewing the signal in case Ms. Cortez needed help. The clinician asked the mother whether she crafted an answer in the event Maria asks how the sperm and egg are able to join to create a baby. Ms. Cortez nodded her head and said she would tell Maria, "A mom and dad decide they want to have a baby and then they join their bodies together in a special way that allows the two things to meet." The clinician suggested this opened the possibility of her then asking what the "special way" entailed, and encouraged Ms. Cortez to consider her answer to that question. She declined to further discuss the topic but agreed to think more on how to explain the issue.

Session 4

Ms. Cortez and Maria entered the session together. As the mother took her seat, Maria sat down while letting out a sigh. She appeared displeased to be in session and rolled her eyes when the clinician greeted her. Ms. Cortez was clearly frustrated with Maria's behavior and began trying to correct the child, who was undeterred. The clinician provided an overview of the session and placed the selected psychoeducational book on the table. Maria briefly glanced at it and said, "Oh, we're going to talk about sex stuff. You're both gross." The clinician ignored her comment and requested that Ms. Cortez begin reviewing the book, as planned. Ms. Cortez followed the clinician's lead in ignoring Maria's remark and recited her planned opening statement.

"Maria, I want to make sure you have good information that will help to keep you healthy. So, we are going to review some things. I hope you will ask questions when you have them." Maria immediately shot a stern look at her mother, "Whatever, Mom, you know you don't want to talk about this stuff." Ms. Cortez responded without prompting, "I want to do whatever is necessary to keep you safe and healthy. If that means talking about private areas, then that's what I'll do." Maria sat back in her chair and Ms. Cortez began to read.

The mother's voice trembled at various points and her anxiety with the material was clearly visible. Nonetheless, she did an excellent job with the first portion of the book, which provided sketches of various internal and external body parts. Maria, looking wary, pointed to a part of one picture that Ms. Cortez did not discuss and quickly asked, "What's that thing?" Ms. Cortez calmly responded, "That's called a fallopian tube." Maria's face scrunched up in a confused look and she antagonistically whispered, "Okay." Ms. Cortez then continued with the book. A few pages later, the mother discussed how females hold eggs and they are what the woman contributes to the process of reproduction. The clinician paused Ms. Cortez and pointed out that a fallopian tube was also present in that picture and asked her to describe for Maria its function. Maria sat up and looked at the clinician. After the mother described the job of the fallopian tube, Maria stated, "I didn't think you would actually talk about that." To help Ms. Cortez grasp what had occurred in session, the clinician opined, "Oh, so you were just testing mom to see if she would discuss something?" That comment elicited a response from Ms. Cortez, "I'm happy to answer any questions you have." Maria let out a small smirk.

Ms. Cortez continued reading the book and, as planned, emphasized that reproduction is only to occur within the confines of marriage. Although Maria did not ask about intercourse, the question to which Ms. Cortez previously developed a response, she did ask her mother, "Why is this so hard for you to talk about?" Ms. Cortez looked at the clinician and appeared lost. Although she did not use the phrase that was a previously agreed upon signal for help, the clinician noticed Ms. Cortez struggling and stated, "I think Maria is noticing these are difficult topics for you. They're difficult for a lot of people. How would you describe your feelings on this?" Ms. Cortez continued to look uncertain and said, "These issues weren't talked about when I was a kid. So, I think it just makes it uncomfortable for me." The clinician empathized with Ms. Cortez and asked a follow-up question, "So, who did you talk to when you had questions about these things?" Ms. Cortez understood the hint and used her answer to open a door for Maria: "Nobody. I heard about things from friends, and that wasn't usually very helpful. But that's why we're talking about it now. I want you [looking at Maria] to feel comfortable coming to me with questions. It might make me nervous, but that's because I want to help you and not mess it up." Maria nodded her head and leaned back in her chair.

Ms. Cortez continued reviewing the book, including a section where she urged Maria to treat her private areas delicately, stating that touching one's own private parts in a way other than intended can lead to infections and injuries. She paused and looked at Maria, asking whether the girl understood or had questions. Maria did not respond. Ms. Cortez finished reading the book and then praised her daughter for her attention and participation. The clinician made a point of similarly praising the mother for her ability to discuss the material. Ms. Cortez asked to speak with the clinician alone for a few minutes to address a few questions. Once Maria left the room, Ms. Cortez asked, "Did I really do okay?" The clinician smiled and responded, "You really did an excellent job." Ms. Cortez appeared relieved and conceded, "That wasn't as bad as I thought it would be." The clinician relayed that many caregivers share her perspective and urged her to remember that this is the beginning of the conversation and future discussions were encouraged.

Alex J., 10 Years Old, Coercing a Sibling

Session 1

Mr. James arrived to session appearing both hesitant and eager. The clinician labeled and normalized the apparent feelings: "You look a little unsure, dad. That's pretty common at this point, but you're welcome to say whatever you might be thinking." Mr. James replied, "I know we need to do this; I just don't like it. It doesn't seem right." The clinician empathized with his response and reassured him they were going to proceed in a way that both provided Alex the information he needed and respected the family's values. The father nodded his head but remained relatively quiet and avoided eye contact.

The clinician decided to start off the conversation with a broad question: "Let's just start by talking about your family's values when it comes to sexual behavior. How would you describe those values?" Mr. James shook his head, with his eyes looking around the room. After a few seconds, he simply replied, "I don't know." Given the significant anxiety Mr. James displayed in previous sessions, the clinician assumed that a significant amount of reassurance and support would be necessary. Reflective and empathic statements were used to normalize for Mr. James the fact that many parents have not given much thought to their family's views on sex, which can compound the uncertainty and frustration they feel when a child has PSB.

The clinician then attempted to provide a more specific question that might be easier to answer, "When is sexual contact allowed?" Again, Mr. James was unsure. He vacillated widely in his beliefs, originally suggesting that sexual behavior should be confined to marriage and then quickly changing his mind to a belief that a person need only be a responsible adult. The clinician noted that it seemed Mr. James was searching for an answer and none of his propositions sat well with him. The father agreed with the clinician's statement, which prompted the clinician to try a new approach. Instead of anchoring sexual behavior to a certain time or event, the clinician asked Mr. James to consider the conditions under which he would view sexual behavior as "unhealthy." This simple question resulted in Mr. James rapidly identifying several aspects, including being a child, coercing the other person, and not using a condom. The clinician then rephrased these comments by using their opposite, summarizing that Mr. James viewed "healthy" sexual behavior as occurring among adults, when consensual, and using protection to prevent pregnancy and the spread of sexually transmitted infections (STIs). Mr. James thought for a moment before responding, "Yes, I think that's it." The clinician used this feedback to begin drafting the Should Know and Should Not Know lists.

Building off of this initial discussion, the clinician reminded Mr. James of something he said in the first session of treatment, that Alex engaged his sister in oral sex because "it probably felt good." The father again restated his belief that this was probably one of the reasons behind the behavior. The clinician asked Mr. James what he believed Alex should learn about how this sensation relates to sexual behavior. The father's eyes grew wide and he stumbled to find his words, eventually saying, "I don't know. Do we need to say anything about it? I guess maybe we do, right?" The clinician noted that Alex probably has learned that stimulation to the genitals creates a pleasurable sensation but that he most likely has not assigned meaning to that feeling. This was an opportunity for Mr. James to frame Alex's interpretation of sexual arousal and teach him how to respond to that sensation. Through some discussion, Mr. James decided to integrate into his list of Should Know topics that genitals respond to touch, and this is how they prepare for reproduction (the function of genitals for reproductive purposes also was added to this list).

Before ending the session, Mr. James expressed concern about how his son would respond to this kind of discussion. He was particularly concerned about whether he would shut down, as occurred in an earlier session. The clinician pointed out that Alex was very engaged in discussions during the prior two sessions and the chances were high that he would engage again. This prompted Mr. James to ask what happens if Alex asks too many questions. The clinician responded that, if a child asks a question, it is generally best practice to provide a developmentally appropriate answer. Responses such as "You don't need to worry about that" or "I'll tell you when you're older" are generally discouraged. These types of answers send the message that the caregiver is not comfortable talking about sexual topics and may close, rather than open, the line of communication. Also, if a child asks a question and does not receive a sufficient answer, they might seek the answer elsewhere (e.g., peers, internet), in which case the caregiver has lost control of the message. The clinician conceded that it is not possible to prepare for every conceivable question a child might ask, but the next session would discuss more about responding to surprising questions.

Session 2

The clinician entered session with two handouts on typical sexual development of preadolescent- and adolescent-aged youth. The clinician reviewed these with Mr. James, highlighting that it is common at these ages that sexual interests become more pronounced. Mr. James listened quietly and occasionally remarked that he remembered experiencing some of these changes when he was Alex's age. Then, revisiting a comment he made in an earlier session, he mentioned that he never performed such behaviors on a sibling and still did not understand why Alex initiated this behavior with his sister. The clinician acknowledged that Alex's behavior was concerning but used this as an opportunity to stress the importance of teaching him healthy information.

Remembering that Alex's behavior included bribing his sister with money and agreeing to play games with her in return for performing sexual behavior, the father's comment referencing the PSB provided an opportunity to emphasize the importance of discussing consent with Alex. Mr. James agreed and expressed concern that such coercion may portend repeated incidents. The clinician assured Mr. James that many children are open to learning about consent, considering the impact their behavior had on other children, and changing behavior. Again, the clinician emphasized that Alex displayed significant remorse for his actions and, in all likelihood, did not intend to harm his sister. For Alex, it was not a scary or negative experience but, rather, one of curiosity, and it is likely he did not adequately consider his sister's perspective. As such, helping Alex better understand the autonomy of other individuals and the importance of consent might be effective at preventing such recurrences. This reframing of the child's behavior from one of willful perpetration of sexual abuse to one that considered developmental concepts of curiosity and lack of perspective taking helped Mr. James see his son's behavior in a different light. The topic of consent was added to the Should Know list.

The clinician reviewed the concept of healthy sexuality with Mr. James, including both the Should Know and Should Not Know lists. Mr. James approved of the concept and the clinician presented various materials that might be used to teach Alex the different pieces of information on the Should Know list. Mr. James selected a psychoeducational book designed for preteens. The book provided details on anatomy, physiological changes that occur during that stage of development, and the growth of interest in sexual topics. However, the book did not include the topics of sexual arousal, oral sex, or consent, all of which were designated on the list for inclusion in the upcoming conjoint session. The clinician worked with Mr. James to develop a script for reviewing these topics at designated points within the book.

After the plan was sufficiently defined, the clinician discussed Mr. James's concern from the previous session that Alex might ask questions that are difficult to answer. The goal in responding to such questions is honesty and reliance on the values the parent wishes to teach. Mr. James was presented with a hypothetical situation where Alex asked whether Mr. James and his wife engage in sexual behavior. After the clinician finished asking the question, the father's face dropped and he muttered, "That's an inappropriate question." The clinician agreed that many parents share Mr. James's sentiment. However, in this context, the discussion involves teaching the child about reproduction and Alex may merely be putting the pieces together to arrive at the conclusion that his parents engaged in sexual intercourse that resulted in his conception. Mr. James understood and noted, "Yeah, I guess that makes sense. How else would he be here?" Answering this question in a truthful manner would merely acknowledge Alex's thought process and validate his understanding of the topic. However, if Alex persists or asks whether such sexual behavior occurs in the present time, it can be helpful to reiterate the values the family wishes to teach. For instance, it was suggested that Mr. James respond, "Your mother and I are consenting adults and we are free to engage in sexual behavior if we choose." This is an honest answer that reinforces the family's values (i.e., consenting adults) and allows the parent to deflect answering questions about their own sex life. Continued persistence by the child on this topic may present the opportunity to teach about privacy and that sexual behaviors of other individuals is not generally a suitable topic for discussion.

Before ending the session, Mr. James and the clinician role played the conjoint session by having the clinician play the role of Alex. Mr. James effectively presented the material, including pausing at points in the book to insert the additional pieces of information. The clinician provided some pushback on particular aspects, including asking Mr. James questions like "Why do people have oral sex?" and "Does sex always result in a baby?" The father handled these questions exceptionally well, turning to the previously discussed information. For instance, when asked why people might engage in oral sex, Mr. James reverted to the discussion of the physiological sensation that occurs during sexual behavior and that oral sex can create a similar sensation. He quickly clarified that even oral sex is restricted to the confines of the values being taught about sexual behavior in general. The clinician ended the session by defining a signal that Mr. James could give the clinician in the event he needed help.

Session 3

The session began with Alex and the clinician discussing the past several weeks. Alex acknowledged that it is difficult to discuss the PSB because of the negative feelings he has toward it and his affect was generally sad. The clinician acknowledged the boy's emotions and reframed them as signs that he regretted what happened, a statement with which Alex agreed. This allowed the clinician to present the following session as an opportunity to learn and grow, which might help him consider more appropriate responses in the future. Alex nodded his head to indicate he understood. The clinician decided to ask a question that might lighten Alex's mood: "You know, when I was in fifth grade, people would make jokes about private parts all the time, but we had a bunch of funny names for private parts. I'll bet that's still the case. What funny names do they use these days?" Alex looked at the clinician and smirked but did not speak. "It's okay, you can say it. You won't get in trouble. I'm curious." Alex continued to grin and said, "The worm." The clinician smiled and admitted having not heard that term before. Alex then provided a few other terms and the clinician engaged in simple banter with each one.

Noticing that Alex appeared more relaxed, the clinician asked him what kids at school say about sex. Alex quickly answered, "I don't know." The clinician reflected this statement and then said, "But I know you've heard that word before. I'm just wondering what you think it means." Alex then placed both of his hands together, interlocked his fingers, and started clapping the palms of his hands together. The clinician asked Alex to describe what was happening with this hand gesture. He clarified that sex involves two people taking off their clothes and performing the motion displayed with his hands. The clinician feigned confusion: "I don't understand. Two people take off their clothes and then slap their hands together?" This elicited a laugh from Alex before he stated, "No. You know, they do it." The clinician again provided a look of uncertainty and calmly asked, "Do what?" Alex responded with "Sex," before realizing he had talked himself into a circle. Upon further questioning, Alex was unable to say what exactly sex involved other than knowing it involves a penis and a vagina. Preferring the psychoeducation come from Mr. James, the clinician did not provide information on the topic.

The clinician then transitioned to discuss the phrase that Alex heard children say at school, "Suck it." Alex stated that he knew it referred to having a person place their mouth on the genitals of another person, but he could not answer the question as to why someone would do that. Within the conversation, he admitted that the behavior with his sister was largely the result of wanting to understand why such behavior was a topic at school. Alex became emotional at this point and the clinician thanked him for discussing these topics and acknowledged it can be difficult. After a few moments, the clinician recentered the discussion by clarifying that the next session was designed to make sure Alex gets good, honest answers to his questions from his father, and this was an opportunity to ask anything he is wondering about related to private areas or sexual behavior. Alex looked uncertain for a moment and then asked, "I can ask anything?" The clinician nodded and restated that any question was acceptable. Alex then quietly said, "There's a boy at school who keeps telling other kids they like things in a back door. I think that has something to do with private parts. Do you know what that means?" The clinician thanked Alex for asking the question and said he would make sure his father answered that question in the next session.

After Alex left the room and Mr. James joined session, the clinician reviewed that the boy appeared to have a significant level of misunderstanding about sex. The clinician conceptualized it for the father as Alex knowing a number of different sexual words but not necessarily how those words are related. Mr. James was surprised to hear that Alex's understanding of sex involved a penis and vagina and some sort of physical motion, as he assumed Alex's understanding was more limited. The clinician also noted that Alex's curiosity around oral sex was the result of hearing these words at school but not understanding why the behavior received so much attention. Mr. James engaged readily in this conversation and asked appropriate questions about how to best present information to Alex.

Using the discussion of hearing things at school as a preface, the clinician then informed Mr. James that Alex heard a boy at school reference behaviors involving the "back door" and seemed to know it had a sexual connotation. Mr. James was shocked and immediately suggested he should contact the school to report the boy. The clinician empathized with the anger while also noting that children hear many things at school, and sexual comments tend to increase in the middle school years. Mr. James collected himself and asked, "Well, we're not going to discuss that, right?" The father referenced the fact that anal sex was one of the items on the Should Not Know list. The clinician reiterated that Alex may seek the answer somewhere else and this was a similar situation to what led to the PSB: Alex heard something at school, had a vague sense of what it meant, and then engaged his sister in the behavior. Mr. James sighed heavily and said, "We need to talk about it, don't we?" The clinician agreed but said it would be best to place it into context. For instance, the plan as previously designed called for discussing the pleasurable sensation that can accompany genital stimulation. This background provided the context for discussing oral sex and, in a similar manner, anal sex can be included in that discussion. In this way, Alex's question can be answered without making the topic of oral or anal sex a prolonged conversation. Mr. James liked this plan and agreed to integrate an answer to this question into his review during the conjoint session.

Session 4

Mr. James and Alex walked into the treatment room both looking hesitant and nervous. The clinician thanked them both for coming and pointed out the beginning of this session usually is uncomfortable for people. Nonetheless, it is often helpful to have this session and it is common for people to feel more comfortable as the session progresses. It was reiterated that Alex would not be in trouble for asking questions or saying sexual words, and Mr. James verbally concurred with this statement, as previously planned. Alex nodded his head to indicate that he understood, and Mr. James opened the psychoeducational book to begin the discussion.

Mr. James read the material in a relatively slow manner and his voice quivered at moments, indicating his anxiety. The clinician paused the father after the first few pages to praise him and point out that Alex seemed engaged throughout. This was the first moment Mr. James had looked up to see his son's reaction, which was fairly emotionless as he was listening intently. Mr. James quietly asked whether his son had any questions so far, which he did not. Mr. James then continued for a few more pages before arriving at the first point for providing supplemental information. He paused, as planned, and told Alex, "When the penis is rubbed or sometimes just touched a lot, it becomes hard. This usually feels good to a guy." Alex nodded his head and said, "Why does it do that [become hard]?" Mr. James's eyebrows raised, as if surprised by his son's willingness to discuss the issue. Given a slight pause in the father's response, the clinician suggested this might be a question best answered on the next page of the book. Mr. James immediately understood the suggestion and responded, "Oh, yeah."

The next page of the book described the act of intercourse, ending with a review of sperm, eggs, and the process of conception. Alex shook his head and blurted out, "Wait, stop. Girls have eggs?! Like chickens?" Mr. James smiled and replied, "Yes, sort of the same thing. They don't lay them though. They're stored inside their belly. An egg is their part of making a baby." The clinician then prompted Mr. James to return to the previous question, "Dad, maybe this is a good time to answer Alex's question about erections." Mr. James, without hesitation, explained to his son that the penis must be sufficiently hard so that it can enter the vagina and allow the sperm to get to the egg. He then defined for his son that the penis becoming hard is called an "erection." Alex smiled and said, "That's so weird."

This point in the book also marked the next designated stopping point to allow the father the opportunity to teach Alex the conditions under which the family finds sexual behavior acceptable. Mr. James effectively reviewed the boundaries of sexual behavior and Alex had no questions. The issue of consent was emphasized by the father in accordance with the previously designed plan, which included examples of what qualifies as consent and what does not. During this discussion, Mr. James included paying someone or playing with them in exchange for sexual acts as implying the person did not want to perform the behaviors and, thus, the behavior was not consensual. Alex understood his father's allusion to the PSB. The boy put his head down and he said, "I know, Dad. I'm really sorry. I didn't know. How do I make it up to her?" Mr. James was taken aback at his son's response and request for making amends. Mr. James rubbed his son's back again and said they could figure out some way to apologize.

Sensing the mood in the room was both sad and hopeful, the clinician took the lead in transitioning to the next topic. "You know, dad, there were a few other things we were going to discuss. Earlier, you talked about when the penis is rubbed or touched that it can create a pleasurable sensation." Mr. James understood the hint and quickly transitioned back into the psychoeducation, now appearing more at ease. He started, "Oh yeah, that's right. When the penis is touched, it can feel really good. That's what makes some people want to do sexual things. And that's not a bad thing, necessarily, because it can result in babies. If sex hurt, there would be no babies." Alex then asked a question, "Does it feel good for girls, too, because it seems like it would hurt?" This was not a question previously discussed with Mr. James, but he responded effectively, "It does hurt for girls sometimes, especially if they've never had sex before. But it can feel good for them, too." Almost as if fearing he made sex sound too positive, Mr. James quickly added, "But you can get diseases from sex and end up with babies; that's why we have those rules we talked about." This led to a brief conversation with Alex, who asked more about the diseases and whether babies always resulted from sex.

Given that time was running low in the session, the clinician prompted the father again to answer the question Alex raised in the previous session: "So, remember, dad, there were a few other things you wanted to discuss around it feeling good when the penis is rubbed." Mr. James again perked up, "Oh yeah. Sometimes, when people want to do sexual things, they do something else with the penis to create that feeling, like put it in someone's mouth or put it in someone's rectum," (note: "rectum" was previously defined with the anatomical names of body parts). Alex's eyebrows raised and his mouth dropped open as he exclaimed, "What!? They put a penis in someone's butt?" Mr. James then continued, "Yes, and people sometimes refer to the butt as the back door." With that comment, Alex slowly nodded his head and let out a long "Oh" sound as he connected it to the comment overheard at school. Mr. James hurriedly commented that even these types of behaviors are subject to the rules established previously. Alex asked one final question, "Do a lot of people do the mouth and butt stuff?" Mr. James thought for a second, but did not initiate the signal that would elicit the clinician's help. He then replied, using a previously discussed response, "Well, when people are consenting adults, they can choose to do whatever they want." Alex quickly retorted, "Well, I'm never doing those things." Sensing one last opportunity to reinforce the concept of consent, Mr. James commented, "And that's your right. If you don't consent, then no one can make you."

The clinician escorted the dyad out of session. As Alex entered the restroom, Mr. James turned to the clinician and said, "Wow, that went a lot better than I thought it would." The clinician smiled and told the father that people say that sometimes; their fear of what will happen is almost always worse than what actually unfolds. The clinician reminded the father to view this session as the beginning of the conversation and not the entirety of the conversation. Mr. James agreed to maintain an open line of communication and to occasionally ask Alex if he has heard any new terms at school. As Alex exited the restroom, the clinician praised the father one more time for his efforts and congratulated him on his success.

SUMMARY

This second phase of PBT involves teaching the caregiver and child psychoeducation regarding sexual topics. This activity allows the caregiver to better understand the child's behaviors and respond appropriately not just at the time of treatment but also for the years to come. Providing psychoeducation to the child counters faulty or unhelpful information learned from previous social learning experiences. The process used during this phase is designed to provide an ongoing developmental impact as the caregiver improves their skills in discussing sexual topics and develops confidence in this ability, while the child learns that discussing these topics with the caregiver is allowed both now and in the future.

6 PHASE 3

Skill Development

A number of child-focused and caregiver-focused skills are relevant to the treatment of childhood problematic sexual behavior (PSB). In particular, empirical evidence suggests that child-focused impulse control skills may be beneficial for some children. Similarly, there is evidence that children with PSB may develop unhealthy cognitions related to sexuality and might benefit from cognitive change techniques. As with any intervention designed for children, it is useful for caregivers to learn these same skills and to encourage their use in the home. There are also noted concerns that children with PSB may be at increased risk for later sexual victimization as a result of their behaviors or interests. It is good practice to review basic safety skills with children and caregivers before completing treatment. These applied skills are the focus of Phase 3. A session-by-session summary of the techniques used in this phase is provided in Table 6.1.

---

https://doi.org/10.1037/0000516-007
Children With Problematic Sexual Behavior: Theory, Research, and Evidence-Based Practice, by B. Allen

TABLE 6.1. Techniques of Phase 3, by Session

Session	Participants	Techniques
1	Child	a. Orient child to the purpose of Phase 3, its activities, and structure
	Child	b. Teach awareness of physiological bodily cues
	Child	c. Teach impulse control skills
	Caregiver & Child	d. Review the skills taught to the child and encourage their use at home
2	Child	a. Explain the relationships of thoughts, feelings, and behaviors
	Child	b. Teach cognitive coping skills and modify unhelpful thoughts
	Caregiver & Child	c. Review the skills taught to the child and encourage their use at home
3	Caregiver	a. Teach the caregiver safety skills that might be implemented
	Caregiver	b. Discuss how to teach safety skills to the child
	Caregiver & Child	c. Facilitate a conversation where the caregiver teaches the skills to the child
4	Child	a. Identify peer influences and preferred qualities of friends
	Caregiver	b. Review how to monitor peer groups and encourage interaction with positive influences
	Caregiver	c. Evaluate treatment outcome and refer for additional services, as needed

SESSION 1

The first session of this last phase is focused on teaching the child impulse control skills. For younger children, it may be advantageous for the caregivers to be present throughout the session to ensure comprehension of the material. For older children, caregivers typically join later in session.

Objective

Teaching the child impulse control skills in this session is a multistep process. First, the clinician helps the child understand bodily sensations and arousal, attempting to tie these physiological states to the display of PSB, if possible. Next, the clinician uses this awareness to teach the child to inhibit impulsive behaviors. Finally, the information learned by the child is shared with the caregiver if they were not already in session.

Techniques

Orienting the Child to Phase 3

This phase represents a departure from the first two phases that centered heavily on caregiver-focused techniques and rarely involved the clinician meeting alone with the child. It is often beneficial to introduce this change in structure to the child. This discussion is commonly brief and emphasizes shifting the focus of sessions more to teaching the child various skills they can use. As a result, the clinician intends to meet more frequently with the child to work on the development of these skills. This simple discussion typically leads naturally into the next technique, which begins the process of skill development.

Fostering Bodily Awareness

It is not uncommon for children with PSB to describe their behavior occurring in a seemingly involuntary manner. This may be the result of impulsive behavior that is difficult to control or because the behavior is habitually used as a coping skill during times of sadness or boredom. Indeed, children often describe their behavior as beginning with some form of internal process, which they poorly understand and do not know how to control. Helping children learn their own physiological cues is the first step in reducing this type of impulsive or reflexive behavior.

Children are asked to describe any sensations they experience in their body that tells them to perform the PSB. This is sometimes a difficult task, especially for younger children, and it is suggested that concrete examples be provided to demonstrate the concept. One useful example is to ask the child how they know when it is time to use a restroom, as this is typically easily answered. Regardless of how the child responds, the clinician can rephrase to emphasize that this example describes a biologically based signal (e.g., drive, urge, impulse) that tells the child to perform a certain behavior (e.g., urinate). The analogy can then be made to the PSB; in a similar manner, there is often a biologically based signal that encourages or prompts the child to perform the sexual behavior. Another example involves an in vivo demonstration of this principle. Using a modified version of the cold pressor task, the clinician can place ice cubes in the child's hand and ask the child to describe their sensations, such as the coldness or the feeling of water that begins running down their hand. This then leads to the natural conclusion that the child is prompted by this signal to drop the ice cubes, which will effectively relieve the unpleasant feeling. Several other such exercises are available in the literature and may be applicable (see Clinical Tip 6.1). Once the child understands the basic idea of a biological drive or impulse, the

CLINICAL TIP 6.1. Conceptualizing Mindfulness in PBT

Many clinicians favor and are trained to use a variety of mindfulness-based techniques, and the description provided here for teaching the child about the body's cues may be interpreted as encouraging the use of mindfulness techniques. Indeed, mindfulness techniques may be helpful for many children. However, there are a few issues to consider when selecting exercises. First, mindfulness approaches are often conceptualized from an "emotional awareness" perspective where the body's cues are associated with specific emotions and regulating physiology is viewed as a key to improving emotional states. However, while there are some instances when a child's sexual behavior serves as an emotion regulation strategy, far more common is the child who describes an urge or impulse that originates separate from any emotional state. Within PBT, it is best to think of impulse control as a behavior regulation technique, and not as a form of emotion regulation. Second, the ideas used to teach impulse control in PBT reflect this conceptualization and closely link bodily awareness with the child's ability to inhibit a response. For example, the cold pressor task suggestion yields an unpleasant physiological experience (i.e., coldness, water), which leads to a clear physiological drive (i.e., drop the ice cubes), which then can be used to demonstrate the child's ability to control that impulse (i.e., not to drop the ice cubes). Mindfulness exercises that do not demonstrate this complete sequence of behavioral control are not indicated at this point in treatment.

question can be restated to ascertain whether the child can identify specific sensations in their body that may lead to the PSB. Some children are quite adept at this exercise while others struggle; some children are never able to identify a bodily sensation connected to the PSB.

After discussing the concept of bodily sensations, it is important to emphasize for the child that these impulses or urges can be controlled. Returning to the example of needing to use the restroom, the child can be asked to describe a suitable solution to the bodily discomfort. Of course, most children respond that they need to tolerate the unpleasant sensation, or "hold it," until finding a restroom. However, this demonstrates that the child can and often does control an unpleasant bodily urge until finding the appropriate time and place to perform a behavior to relieve that sensation. Similarly, with the modified cold pressor task, the clinician can have the child drop the ice cubes into a bathroom sink instead of on the treatment room's floor, demonstrating the child's ability to control their behavior in response to a negative physiological state. Again, this analogy can be applied to the child's PSB. The child is capable of controlling the impulse to perform the behavior and may search for a more appropriate time and place to perform the behavior. For instance, a child who is self-stimulating in front of others may be encouraged to find moments when the behavior is more acceptable, such as when alone in the restroom or bedroom with the door closed. Caution is urged in this situation, however, as family cultural values must be considered and this plan must be discussed with the caregiver beforehand (e.g., during Phase 2 discussions of acceptable behavior; see Chapter 11, Point 10). For some children, there is no acceptable time and place for performing a given behavior (e.g., touching the private areas of other children) and this part of the conversation can be omitted.

Teach the Child Impulse Control Skills

After the child understands the concept of bodily sensations and the ability to control acting on those impulses, it can be validating to recognize that it is often difficult to control the behaviors that follow. This simple acknowledgement is used to engage the child in the development of skills designed to increase their ability to control impulses and, thus, reduce PSB. These skills typically emphasize three elements: initial inhibition of the behavior, calming techniques, and problem solving. There is no shortage of recommendations available in the literature on how to teach these techniques. It is recommended that the clinician spend time attempting to enhance the child's ability to utilize each component with a focus on experiential practice.

One prominent approach to teaching impulse control skills is known as the "turtle technique." The clinician tells the child a story about a turtle that often experiences bodily sensations or thoughts that get him in trouble (scripts, drawings, and other resources for this story can be found online). The turtle learns that, instead of acting on these prompts, he tells himself "STOP" and mentally imagines a stop sign (i.e., thought-stopping techniques) before pulling his head into his shell to calm down. This provides the opportunity to teach the child assorted relaxation skills, such as controlled breathing, positive imagery, and/or progressive muscle relaxation. While in his shell, the turtle thinks of various alternative behaviors that may be performed in the moment, including the consequences of those behaviors (i.e., problem-solving skills). The turtle then selects one of the options, emerges from his shell, and performs the behavior, thus resolving the unpleasant impulse. Caution is warranted, however, as older children may view the analogy of the turtle as condescending. In these cases, the clinician can present the techniques in a more straightforward manner while omitting the story of the turtle. Nonetheless, the techniques should be presented as an integrated behavioral response to an impulse and not as individual response options to try.

A few notes are worth mentioning as it relates to teaching impulse control skills. First, how to effectively teach each of these skills to a specific child is a decision best left to the clinician and should consider the child's age, cognitive sophistication, preexisting skillset, and presenting concerns. Second, each of these individual elements (i.e., initial inhibition, calming, problem solving) may require more or less attention depending on the child's ability to master them. Third, it is critical that the development of these skills be linked to the previous discussion regarding awareness of bodily sensations and related specifically to the child's PSB. By the end of the session, clinicians should walk the child through a complete sequence: onset of bodily sensation that precedes PSB, initial inhibition using a specific skill, implementation of relaxation skills, and an identified problem-solving technique.

Caregiver Participation

After completing these techniques, the caregiver joins the session and the clinician provides a brief overview of the third phase of treatment. This transitions into an introduction to the concept of impulse control. It is preferable for the child to teach the learned information to the caregiver, which both reviews the material for the caregiver and provides the opportunity for the child to rehearse the skills. The clinician can ask whether the caregiver has identified any signs or situations that suggest an increased possibility of PSB. If so, this information can be integrated into the beginning of the sequence demonstrated by the child with the direction that the caregiver prompts the use of the skills in that moment. The session ends with the recommendation that the caregiver practice these skills with the child at home over the coming week.

SESSION 2

While many children with PSB describe their behaviors as occurring as a form of automatic process that occurs outside of conscious awareness, for a minority of children, there may be identifiable and deliberate cognitive processes that predispose them to acting in sexual ways. These may include rumination, faulty assumptions, and curiosity, among others. As with the first session of this phase, the clinician begins by meeting individually with the child, and the caregiver joins later in session, unless there is a reason to implement a conjoint session throughout the time (e.g., age of the child). For preschool-aged children (ages 3–5), the clinician may decide to omit this session from treatment, as the concepts may be too abstract for younger children to comprehend.

Objective

This session is designed to help children identify maladaptive cognitions that may be connected to their PSB and teach effective cognitive coping skills that may aid in preventing the occurrence of problematic behavior.

Techniques

Identify Potential Maladaptive Thought Processes

Teaching children how thoughts impact behavior can be a difficult task and asking them to identify their own thoughts is often even more challenging. A helpful tool, which is used in various clinical interventions with children (e.g., Cohen et al., 2017; Southam-Gerow, 2013), is the concept of the cognitive triangle. The child is shown a triangle with each corner labeled as thoughts, feelings, and behaviors, as shown in Figure 6.1. The clinician then uses practical examples to explain to the child how any one point on the triangle (e.g., thoughts) can influence the other points (e.g., feelings and behaviors). For instance, a child who is pushed from behind while walking in the hallway at school may believe the other person did so intentionally. This is a common automatic thought for children with behavioral problems. The clinician can then ask the child how that thought influenced their feelings (e.g., angry) and the behaviors performed (e.g., punch the other child). A multitude of other such examples may be presented to the child to demonstrate the concept. Another commonly utilized demonstration involves the child not being picked by peers for a game or activity. The automatic thought for children is often that they are disliked by the other children, which leads to them feeling sad and behaving in a rude manner toward the other children or crying.

It is recommended the clinician utilize at least two or three such examples to help the child understand the concept. First, provide the initial event

FIGURE 6.1. The Cognitive Triangle

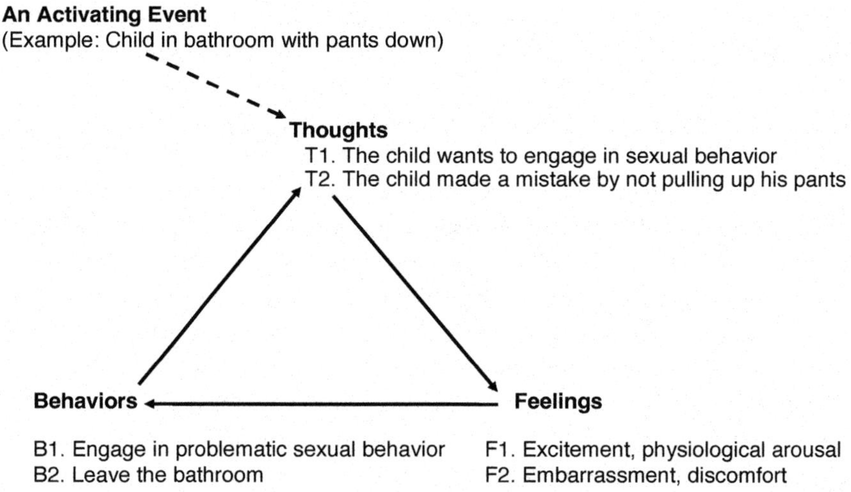

(e.g., pushed in the back, not picked for activity) and, second, ask the child to identify their thoughts as to the reason for the event. Third, ask the child to provide the feelings and behaviors that accompany these thoughts. Note that while it is possible to start at a different point in the triangle (e.g., how behaviors might influence thoughts and feelings), for the purposes of this technique within phase-based treatment for PSB (PBT), the emphasis is placed on using thoughts as the starting point.

After the concept of the cognitive triangle is understood by the child, introduce selected and relevant sexual situations into the examples and ask the child to respond in a similar manner. For a child whose PSB included intrusively touching others, an appropriate situation may involve entering a school restroom and seeing a child turn away from the urinal with their private areas exposed. When asked why the other child may have done this, a common answer involves a belief that the other child is interested in engaging in sexual touching. For a child who previously touched their own private areas while around others, the presented scenario might ask about the automatic thoughts that occur when observing another child scratch their private areas. A child's answers to these more sexually based scenarios provide clues into the thought processes that may be underlying the PSB. They also serve as the basis for helping the child monitor and modify maladaptive cognitions, which is the focus of the next technique.

Modifying Maladaptive Thoughts

After the child clearly understands the concept of the cognitive triangle, the clinician can encourage the child to consider potential alternative thoughts that might be possible given the scenarios. For instance, in the scenario of the child being pushed in the back, a child might identify the possibility that the other child tripped and fell as opposed to being the victim of bullying. Similarly, in the scenario where the child is not selected for an activity, some may quickly argue that they were not very good at the activity or did not display an interest. While some children excel at this task and easily identify several possible attributions for the events, others struggle and are unable to provide alternate thoughts. The clinician must be prepared to provide direction to a child who rigidly adheres to the original thought. It may be helpful to reverse the identification of the child in session with the child in the scenario. For example, instead of asking the child what the automatic thought might be when pushed in the back, the clinician may prompt the child to identify if they have ever pushed someone in the back and why this occurred. It is not uncommon that children identify other potential explanations when they are placed in the role of the presumed aggressor.

After demonstrating this process of identifying alternative thoughts, revisit the scenarios that used the sexually based situations and repeat the process. Clinicians must be aware that the explanations a child provides may be multilayered or dismissive. Consider a child who stands in front of a mirror and takes nude pictures of themselves. The child's initial thought may be "It's not a big deal," which leads to no particular negative feeling and a behavior of taking the picture. This thought does not provide any rationale of why the child does not consider the behavior a concern and does not offer sufficient material for changing the thought. At this point in the process, it is important to elicit a more defined attribution or explanation. A useful approach might be to restate the child's answer by following it with the word "because." The exchange below demonstrates a larger conversation with the child taking naked self-pictures:

CLINICIAN: Earlier you said when you get a camera and are looking in the mirror, that you don't really have any thoughts about it at that time. I think you said you don't care. Is that right?

CHILD: Yeah. Who cares? It's not a big deal.

CLINICIAN: Maybe you can help me understand that more. Some people think it's a big deal, but you don't. So, I'm wondering, it's not a big deal to you because . . .?

CHILD: Because everybody does it. I'm not the only kid taking these pics. No one cares but adults.

This type of an answer provides sufficient detail for challenging maladaptive thoughts. This process can be facilitated by identifying faulty assumptions that can be modified. For instance, the child taking self-pictures demonstrates all-or-nothing thinking by stating that "everybody does it." By leading the child through a series of questions and responses, it is likely the case that exceptions will be identified and the conclusion will be reached that relatively few children are engaging in this behavior. Similarly, the child who believes a bully deliberately pushed them from behind may exhibit a hostile attribution bias. Demonstrating that other causes may explain the behavior can undermine this assumption. The child who believed the other child in the restroom at school exposed his private areas because he wanted to engage in sexual touching may be making an arbitrary inference, immediately ascribing his own thought processes to the other child. Considering the possibility that the child was not aware that another child entered the restroom, or the child was impulsive and turned away from the urinal too quickly, can help address this type of faulty assumption. The goal of this process is to demonstrate for the child that automatic cognitive explanations resulting in PSB often are maladaptive, if not incorrect, and in need of revision.

Another approach to creating change in maladaptive cognitions is to have the child weigh the evidence supporting different thoughts. This is most often accomplished by creating a "pros and cons" list or identifying longer-term goals that may be hindered by the behavior. For instance, the child who was taking naked pictures of themselves may be asked to identify long-term goals (e.g., job, dating relationships) and how accomplishing those goals may be affected if someone saw the pictures. Of course, this example works more effectively with older children. For younger children, the outcomes may relate more to social ostracism or school consequences. This process forces the child to consider more helpful thoughts that suggest greater benefit in not performing a given behavior. Additional examples of these types of thought changing activities are discussed in the case examples in this chapter.

Caregiver Participation

Following the implementation of these techniques, have the caregiver join the session and allow the child to teach these cognitive coping skills to the caregiver. This should include having the child demonstrate the structure of the cognitive triangle and the thought changing techniques the clinician implemented. A point of caution is due here, however. Children may sometimes provide rationales that are upsetting to the caregiver, and it may be prudent to not provide the caregiver with these details. For instance, a 12-year-old child once described a mutual sexual relationship with a same-age peer as the result of being "in love" with the other child. However, she also stated that her father previously made comments about wanting to physically harm the other child involved and became extremely angry when the girl stated that she loved him. She displayed understandable anxiety about discussing her thought processes with her father, even though she believed after the session that the sexual contact was not in her best interests. This is a logical request and the clinician looked for an alternative arrangement, gaining the girls' consent to share the contents of the session with the father after the child left the room.

Sometimes the cognitive change techniques may benefit from a longer-term process, such as asking the child to identify pros and cons throughout the course of the week, or identifying situations where the thoughts are most likely to occur. In these types of situations, it is often beneficial for the caregiver to play an active role in prompting the child to record such information throughout the week. This directive can be made during this last part of the session after the child and/or clinician taught the techniques to the caregiver.

SESSION 3

It is generally recognized that the child's display of PSB places them at increased risk for prematurely experiencing sexual situations and sexual abuse. It appears prudent to provide information and develop skills designed to protect the child from these outcomes. This session typically begins with only the caregiver present; the child joins in the middle.

Objective

The goal of this session is improving future developmental trajectory and safety as opposed to eliminating problematic behavior. However, the themes from the previous sessions continue, including fostering an open line of communication between the caregiver and child and encouraging skill development.

Techniques

Teaching Safety Skills to the Caregiver

It is often advantageous to explain to the caregiver the reason for teaching various forms of safety skills to both the caregiver and child, and clinicians can rely on the explanation provided earlier, as well as mention some of the adverse outcomes mentioned in Chapter 1 (e.g., earlier sexual debut, preoccupation with sexual topics, sexual risk taking). Throughout this discussion, the clinician can emphasize the role of the caregiver in helping to prevent negative outcomes and transition into a discussion of how to foster safety for the child. Although the goal of this session is to increase safety, broadly conceived, it is typically most effective to focus on the specific topic of preventing sexual abuse, as this is a commonly accepted outcome that does not transgress cultural values.

A suitable starting point is to ask the caregiver if they have taken any steps in their home or in the child's life designed to reduce the likelihood of sexual abuse. Some caregivers respond with a list of actions they have taken while others are uncertain or respond by stating they have never thought of it before the child's PSB. The clinician can build the discussion around this initial response of the caregiver. An easy first topic is to review who is allowed around the child unsupervised. The point of this simple question is to help the caregiver develop a discriminating process where not all individuals are automatically entrusted with the care of the child. Many caregivers limit their consideration only to those individuals they think might directly abuse the child and, of course, most do not believe close family or acquaintances would perpetrate such behaviors. However, a second consideration is identifying people that might act in sexual ways, encourage inappropriate boundaries, or otherwise teach the child undesired information (e.g., making sexual jokes, accessing inappropriate websites) and limiting their unsupervised access to the child. Caregivers are typically more capable of identifying individuals that might influence the child in this way. Clinicians can help caregivers think through how to limit the child's exposure to these individuals while not negatively impacting personal relationships.

A second point of emphasis for the caregiver is identifying what is told to individuals who do have unsupervised time with the child (e.g., babysitters). Caregivers are encouraged to establish expectations and limitations with such individuals as a common course of practice. For instance, the clinician might encourage the caregiver to foster a home environment where "secrets" are not permitted, in preference to "surprises." The distinction is that secrets are meant to exclude people and the information is designated not to be discovered. However, surprises are commonly considered to be fun and meant for eventual discovery by others. Establishing this perspective in the home allows the caregiver to convey such a practice to individuals who might be alone with the child. After providing an example such as this, many caregivers are able to identify other aspects of the home environment that can be established and/or relayed to individuals who may have unsupervised time with the child.

Next, the clinician shifts the focus to discussing the material that will be taught to the child by asking the caregiver what information the child previously received related to sexual abuse. In our current society, on average, caregivers are more attuned to this topic than in previous decades and is it increasingly common that the child learned something about sexual abuse from caregivers, school assemblies, or elsewhere. However, some caregivers believe, either rightly or wrongly, that no such discussions have occurred with the child. Identifying the child's previous exposure to the topic of sexual abuse prevention can help with crafting the message the caregiver will send to the child later in the session.

After orienting the caregiver to this task, the next step is developing a suitable definition of sexual abuse. This is challenging for some caregivers (and clinicians), as sexual abuse is often thought of in legalistic terms or in an "I know it when I see it" manner. However, for discussing this topic with the child, it is necessary to provide a more concrete definition. An effective approach is to return to the rules developed during Phase 1 that defined limits around sexual behavior. An individual breaking these rules against the child is inherently not behaving in an appropriate manner toward the child, and this behavior can be labeled for the child as "abuse." Additional behaviors can be supplemented as necessary. For instance, if the child's rules primarily defined limits on self-focused behaviors, a few new rules related to interpersonally intrusive behavior might be added to further define sexually abusive behavior.

Once the caregiver agrees on how sexual abuse will be defined for the child, the discussion turns to identifying ways to teach this definition and the prevention skills to the child. Again, the clinician can emphasize the importance of the caregiver providing this information to the child as furthering the goal of keeping the dialogue open regarding sex and sexual behavior. How to teach sexual abuse prevention skills to the child is a decision best left to the clinician, who should take account of the unique characteristics of the child (e.g., age, cognitive sophistication). There are countless ways of teaching these skills to a child, such as reviewing the differences between surprises and secrets and safe and unsafe touches, as well as developing a list of trusted adults who will always listen to the child's concerns, with the caregiver at the top of this list. There are many games, books, and online resources available for this process, and several of them are listed in Appendix A (see also Clinical Tip 6.2). The clinician should come into session having already selected these materials. Before having the child join the session, it is advisable that the clinician and caregiver sufficiently review the designed process and materials to ensure the caregiver feels confident in the task of teaching the information to the child.

CLINICAL TIP 6.2. Selecting Abuse Prevention Skills Materials

As discussed in Chapter 5, it is critically important for the clinician to sufficiently review potential psychoeducation materials before presenting them to the caregiver. Recent years have seen a proliferation of published resources on the topic of childhood sexual behavior and abuse, often embedded within a specific perspective and providing corresponding recommendations for caregivers. On several occasions, clinicians have utilized a book or pamphlet on the recommendation of a colleague, only to realize in session with the caregiver that the material contained several religious references the caregiver found offensive. Situations such as these may undermine therapeutic rapport with the caregiver and cause disruptions to the clinical process. While some materials may be appropriate, or even ideally suited, to a specific family, they may not be as applicable to others. This underlines the importance of clinicians sufficiently vetting and carefully selecting the materials to be used in session, and encourages clinicians to tailor treatment to the unique considerations of a given child and family.

Teaching Safety Skills to the Child

Once the child joins the session, the process unfolds similar to the conjoint session in Phase 2. The clinician remains in a facilitative role and supports the caregiver sharing the information with child, beginning with a brief review of the types of behaviors being considered and defining the behaviors committed by another person as abusive. It is not necessary to use the word "abuse," as some caregivers find it objectionable or believe it unduly frightens the child, particularly in the case of younger children. However, the types of actions being considered must be presented in a serious manner with the child clearly understanding the gravity of the topic.

The materials used are presented to the child to build specific safety skills, including the explicit directive of telling the caregiver or another trusted adult in the event the child is exposed to abusive behaviors. While the teaching of the skills often involves books, games, or other activities, as mentioned earlier, it must be clearly stated that the child will never be in trouble for reporting such concerns to the caregiver. To demonstrate that this is not a burden being placed exclusively on the child, it is appropriate for the caregiver to share the steps they will take to protect the child, including those topics reviewed earlier in session with the clinician (e.g., being selective with who is allowed around the child unsupervised). It is important that the child be given the opportunity to ask questions throughout this discussion. As before, it is not possible to predict the types of questions a child may ask, but the clinician should be ready to interject, if needed, to assist the caregiver. After the conclusion of the conversation, the clinician should encourage the caregiver to begin implementation of the safety plan at home.

SESSION 4

PSB can be related to negative peer influences, as children often learn about sexual topics from peers, whether it be at school, during activities, or in the neighborhood. Caregivers, however, are often unaware of the impact of peers and may be unfamiliar with the child's friend group. This session begins with the clinician meeting alone with the child and the caregiver joins later.

Objective

This session aims to identify the role of the child's peers, improve the caregiver's ability to monitor the child's interactions with peers, and guide the child toward positive friendships.

Techniques

Identify Peer Influences

Beginning the session by discussing the child's preferred activities is often an easy task in which the child readily engages. This also allows the clinician to ascertain the other children engaged in these activities. More straightforward queries, such as "Tell me about your friends" or "Tell me about the kids you like to play with" also may be effective. Once the child's friends are identified, the clinician can turn the conversation toward a more focused examination of those aspects of these friends the child finds appealing. For instance, the clinician might ask what the best thing is about a particular friend or why they are friends. The child's answers to these questions often yield clues as to the type of traits or qualities the child looks for in friends. Common answers typically indicate some form of shared interest (e.g., video games, a sport, an activity), preferred attribute (e.g., friendly, smart, good athlete), or social standing (e.g., the child is popular).

Next, the clinician can explore the impact of the peer group on the child. After identifying why the child is drawn to a particular other child, ask about the last time the two interacted or a favorite memory the child has with that friend. These concrete examples may allow for the identification of social processes exerting an impact on the child. Clinicians should be acutely aware of signs of peer pressure, a need for belonging, or rejection. The child may not present the interactions as suggesting such processes are at work, but it may be obvious nonetheless. It is important to note both positive and negative influences of friends, as children may become defensive if they perceive the discussion is designed to criticize their peer group. Also, identifying positive aspects of peer interactions may provide ideas of how to leverage peer relationships for improving developmental outcomes.

Children frequently are defensive when it comes to discussing their friends, and they may have past experiences of hearing caregivers criticize their peers. Clinicians are encouraged to maintain a neutral stance during this conversation and provide both empathic and supportive comments to the child. Despite a clinician's best efforts, the child may remain quiet. In such situations, it might be helpful to pivot the discussion toward the child's favorite activities and omit any reference to friends or peers. Alternatively, the child's silence may be the result of a lack of friends, in which case the discussion may be oriented toward trying to identify ways of promoting a positive peer group as opposed to defining the influences of a current peer group.

Teach Caregivers to Monitor Peer Groups

After the discussion with the child is complete, allow them to leave the session while the clinician talks with the caregiver. The first task of the clinician in this part of the session is to provide psychoeducation to the caregiver on the influence of peers. This may take many forms and clinicians are free to use handouts or other materials if they so desire, but a simple conversation about the topic with the caregiver is usually sufficient. Many caregivers are well acquainted with this topic while others have given little thought to the child's friends. The clinician can tie this conversation back to previous topics within PBT, such as social learning influences discussed in Phase 1 or countering misinformation within Phase 2. The goal is for the caregiver to understand the need to monitor the child's interactions with peers (to the extent possible) and promote positive friendships.

The clinician should review with the caregiver the results of the conversation with the child, including who the child identified as friends, the activities in which they engage, the qualities of those friends the child finds appealing, and the social processes that appear at work. It is important the caregiver recognize the child's perspective and caregivers should be allowed to express their own views on the topic (see Clinical Tip 6.3). The goal of this conversation is twofold. First, if positive peer influences are noted, the clinician can help the caregiver consider ways of increasing those interactions. This may involve scheduling more activities with those peers (e.g., play dates) or fostering the child's development in their shared interests (e.g., music, sports, reading). In this manner, there is a clear attempt to increase the frequency of identified positive peer influences.

CLINICAL TIP 6.3. Caregiver Perceptions of Friends

Caregivers often have their own perceptions of the child's friends, and sometimes, these are quite negative. Although it is important to allow caregivers the opportunity to voice their concerns, the clinician should take steps to prevent the session devolving into the caregiver airing a list of grievances. This may be a sensitive area for some caregivers, and the clinician must ensure both that the caregiver feels heard and that the caregiver understands the child's perspective, including the characteristics of the peers the child finds appealing, as this provides direction on how to identify a more positive peer group. Overly restrictive responses by the caregiver related to the child's peer interactions may inadvertently result in social isolation, and the clinician must be prepared to address such issues. For instance, one caregiver so disapproved of the child's friends that the child was forbidden from all peer contact outside of the school environment until he developed friends whom the caregiver approved. This same parent simultaneously complained that the child spent most days inside the house instead of playing outside. In this situation, the caregiver provided no opportunities for the child to develop suitable friendships, resulting in social isolation. This situation is not uncommon; when a caregiver disapproves of a child's friends, the typical response is to forbid interactions with those friends, but rarely does a caregiver take steps to help the child develop a more positive peer group. Depending on the caregiver's responses, the clinician may need to be more or less directive in focusing the caregiver on actionable steps that can be taken to encourage more positive peer interactions.

The second goal of this technique is to steer a child away from negative influences and toward more positive ones. If negative peer groups are identified, it is critically important to attend to what the child described as attracting them to those peers (e.g., peer is friendly or enjoys a similar activity). These answers provide clues of what the child is looking for in friendships. The clinician can work with the caregiver to identify ways of introducing the child to peers who share the same interests and will provide a more positive influence. For instance, if a child is being negatively influenced by peers at the neighborhood park while playing basketball, the caregiver can explore other avenues for the child to play basketball in a more constructive environment (e.g., church, school, local club). As the child becomes more invested in the new milieu or activity, the limited time available often results in less interaction with the negative peer influences. To this point, the caregiver can restructure the child's schedule to reduce, if not eliminate, the opportunity to interact with the negative peer group. Responding in this manner also requires the caregiver to take a more active role in identifying and promoting positive peer interactions.

Evaluate Outcome and Need for Further Services

Before ending treatment, it is advised that clinicians examine the outcome for PSB. This may involve administering the Assessment of Sexual Behavior-Child Version (ASB-C) or a similar measure to provide an index of effect. If ongoing concerns are noted, the clinician may want to review with the caregiver those endorsed behaviors and revisit aspects of the PBT protocol that appear relevant. However, if regular progress monitoring was occurring as suggested, it is uncommon for these concerns to emerge only near the end of treatment. Typically, ongoing problems are the result of poor adherence to the monitoring plan or caregiver difficulty with implementing consequences when the child breaks the rules. If such concerns are not adequately addressed by the end of treatment, the clinician might want to consider the need for a behavioral parent training program to enhance parenting skills.

In the vast majority of cases, PSB is the clinical priority whether because of suspension from school, significant disruption to the family home, the potential for self-injury, or exposing other children to sexual behavior. However, as reviewed in Chapter 1, many children with PSB present with other significant emotional and/or behavioral concerns. Before ending PBT, it is important to assess the need for further treatment services. The clinician may wish to explore ongoing concerns with the caregiver, either through an informal discussion or by administering a larger battery of assessment measures. Appropriate referrals may then be made if the clinician does not have the training or ability to provide the recommended intervention.

CASE EXAMPLES

The examples that follow demonstrate the conclusion of treatment with the cases that have been followed since Chapter 2. Not only are Phase 3 activities described, but also clinical outcomes are assessed.

Lydia E., 5 Years Old, Sexual Abuse Survivor

Session 1

Given Lydia's age and her quiet nature around the clinician, Mr. and Mrs. Thomas accompanied her into the session. However, in a first, Lydia chose to sit in her own chair this session. The clinician began by telling Lydia that sessions were going to be a bit different from this point forward in that they were going to involve more games and discussions. Lydia seemed interested when the clinician referenced games, which provided an opening to begin teaching the concept of impulse control. The clinician described the first game as the "ice cube challenge" and presented a small bowl full of ice cubes. Lydia looked confused and cautiously held out her hand when requested to do so by the clinician. The clinician then placed two ice cubes in her hand and said the challenge was to see how long she could hold them before feeling like she needed to drop them into a waste basket placed underneath her hand. Lydia closed her hand around the ice and the clinician started a stopwatch. The girl started smiling and giggling, making it just 15 seconds before dropping the ice cubes.

The clinician pointed out Lydia's giggles and that she appeared to find this game fun. She nodded her head and said, "It tickled." When asked how it felt, Lydia turned to Mrs. Thomas and loudly whispered, "The ice cubes made my hand all wet." Mrs. Thomas agreed, and then Mr. Thomas surprisingly requested to do the challenge to see if he could beat Lydia's time. Lydia became excited and emphatically nodded her head to encourage him. Mr. Thomas performed the challenge and made it to 25 seconds before dropping the ice cubes. He then said, "It made my hand tingle and I didn't like feeling the water run down my hand." Lydia agreed, "It made my hand tingle and kind of hurt." Mrs. Thomas politely declined the offer to repeat the activity.

The clinician explained that the ice cubes created a signal in the body, in this case, in the hand, and that told Lydia's brain to do something to make it feel better, which led her to drop the ice cubes. This brief example resulted in a discussion of other ways that the body sends signals. Lydia quietly said, "Like when I'm hungry and my tummy tells me to eat a cookie." Mrs. Thomas chuckled and praised Lydia but clarified that her "tummy tells you to eat something, but it doesn't have to be a cookie." Lydia gave Mrs. Thomas a stern look and said, "I guess." The clinician used this moment to point out that the body is creating the urge to do something, but it is still up to Lydia what exactly she does in response to that urge. For example, she could eat a cookie, or an apple, or wait another 30 minutes until dinner was ready. Lydia nodded her head in agreement. The clinician then connected this discussion to the PSB, taking care not to present the issue as shaming or embarrassing. "Sometimes, those signals come from the hand or the tummy, and sometimes they can come from the foot or the vagina. Any body part really can send a message to the brain to act in a certain way." The clinician here used the word "vagina" taught to Lydia in the previous session, suggesting that an urge may arise in that part of the body and that sexual behaviors may be the result of acting on these urges. Lydia remained engaged without any noticeable negative reaction.

The clinician then transitioned into teaching Lydia impulse control skills by using a scripted sequence of the "turtle technique" (see earlier). This procedure combined a series of thought stopping, relaxation (i.e., controlled breathing), and problem-solving skills. Lydia participated well in this process and Mr. Thomas also joined in to practice the technique. Whenever Lydia was feeling an urge from her body to act in a way that was not appropriate, she was instructed to "do the turtle." To practice, the "ice cube challenge" was repeated. Lydia was told that she would earn five stickers if she could beat her previous time. The ice was placed in her hand and Mrs. Thomas instructed her to "do the turtle." Lydia improved her time to 43 seconds, which resulted in an excited smile and her immediately selecting the stickers she wanted. Mr. Thomas also repeated the challenge and improved his time to 50 seconds. He looked at Lydia and said, "Wow, that really worked!" The clinician instructed Lydia to use the technique in the coming week, whether it be a signal from her "tummy or vagina" so she could follow the rules of the home and not get in trouble. She agreed. The clinician also encouraged the caregivers to watch for any physical signals that Lydia might need to "do the turtle" and to prompt her accordingly. They agreed.

Session 2

Session 2 typically focuses on teaching cognitive coping skills, but the caregivers believed these elements would be difficult for Lydia. Instead, the session was spent teaching Lydia additional relaxation skills (i.e., muscle relaxation, positive imagery) and integrating them into her use of the "turtle technique." As before, Mr. and Mrs. Thomas joined in this process, learned the skills themselves, and agreed to promote their use in the coming weeks.

Session 3

The clinician began the session with only Mrs. Thomas, as Mr. Thomas was again called away for work. The focus was initially on identifying individuals who might come into a caregiving role with Lydia, such as babysitters or grandparents. Mrs. Thomas dismissed any concerns in relation to these individuals, as the grandparents were the only caregivers of Lydia and her sister, other than herself and Mr. Thomas. The clinician reflected this comment and acknowledged the likelihood that there was no need for concern. However, the clinician pivoted and talked about aiming for uniformity across caregivers and clearly conveying safety rules around sexual topics. Mrs. Thomas understood this point and agreed that sharing the body safety rules and events of session with the grandparents was appropriate. The clinician offered the idea of allowing Lydia to teach them the rules, and she agreed, saying, "Lydia would love to do that. She likes to think she is teaching people things." The clinician asked Mrs. Thomas to identify other people that may have a negative influence on Lydia through talking about sexual topics or acting in inappropriate ways, but she was unable to think of any.

The clinician then turned the discussion to developing a suitable definition for the term "abuse." Given Lydia's previous experiences, defining the term was a delicate issue. It required delineating why the experience she had with "mommy's friend" differed from her initiating sexual behaviors with her sister. Mrs. Thomas suggested relying on the deliberate breaking of the body safety rules. This offered a useful method of discussing the topic as "mommy's friend" surely knew his behavior toward Lydia was wrong, but Lydia learned these behaviors from an adult and had not previously learned rules around these types of behaviors. Mrs. Thomas further crafted her definition and defined sexual abuse as "touching the private parts of another person when they don't want to and you know it is wrong." She further clarified that this behavior also related to coercing the other person to touch one's own private parts. This allowed for clarifying that adults touching the private areas of children is always abusive.

After defining the term, she identified several different skills she wanted to teach Lydia around the topic of sexual abuse prevention. First, she wanted to include grandparents on the list of safe people to tell in the event that someone attempted to touch Lydia's private areas or force her to touch them. The clinician recommended reviewing the four body safety rules developed in earlier sessions and to couch this discussion within the framework of that rule. Second, she wanted to emphasize to Lydia that it is never acceptable to keep secrets about sexual topics, as this was something mentioned to Mrs. Thomas previously in relation to the sexual abuse experiences with "mommy's friend." The clinician introduced the concept of separating "secrets" from "surprises" and how the two terms differ. Mrs. Thomas liked this distinction and related it to a third skill she wanted to teach Lydia, assertiveness. She stated that Lydia is often reserved and may lack the confidence to speak up when necessary. This made the clinician think of a psychoeducational book that teaches the concept of self-assertiveness; the clinician stepped out of the room to retrieve the book and then presented it to Ms. Thomas. She liked the book and decided to use it to teach this skill to Lydia.

Lydia then joined the session. Mrs. Thomas started the discussion by continuing the theme of keeping Lydia safe. She then reviewed the term "sexual abuse" for Lydia using the developed definition. Lydia looked more serious than when she first entered the session and again whispered in Ms. Thomas's ear, who responded, "Yes, like what [biological] mommy's friend did to you. That would be sexual abuse." She then reminded Lydia of the fourth body safety rule that required her to tell either her or Mr. Thomas in the event any such behavior occurred. To this, she added that Lydia is now free to tell one of her grandparents, as well as a teacher or doctor, and defined this group as "safe people." Mrs. Thomas shared that Lydia may teach the rules to her grandparents if she wished, to which Lydia smiled and nodded her head emphatically. Mrs. Thomas smiled and notified Lydia that she could teach them when they next came to visit.

Mrs. Thomas then discussed the difference between secrets and surprises by using the example of a birthday present. If the present is never given to the person and never discussed, it becomes a secret. That is not fun and the person may feel sad when they do not receive a present on their birthday. However, wrapping the present and giving it to the person is exciting and is a great moment for everyone. Thus, surprises are acceptable, but not secrets. She described sexual abuse in similar terms; keeping it a secret means people feel bad and are unsafe. If she tells someone, they may be surprised, but at that moment, people can start to feel better and take steps to ensure safety. This basic analogy transitioned well into the psychoeducational book, which described a young child being upset about an uncle that tickles him (in a nonsexual way). Once the child tells his mother that he dislikes that form of touching, the mother helps the child confront the uncle, who apologizes and refrains from such behavior in the future. Mrs. Thomas emphasized that Lydia similarly has a right to decide who can touch her body and, just like the boy in the book, she should let one of the "safe people" know what is happening as a way to protect herself.

Session 4

Given Lydia's age, there are relatively few peer influences not under direct adult supervision. Nonetheless, given Lydia's reserved nature around the clinician, it was decided to spend the session reviewing with the caregivers how to monitor peer influences moving forward in Lydia's life. The clinician emphasized that Lydia's prior experiences might make her susceptible to peers who discuss sexual topics, as she may believe she has a unique perspective on the topic or more advanced knowledge to share. It was recommended that the caregivers occasionally revisit with Lydia the discussion about how to maintain safety and apply the skills specifically to peer relationships. For example, they might process how Lydia can best respond if she hears a peer make a sexual joke or comment. Mr. Thomas asked about potential internet influences, such as pictures or pornography sites. The clinician agreed that internet activities should be monitored and provided a handout on how to keep children safe online. Mr. Thomas stated he would look into potential monitoring software to assist in this effort.

The clinician conducted a posttreatment evaluation with Mr. and Mrs. Thomas. Neither caregiver identified seeing any of the targeted sexual behaviors over the past few months, with the last instance occurring just days before the initial assessment. However, the caregivers noted ongoing posttraumatic stress symptoms during the discussion, including nightmares, an exaggerated startle response, and noted negative emotion when reminded of the sexual abuse. This last concern was observed in sessions with the clinician, who discussed the potential need for a trauma-focused treatment to target posttraumatic stress symptoms. The caregivers agreed to this new plan of treatment.

Maria C., 8 Years Old, Self-Stimulating at School

Session 1

The clinician chose to begin this session by meeting with Ms. Cortez to assess Maria's progress. The mother stated that she has not seen any PSB from Maria at home since the incident where she walked into her bedroom. However, about 2 weeks prior to this session, Maria was observed by the teacher self-stimulating in class in the same manner as before. The teacher redirected Maria and notified the mother via email, and consequences were applied at home. This equated to roughly 2 weeks without a known incident of PSB and, even before that, the frequency was significantly reduced. Ms. Cortez stated that no further discussions with Maria took place regarding sexual topics and she appeared content to allow Maria to initiate any future conversations. The clinician also inquired as to whether she made any attempts to catch Maria self-stimulating in private, and she said she decided to allow her to maintain a level of privacy in her room when the door is closed. The clinician reviewed with Ms. Cortez the plan for the session, including teaching Maria impulse control skills.

When Maria joined session, Ms. Cortez went to the waiting room. True to form, Maria appeared irritated by attending session. The clinician decided to use Maria's negativity to develop an incentive program, by asking her what she would rather be doing instead. "Listening to music, watching videos. Fun stuff like that," she replied. The clinician then made Maria a deal: If she engaged in treatment for 20 minutes, then the last 10 minutes would be left for her to show the clinician videos of her choosing. Maria smiled at that prospect and agreed to the terms.

The clinician began the conversation by asking the girl how she knew when it was time to use the restroom. Maria quickly sat back in her chair and said, "Yuck, why would you ask that?" The clinician reminded her of the deal they just made and restated the question, pointing out that it was not a trick or a particularly complicated question. Maria continued with her disgusted look and answered, "I don't know. I feel something in my body and it tells me I have to pee. Is that what you mean?" The clinician acknowledged the answer and then followed by saying, "So, when you get that feeling in your body, do you just drop your pants and pee on the floor?" Maria's mouth dropped open, "That's gross. Is that what weirdos like you do? I go to the bathroom." The clinician smiled and then summarized the girl's answers, "Okay, so you're saying you get a feeling in your body, you then stop yourself from immediately acting on that feeling, and instead find a more acceptable place to pee . . . in the bathroom."

Having established Maria's inherent ability to inhibit her behavior in response to a biological drive or internal sensation, the clinician turned the discussion to her self-stimulating behavior. Of course, the clinician approached the topic delicately, "You know the reason you have been coming in here is because of the behavior that occurred in school, with you touching your private areas. Can you explain for me what the feeling was you had before you would do that?" Maria immediately glared at the clinician and answered, "I don't know. I wanted to, so I did it." The clinician empathized with Maria, "Yeah, sometimes it's really hard to describe that kind of feeling, but you said you 'wanted to,' so at least you know there was something inside creating that urge for you." Maria shrugged her shoulders, "I guess." With Maria's recognition that something internal gave rise to the self-stimulatory behavior, the clinician linked this to the previous discussion: "It sounds sort of like the bathroom situation. You have some kind of signal or feeling inside your body that tells you to do something and you have the option of immediately performing the behavior or waiting until a more appropriate place." Maria smiled and said, "I guess so. You're saying I can wait to do things I'm thinking, just like peeing in the bathroom instead of on the floor." The clinician agreed and praised Maria's participation. Not wanting Maria to view the process as necessarily an easy one, the clinician qualified her statement, "But, it's easier to control some behaviors. Waiting to pee in the bathroom might be easy, but waiting to touch your private areas behind closed doors might be more difficult. The good news is there are things I can teach you to make that easier." For the first time in any session, Maria leaned in as if interested to hear what the clinician had to say.

The remainder of the session with Maria was spent teaching her controlled breathing and positive imagery skills. Maria engaged well in the activities, but she stopped short of agreeing to use the skills. Nonetheless, the clinician helped her connect relaxation skills to various types of behaviors, with a special emphasis on the self-stimulation. When asked to practice them in the coming week and use them when necessary, Maria retorted, "Yeah, I probably won't." Maria also declined to demonstrate them for her mother. The session ended with Maria showing the clinician various videos of dogs performing tricks and listening to a song by her favorite singer. The clinician briefly talked with Ms. Cortez on the way out of session, letting her know that Maria learned some skills to help control her behavior and that Ms. Cortez may wish to prompt her implementation of the skills if she notices any behavioral concerns, whether sexual or not.

Session 2

The clinician met with Maria first and established the same bargain as the prior session; if she engaged in session, the last 10 minutes could be used at her discretion. Maria agreed and the clinician began reviewing the previously learned coping skills. Maria was able to sufficiently demonstrate their use but denied employing them over the past week, claiming no opportunity presented itself that required them. The clinician transitioned this discussion into a review of the cognitive triangle, as described earlier. Maria easily learned the concept but struggled when the clinician tried to apply it to sexual thoughts. When asked, "What's the first thought that comes to mind when you get that feeling or signal from your body that might lead to touching your private areas?" Maria was unable to answer, asserting that she does not think anything.

The clinician used this same method to examine maladaptive cognitions that might be present as a result of her PSB: "When the teacher points out that you are touching your private areas, what's the first thought you have?" Maria put her head down and said, "Embarrassed." Given that Maria confused a feeling for a thought, but obviously appeared sad in the moment, the clinician decided to gently reword the question. "I understand. People saw you performing that behavior and that's embarrassing. Why is it embarrassing and not, I don't know . . . make you happy?" Maria appeared confused by the question. She cautiously said, "Because I'm not supposed to do that, and I don't want people to see it. They probably think I'm weird." The clinician nodded and began writing down on a piece of paper the sequence, starting with the thought of other people evaluating her in a negative way, which leads to the feeling of embarrassment. Maria was then able to complete the triangle by noting that she puts her head down and later yells at students on the playground.

The initial cognitive triangle completed by Maria is an accurate representation of the situation occurring within the classroom as it is likely that other students notice her self-stimulating behavior and it results in negative peer evaluations. Instead of attempting to change her evaluation of the situation, the clinician decided to pivot to emphasizing more adaptive thoughts. The clinician discussed how Maria had not displayed any PSB in the classroom for over 3 weeks at the time of the session (as reported by her mother during a brief check-in at the beginning of session). Maria looked at the clinician and nodded her head. The clinician asked Maria to complete another triangle based on this piece of information. The girl quickly finished the task, stating that she believed she was able to control her behavior around others (thought), it made her feel happy to know she was able to control her behavior (feelings), and she did not shut down as much in class as a result (behavior). The clinician praised Maria's ability to complete the triangle and encouraged her to take pride in her accomplishment. Although this is not the standard use of the cognitive triangle in terms of altering maladaptive thoughts, Maria certainly recognized that inhibiting her behavior led to more positive outcomes in terms of feelings and behaviors.

Ms. Cortez then met with the clinician for a brief time to learn the different skills Maria was taught over the past two sessions. She had relatively few questions and agreed that Maria is making significant progress toward controlling the PSB. However, Ms. Cortez was concerned about ongoing behavioral challenges, including oppositional behavior and a negative attitude. The clinician reflected Ms. Cortez's concerns and noted that only two sessions remained of PSB treatment and then it would be appropriate to shift focus to the larger behavioral concerns. Ms. Cortez understood and the clinician urged her to continue implementing the plans previously established for treating PSB, and to encourage Maria's use of the learned skills.

Session 3

The mother came into session continuing to express concerns about Maria's nonsexual behavioral problems. The clinician reviewed the importance of ensuring that Maria understands the concepts of sexual abuse and the need to teach her appropriate responses in such instances. Ms. Cortez agreed to provide this instruction to her daughter and defer a larger discussion of her behavioral concerns to the next session. The clinician reviewed much of the same material as discussed with the caregivers of Lydia E. One unique aspect in this case, however, centered on Ms. Cortez's hesitancy to allow any babysitters or family members to supervise Maria. She discussed that her family lives some distance away and she does not trust babysitters whom she does not know. Despite the clinician's attempts, Ms. Cortez was unable to identify any situation where a surrogate caregiver would be required for Maria. The clinician then turned the issue to one of teachers at school and the extent to which she trusts them with the care of her daughter. Ms. Cortez believed this was a different situation, as there are several children around at the same time and teachers are trained to care for children. Attempts to identify the reasons for Ms. Cortez's reluctance to other caregivers were largely unsuccessful as she repeatedly reverted to it being an issue of safety.

Defining the concept of abuse proved somewhat challenging as Ms. Cortez specified that any sexual behavior with any individual was abuse, given Maria's age. While this is likely the case in most instances (except, potentially, noncoercive behaviors with a same-age peer), this definition held the potential of stigmatizing all sexual behavior. The clinician helped the mother provide more context to the definition and reviewed how to teach the concept in a way that coincided with previous discussions. In effect, Ms. Cortez was encouraged to review the safety rules that previously defined the limits around Maria's behavior and then to expand on them by discussing behavior by other individuals. Within this context, it became much easier to discuss interpersonal forms of behavior that are clearly abusive. This conversation allowed for an opening to discuss the steps Maria can take if she is exposed to such behavior. Ms. Cortez practiced this conversation with the clinician and felt comfortable providing the information to her daughter.

When Maria joined session, the conversation quickly derailed. Soon after her mother began speaking, Maria interrupted her, "Are you talking about 'unsafe' touches?" Ms. Cortez was taken aback and agreed this was the topic of conversation. Maria then sighed and said, "Ugh, we already did this at school." It seems Maria recently had a presentation at her school where the presenters used puppets to teach concepts such as personal space, "safe" and "unsafe" touches, and who to tell in the event someone attempted an "unsafe" touch. Ms. Cortez was unaware of this presentation and listened intently as Maria explained the content. Indeed, most of what Ms. Cortez planned to teach Maria was already covered during the performance at school. Ms. Cortez praised the girl for her recall and participation, to which Maria responded, "Good. Are we done with this now?" The clinician praised Ms. Cortez for speaking directly with Maria about these topics and similarly thanked Maria for sharing. Maria bobbed her head and asked, "Since Mom is here, does she have to watch my videos too?"

Session 4

Maria reluctantly entered session, complaining that she thought treatment was finished. The clinician suggested that there are still a few more topics to discuss and that it was understood she did not enjoy attending session. The clinician allowed Maria to pick a game she wanted to play, and the two of them played while they talked. The clinician started the conversation by asking Maria to identify her best friends, but she struggled with this task. She did mention the names of two individuals but was unable to identify any activities in which she participated with them. Her interactions with these peers appeared limited to the classroom and her identification of them as friends owed to the two treating her in a kinder manner than many of the other children. Maria displayed a sad affect while trying to discuss friendships and it became quickly apparent that she did not have any significant peer relationships. The clinician refocused the conversation to ask Maria about the types of friends she would like to have. She related that it would be great to find other children who liked dolls and the same music as her. The clinician empathized with this comment and asked if there are any other activities she would like to try. Maria thought for a moment and then stated that she has always believed she would make a good dancer. The clinician thanked Maria for talking and praised her participation.

The clinician reviewed with Ms. Cortez the contents of the discussion with Maria, including her demeanor and the likelihood that she had no close friends. Ms. Cortez agreed this was the case and said Maria never displayed any interest. The clinician shared that Maria's comments suggested that she does, indeed, have an interest in friends, but she seemed to be ostracized by the other children at school. Ms. Cortez was surprised to hear this as Maria never talked to her about her peers. The clinician mentioned that children who display behavioral problems are often not well liked by other children and her behavioral concerns may at least partially be the cause. However, Maria did provide some indications of how she might improve her peer relationships. The clinician discussed her interest in dance and the possibility of enrolling her in a dance class. Ms. Cortez asked how a dance class might improve her behavioral problems and whether it would have any impact on her PSB. The clinician discussed how exercise and positive, enjoyable experiences are often associated with improved mood, which may then help with the negative attitude she frequently displayed. Similarly, if her PSB was the result of attempting to regulate negative emotions, then a dance class may have a positive impact on the self-stimulating behavior. Also, she might meet peers who share common interests. Ms. Cortez agreed to explore this possibility and the clinician promised to identify classes that might fit within her budget and time constraints.

Before ending treatment, Ms. Cortez completed the ASB-C and noted that no self-stimulating behavior was observed in the prior month; the score for the ASB-C was within normal limits. Although she still worried about a potential return of the PSB, Ms. Cortez believed she was more capable of responding in the event it reappeared. Her primary concern remained the oppositional behavior and negative attitude that Maria displayed on a somewhat regular basis. The clinician recommended implementation of a parent training program designed to teach Ms. Cortez how to shape Maria's behavior in a more positive direction. The mother agreed and, given that the clinician was trained in such a model, the clinician planned to change treatment approach at the next session.

Alex J., 10 Years Old, Coercing a Sibling

Session 1

Alex and the clinician began session by playing a game together, allowing Alex the opportunity to discuss topics of his choosing. He mentioned various aspects of his life, including his basketball team, violin lessons, and events happening at school. On this last topic, the clinician asked whether he heard any additional sexual comments at school since the prior session. He said such comments occur on an almost daily basis from a few children he described as "the ones always in trouble." The clinician followed up by asking how he responds when he hears these sexual comments, to which Alex replied, "I usually just ignore them."

The clinician transitioned into reminding Alex about some aspects of the previous discussion with his father. Specifically, the physiological arousal that can occur as a result of sexual exposure or thoughts. Alex nodded in agreement and said he remembered that part. The clinician explained that our bodies can have a lot of different sensations that tell us to do something. For instance, Alex was asked how he knows when he is thirsty. He accurately described a feeling of a dry throat or feeling hot, and stated that these sensations prompt him to seek out water. The clinician asked the boy to identify other physiological states and the behaviors they elicit. He was able to report that feeling hungry is a stomach pain that makes him eat, that a pressure in his bladder results in urination, and a feeling of tiredness marked by drooping eyes and difficulty concentrating encourages sleep. To this list the clinician added that a feeling of sexual arousal in the body can foster a desire to touch one's private areas or engage in other sexual behavior. Again, the clinician deliberately related this back to the explanation provided by Mr. James in the previous session with the goal of demystifying and normalizing such physiological sensations.

Once Alex understood the concept, the clinician talked about the ability of individuals to control these biologically based impulses, using the example that Alex learned to use the restroom when feeling the need to urinate and to identify appropriately edible objects when he is hungry. The sexual impulses were then cast in the same perspective, that individuals can control them and find acceptable outlets. With this, the clinician taught Alex controlled breathing and decision-making skills. Making lists of positive and negative consequences and potential solutions that prevented negative outcomes was particularly appreciated by Alex. Interestingly, one of the options he identified that might yield positive outcomes was removing himself to a private area (e.g., bedroom, bathroom) if he felt the need to touch his private areas. Having previously discussed with Mr. James his acceptance of this behavior, the clinician agreed with the child.

Alex performed exceptionally well throughout this session, as expected. His PSB appeared neither impulsive nor the result of significant emotional dysregulation, and he possessed sufficient self-regulation skills. Nonetheless, Alex agreed to demonstrate the use of the skills for his father so he might encourage their use in the home. When Mr. James joined the session, the clinician showed him the paper where it was written that Alex identified the potential solution of removing to a private area when feeling physiologically aroused. He nodded his head, understanding that this would be a topic of conversation. Alex proceeded to teach the skills to his father. When the solution of going to a private area was raised, Alex looked at his father and said, "That's okay, right? It doesn't break any rules." Mr. James concurred, adding, "You're allowed to touch your private areas when you're alone. Just make sure it's not where other people can see." The clinician praised Mr. James's response and noted that discussions such as these are examples of continuing the conversation around sexual topics.

Session 2

Alex entered session in a positive mood and mentioned to the clinician that his team won an important basketball game the night before and he was still happy about it. Sensing an opportunity, the clinician immediately jumped into teaching cognitive coping skills. A cognitive triangle was mapped out with the activating event being winning the game. The feeling of "happy" was also penciled in. The behavior was also easily identified as Alex mentioned jumping up and down with his team and cheering. However, the thought that led to the positive feeling stumped Alex. The clinician engaged him further in a discussion about what winning the game meant to him. The boy was confused at first and simply answered, "It meant we won." The clinician then gave an example of perhaps another boy playing basketball who was being forced into it by his father. In this instance, the boy may think, "If we keep winning, I'll have to play more games." Alex was able to deduce that such a thought would make this boy sad, and this appeared to result in an understanding of the initial question. Alex concluded, "My thought is that we are a good team and might have a chance to win the championship." The clinician agreed that this likely resulted in a happy feeling.

The clinician transitioned to another thought, using the example of a child who is pushed from behind by another child at school. Alex completed this exercise with minimal effort, easily identifying various thoughts and how they impact feelings and behaviors. Having established his understanding of the concept, the clinician returned to what Alex said before regarding his PSB, that he was curious about oral sex and did not believe it would upset his sister. Placing this into the cognitive triangle, the clinician used exposure to the term "suck it" at school as the activating event. Alex identified his most immediate thought being "I wonder what that feels like." The feeling was more difficult to define and he described a state of uneasiness mixed with excitement, what he labeled "weird," which intensified as he began talking with his sister about performing the sexual behavior.

Considering alternative thoughts for this situation proved easy for Alex given the prior discussions. These thoughts included "That is not an appropriate topic for discussion" and "I should talk to Dad about what I heard." Neither of these thoughts resulted in negative emotions or problematic behaviors, but Alex also noted that he did not consider these alternative views at the time. He then abruptly stated, "I should've thought about other people." The clinician empathized with Alex, as his affect became noticeably sadder, before praising him for integrating the concept of consent into the discussion. The clinician reverted to his prior answer, "But, like you said, you didn't think about that and no one had talked to you about these issues before." Alex's mood improved and the clinician taught him how to identify evidence for different thoughts to determine which is the most helpful in a given situation.

Mr. James joined the session and Alex taught him about the cognitive triangle, including the completed examples. Alex's ability to discuss each aspect of the diagram demonstrated his understanding of the concept. When discussing the situation involving the PSB, Alex again apologized to his father and stressed that he simply did not consider other options. Mr. James, for the first time, apologized to Alex for not teaching him the rules earlier and giving him information that might have prevented the PSB. Mr. James transitioned back into praising Alex's efforts and thanked him for working so hard in treatment. When attempting to teach his father how to evaluate the strength of evidence for different thoughts, Alex struggled to provide examples of how that evidence might be gathered, which led the clinician to provide additional ideas. Mr. James suggested additional pieces of evidence that might be useful and agreed to help Alex practice this skill at home.

Session 3

The clinician began the session meeting with Mr. James. Although this session aims to reduce the risk to the child of sexual abuse, the clinician chose to focus on this topic from the perspective of the child. In particular, it was emphasized that Alex displayed some interest in sexual topics, has experienced sexual behavior, and would soon enter a stage of rapid physiological and sexual development. The social setting also would change as the middle school years typically involve increased focus on interpersonal attraction or relationships and sexual commentary. All of these developments suggested the need to teach Alex the appropriate steps to take in the event he finds himself presented with a sexual situation with which he is uncomfortable. Mr. James agreed this was an important topic for his son.

The clinician reviewed with Mr. James several tactics he can try to minimize the chances that Alex would encounter such situations. This included discussions of who is allowed around the children unsupervised, information to share with potential babysitters, and creating an atmosphere of support and openness within the home. The clinician suggested it would be most helpful for Mr. James to teach his son several techniques as the next step in continuing to maintain an open line of communication. He agreed and the clinician discussed different topics for conversation and wrote them down as a visual guide for Mr. James.

Alex then joined the session and Mr. James went directly into the list. He began by stating that he cared about his son and wanted to make sure he remained safe, with some reference to potential sexual topics he might encounter in the coming years. This led into the first point on the list: Alex can talk to Mr. James about anything that concerned him, and Mr. James would listen with a goal of providing help. Examples of this included hearing students at school make sexual comments, seeing nudity or sex in movies or on television, and having another individual proposition Alex to engage in sexual contact. Alex remained quiet throughout and only occasionally said, "Okay."

Mr. James then transitioned into talking about concrete steps Alex could take in the moment if any of these situations occurred. The father did an excellent job of discussing Alex's right to refuse and that it was best for him to leave the setting and find a place with more people. He then reviewed a list of trusted people that Alex can approach for help if needed, including teachers, police officers, and relatives. He, again, emphasized that Alex is always able to approach his parents with any concerns and they would listen and help. Alex continued to nod along with his father's statements, and the clinician sensed Alex was experiencing a level of concern or, possibly, fear. When the father finished with this latter discussion, the clinician asked Alex to discuss how he was feeling in the moment. The boy looked at his dad and said, "A little freaked out. Is this going to happen?" The father, seemingly realizing his stern demeanor elevated the gravity of the situation, leaned back in his chair and said, "No, probably not. I just want you to be prepared." Alex appeared relieved and then volunteered, "I know, Dad. I hear kids talk about this stuff sometimes and I try to stay away from them." The clinician praised both the father and son for their ability to talk about these issues so freely.

Session 4

Alex and the clinician started session by discussing his recent basketball games and this led into a larger discussion about peer groups. Alex described his preferred friends as being athletic and that he likes people who tell jokes and laugh a lot. Given the frequent mentions of negative peer influences at school, the clinician asked Alex to clarify whether the boys who used the term "suck it" were in his friend group. One of these boys, Charlie, was in Alex's class and they typically played together at recess, while the other boys were more acquaintances from other classrooms. Alex declined, however, to describe Charlie as a friend. He also quickly pointed out that he tried to stay away from Charlie since beginning treatment but that Charlie often followed him at recess and wanted to play. When asked, however, Alex denied he had taken any steps to notify teachers or monitors about Charlie.

The clinician met with Mr. James to review Alex's peer groups. He had few concerns with Alex's friends and noted those who visit the home or play in the neighborhood often behave appropriately from what he observed. The same was said for Alex's basketball team, as the coaches and other parents had not voiced any concerns. The boys at school were the only concerning peer influence of which Mr. James was aware. The clinician shared with him the information Alex provided and the problems with Charlie. The father asked about potential solutions to this problem and proposed contacting the school. The clinician acknowledged this may be helpful, but suggested that Mr. James discuss it with Alex first. Also, contacting a teacher is often most effective when done in the spirit of collaboration. It was recommended that Mr. James schedule a time to chat about the concern with the teacher and view it as mutual problem solving. Taking an overly directive tone and attempting to dictate the outcome (e.g., Charlie is not allowed around Alex) was unlikely to yield the desired outcome and may prevent developing helpful solutions. Mr. James agreed to review the issue with Alex and potentially reach out to the school.

Given that this was the final session of treatment, Mr. James completed the ASB-C and reported no concerning sexual behaviors over the past month. However, the clinician discussed that it may be advantageous for Alex and his sister to participate in a clarification process, which would afford Alex the opportunity to apologize to his sister properly and make amends. This would also allow for all members of the family to come together to discuss safety moving forward. Alex's sister and mother engaged in treatment with another clinician at the same clinic while Alex participated in PBT. The sister's treatment primarily focused on learning coping and safety skills, as she did not display any significant emotional or behavioral concerns. Mr. James agreed to this approach and intended to speak with his wife. Greater discussion of the clarification process is beyond the scope of this volume, but the interested reader is referred to Lipovsky et al. (1998).

SUMMARY

The evidence available to date suggests that applied skill development for the child is weakly, though significantly, related to improved outcomes for PSB (St. Amand et al., 2008). Clinical data for PBT demonstrates significant improvement in PSB is typically observed before reaching this final phase of treatment (Allen et al., 2018). As such, some children may show little appreciable benefit from Phase 3, but clinical experience teaches that some children do engage and actively attempt to use impulse control and cognitive coping skills after this phase. It is prudent to deliver these skills even in cases where the PSB appears reduced or eliminated. In addition, concerns about developmental outcomes for children with PSB encourages taking concrete steps to enhance safety and minimize negative peer influences. Taken together, these factors encourage the implementation of Phase 3 techniques for all cases of children with PSB.

7 ALYSSA P.

A Preschool-Aged Child With Self-Focused Problematic Sexual Behavior

ASSESSMENT

The case of Alyssa demonstrates the use of phase-based treatment for problematic sexual behavior (PBT) with a very young child. It incorporates a number of various considerations often encountered with children displaying problematic sexual behavior (PSB), such as a caregiver concerned that her child may have experienced unreported sexual abuse, concerns about potentially injurious self-focused behavior, a caregiver with a pronounced permissive parenting style, and a caregiver under significant stress. The case is further complicated by the fact that the mother's approach to educating her child failed to effectively consider the girl's developmental level.

Background

Alyssa's mother, Ms. Prentice, attended the initial assessment without her 4-year-old daughter. It seemed that Alyssa was having behavioral issues earlier in the day and was left at home with her father. Shortly after sitting

https://doi.org/10.1037/0000516-008
Children With Problematic Sexual Behavior: Theory, Research, and Evidence-Based Practice, by B. Allen

down, Ms. Prentice became emotional and said that she was very concerned someone had sexually abused her daughter, but she did not know who could have done it. The clinician asked Ms. Prentice why she believed this and the mother launched into a discussion of the multiple forms of sexualized behavior displayed by Alyssa. These concerns included the young girl repeatedly inserting objects into her own vagina, attempting to take off her mother's clothing, and frequently touching her mother's breasts. The mother said she tried multiple times to explain why these behaviors were not acceptable, but Alyssa continued to perform them. The young girl recently completed a forensic interview at a local children's advocacy center due to concerns about potential sexual abuse but did not make any allegations and the family was referred to treatment.

Assessment Data

Ms. Prentice endorsed 20 different behaviors on the Assessment of Sexual Behavior-Child version (ASB-C), including self-focused, looking, interpersonally intrusive, and interest-related items. The total score on the measure was 44, well above the cutoff score of 12, suggesting clearly problematic behavior was observed from the girl. However, only four of the items were "critical items": *inserts or tries to insert objects inside own private parts, touches or tries to touch the private parts of others, tries to undress others against their will,* and *continues to engage in sexual behavior after being told to stop.* On the Strengths and Difficulties Questionnaire (SDQ), the mother reported significantly elevated scores for all subscales, implying significant emotional and behavioral dysregulation for Alyssa and/or a significant level of concern and stress for the mother. Indeed, the mother reported significantly elevated concerns on the Patient Health Questionnaire-9 (PHQ-9) and the Parenting Stress Index–Short Form (PSI-SF). When interviewed using the Child and Adolescent Trauma Screen (CATS), the mother reported no identifiable trauma history for her daughter, other than a belief that she was sexually abused, and no significant posttraumatic stress symptoms. Given Ms. Prenctice's heightened emotional state, the clinician chose not to administer the Exposure to Sexuality Scale (ESS) and deferred it to the first treatment session.

Conceptualization

With the data available after the assessment, the most suitable conceptualization of Alyssa's problematic sexual behavior (PSB) relied on a developmental psychopathology perspective. She displayed significant emotional and behavioral concerns and her mother appeared under significant stress. The clinician operated with the assumption that significant time and effort may be needed to support the mother and teach her effective parenting skills to address Alyssa's PSB. However, the role of social modeling was unclear, as Ms. Prentice's frustration resulted in significant time being focused on her belief that the young girl was sexually abused. Little information was gathered about the home environment or larger social influences.

PHASE-BASED TREATMENT

Using the conceptualization, the clinician was acutely attuned to the possibility that the mother would have difficulty implementing caregiver-focused techniques. In response, the clinician took a stance that emphasized supporting the caregiver while still focusing on the delivery of the indicated treatment techniques. Maintenance of rapport with the caregiver was a focus throughout treatment.

Phase 1

Session 1

Ms. Prentice entered session uncertain why her daughter did not also attend. She asked how the clinician could identify who abused her daughter if the girl was not present. The clinician oriented Ms. Prentice to the purpose of sessions and clarified that it was not the role of treatment to investigate potential abuse while explaining that, as a mandated reporter, any disclosures of abuse would be reported in accordance with law. Although she understood the distinction between treatment and investigation, Ms. Prentice continued to question how effective an intervention can be if the root cause of the problem (i.e., presumed sexual abuse) was not identified. The clinician reviewed with the mother that many children with PSB do, indeed, have a history of sexual abuse; however, many children with PSB did not have such experiences. This surprised Ms. Prentice, who asked why else a child would display such behaviors. The clinician discussed that PSB frequently co-occurs with other behavior problems and that social modeling can play a role. With that, Ms. Prentice became strangely quiet and did not ask further questions.

The clinician used this opportunity to transition into the completion of the ESS, which was not administered during the assessment. When handing the measure to the mother, the clinician prefaced it by stating, "This is just a tool we use to see if a child has observed any type of sexual behavior or nudity. Some of these might be 'No,' but some might be 'Yes.' Would you mind filling this out and we can discuss it afterward?" Ms. Prentice nodded and took the form without saying a word. She calmly completed the ESS and then handed it back to the clinician with several items endorsed. The clinician reflected this finding to the mother: "It seems there is a level of openness in your home toward sexual content and nudity. Could you tell me a little about that?" Ms. Prentice looked at the clinician with a straight face and said, "I don't want my daughter growing up ashamed of her body."

The conversation around sexual modeling in the home lasted over 30 minutes, with Ms. Prentice emphasizing that her family does not believe in stigmatizing nude bodies or shaming the display of nudity. Rather, the mother spoke at length about wanting her daughter to learn that human bodies are beautiful and that sex is a natural part of life. Ms. Prentice noted that she provides detailed explanations to her daughter when she asks questions about sexual topics. The clinician asked for an example. The mother recalled a time when Alyssa asked why boys and girls have different forms of genitals and how she answered her by discussing, in detail, sexual intercourse for the purpose of reproduction. When the girl responded that intercourse sounded gross (i.e., "Eww, the penis goes in a girl?!"), the mother's response focused on pleasurable sensations and that sex is often viewed as fun and enjoyable. This mother–child conversation ended with Ms. Prentice noting that the physical sensation can be so pleasing that some people use "fake penises" to create it.

At this point in the discussion, the clinician stopped Ms. Prentice to ask her a rather simple question that led to a larger discussion.

CLINICIAN: Do you think she has ever felt that kind of sensation before?

MS. PRENTICE: Umm . . . Probably not. I hope not.

CLINICIAN: So, what is it you hoped she would do with that information?

MS. PRENTICE: I don't know, but I don't want to lie to my daughter.

CLINICIAN: Yes, of course. I don't want to lie to your daughter either. My question is more about what she understood. Given that she probably never felt that sensation, do you think she understood the idea of sex toys?

MS. PRENTICE: Hmm . . . I don't know. You're saying that she might be too young for that topic?

CLINICIAN: Probably, but it is great that you are so willing to teach her information. What else have you taught her about sex?

This conversation wound through several topics. By the end, Ms. Prentice noted having attempted to teach her daughter about orgasms, sexual attraction, and condoms. Importantly, the mother reported that these lessons involved only discussion and she did not show her daughter explicit videos or other forms of visual aids.

Ms. Prentice stumbled when the clinician asked whether any of these discussions involved teaching Alyssa rules or boundaries around sexual behavior. The mother initially was unsure how to answer, and it quickly became apparent that her lessons did not include topics such as consent, personal space, or safety. The clinician continued to praise her desire to teach her daughter to value her body while emphasizing that teaching limits around bodies are also necessary. Mr. Prentice agreed and then asked whether her openness around sexual topics is to blame for her daughter's PSB. The clinician chose to focus the answer on actionable steps to improve Alyssa's behavior: "It's difficult to say, but since you are so open to discussing these topics, it should be relatively easy to talk about rules." This allowed the clinician to emphasize the importance of making sure that Alyssa does not receive conflicting messages, such as hearing it is not acceptable to look at the private areas of others while the home includes people walking around nude. Ms. Prentice understood the need to place limits on the displays of nudity in the home, but wanted reassurance that the topic would be explored with Alyssa in session. The clinician agreed to the terms and Ms. Prentice agreed to restrict exposure in the home.

Given that the session was quickly drawing to an end, the clinician decided to develop an ABC chain around the one behavior that presented the most significant threat to safety: inserting objects into oneself. Ms. Prentice identified the bathtub as being the location she observed this behavior and noted that Alyssa inserted different types of toys (e.g., legs of a doll, foam letters). Further, the mother stated that Alyssa only inserts the objects when left alone, such as when the mother leaves the bathroom to perform a chore. The result was the mother returning to the bathroom to find an object inserted by the girl. Ms. Prentice said she typically yells at Alyssa, makes her remove the object, and ends the bath. This resulted in the following diagram:

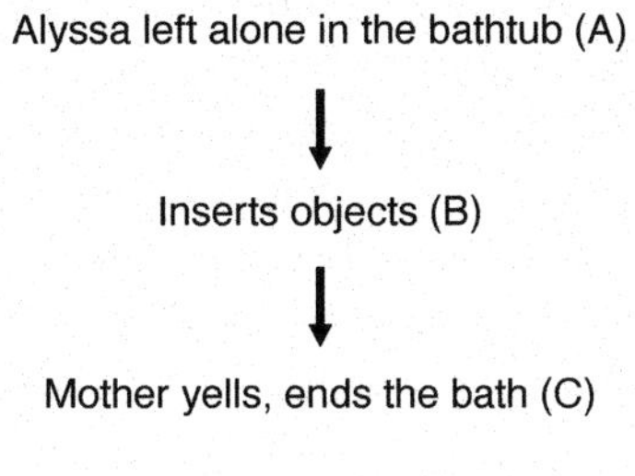

Upon looking at this sketch from the clinician, Ms. Prentice began shaking her head and said, "I probably shouldn't leave her alone in the bathtub anymore." The clinician agreed with her statement and spent a few minutes talking through a monitoring plan that could eliminate this unsupervised time. The mother agreed to implement the plan over the coming week.

It should be noted that the information provided in this session significantly changed the clinician's conceptualization of the case. Certainly, the significant self-dysregulation remained a concern, but it became readily apparent that social modeling of nudity and sexual behavior pervaded the home environment. Although well intentioned, the mother's lessons were too advanced for a child of Alyssa's age. Exposure to this content, combined with her significant self-dysregulation, likely resulted in the PSB displayed by the girl. The clinician quickly surmised that the mother displayed a potential for self-blame, which might contribute to her stress. As such, therapeutic rapport with the caregiver was enhanced through the frequent use of empathic and supportive comments, while sessions emphasized reducing social modeling and establishing appropriate boundaries.

Session 2

The first order of business at the beginning of the second session was to check on Ms. Prentice's progress reducing sexual modeling and implementing the monitoring plan to prevent Alyssa from inserting objects. The mother reported success with ensuring people wore clothing around the house, though she stated she remained uncomfortable with such restrictions. She also noted success with the monitoring plan as Alyssa was not left alone during bath time over the prior week. At one point, as Ms. Prentice remained in the bathroom, Alyssa looked at her and motioned with a toy as if she was going to insert the object, but Ms. Prentice corrected her and removed the toy. The clinician praised Ms. Prentice's efforts and asked her to continue monitoring Alyssa in this manner.

Next, attention turned to the intrusive behaviors mentioned during the assessment, which were not discussed in the previous session due to time constraints. Ms. Prentice noted that these behaviors (e.g., touching breasts, touching other's genitals, trying to undress others) are typically directed at her. Alyssa would find reasons to be close to her mother, such as asking for a hug, and then performed these behaviors while in close proximity. Ms. Prentice stated that her response was typically to break off the contact, express surprise and disappointment, and tell her daughter that such touching is not acceptable. Alyssa commonly responded by either laughing or smiling. The clinician wrote the following ABC chain:

Alyssa gets close to her mother (A)

↓

Touches mother inappropriately (B)

↓

Mother separates, corrects her daughter, girl laughs/smiles (C)

Ms. Prentice agreed that this depiction was accurate but was puzzled. She asked, "Am I not supposed to hug my daughter?" The clinician responded, "Of course, you should hug your daughter. In this instance, we don't want to remove the opportunity, but rather change the consequence."

The clinician used this exchange to review the importance of having clearly established rules for Alyssa, as it allows for an immediate delivery of a consequence in the event the rule is broken. The mother appeared unsure of this discussion, saying she preferred to explain to her daughter why something was wrong instead of being punitive. The clinician agreed that it is important to teach children why something is wrong, but pointed out that Ms. Prentice said she already explained this to her daughter several times and the behavior had not changed. The mother nodded her head in agreement and said, "So, you think I need to try a different approach." The clinician could see the anguish on Ms. Prentice's face and decided to empathize while pressing for a different response: "Again, I think you are absolutely correct that a child needs to understand why a given behavior is not acceptable. And it sounds like you have tried to do that. Sometimes, though, children continue to perform the behavior if they are getting something out of it. We need to change what happens when she performs the behavior."

Ms. Prentice appeared confused and said, "What is she getting out of touching me like that? Are you saying she enjoys it?" The clinician pivoted, "No, I'm not saying she enjoys it like some sexual type of pleasure. But, look at the ABC chain [pointing to the C]. After she touches you, there is a good dose of attention that she receives as you explain the inappropriateness of it to her and your, understandably, shocked reaction." The mother followed this explanation and said, "So, if I don't try to explain what is wrong with it, what should I do instead?" The clinician restated the mother's question in a different way, "Well, if she is performing the behavior because it gets a reaction from you, then what could you do that might reduce the behavior?" Ms. Prentice easily responded, "I need to stop giving her attention." The clinician agreed and reviewed ways to separate after inappropriate touching without providing attention.

The clinician recognized that the mother was opposed to punishments, but emphasized that a negative consequence for Alyssa may prompt her to better self-monitor and inhibit herself in order to prevent that consequence. Ms. Prentice thought about this explanation for a moment, and then said, "I've never thought of it that way." The clinician further clarified that the goal of such consequences is not to punish questions, curiosity, or developmentally typical behaviors, but to help Alyssa learn and apply rules to eliminate undesired behaviors. Ms. Prentice agreed to try implementing natural consequences and removal of privileges in response to breaking rules. She identified the most effective consequences as likely being restriction from watching television and not receiving candy or other treats for a day.

Having defined these consequences, the clinician presented Ms. Prentice with two rules, developed prior to session in anticipation of this discussion:

1. It's not OK to put things in my private areas.
2. It's not OK to touch or look at other people's private areas.

Ms. Prentice reviewed the rules and agreed that they adequately addressed the behaviors she hoped to change. The clinician reviewed the process of teaching these to Alyssa and how to integrate the use of consequences when a rule was broken.

Alyssa joined the session and, as planned, Ms. Prentice showed the girl a drawing of a boy and girl on the beach wearing swimsuits. The mother proceeded to teach her daughter that anything covered by the swimsuits is considered "private areas" and that rules are going to be established about how to treat private parts. Alyssa looked at the picture and said, "Boobs are private areas?" Ms. Prentice confirmed that they were, indeed, included in the definition. Alyssa started laughing and said, "You have boobs, mommy. Me too. See. [lifting up her shirt]" The mother's mouth dropped as she looked at the clinician, who motioned for mom to ignore and continue. Ms. Prentice began reading the rules to Alyssa. After reading the first one, Alyssa interrupted, "I don't do that anymore." The mother acknowledged the behavior had not occurred in a week and praised her daughter. She continued by reading the second rule. Alyssa laughed again and said, "You mean like this? [tried to touch her mother's breast]" Again, the mother looked at the clinician, who motioned for her to ignore the child's behavior and continue. The girl's comments demonstrated that she clearly understood the rules.

Ms. Prentice then explained to her daughter that breaking the rules would result in removing television time or treats. At that point the girl looked confused and asked, "Why?" The mother clarified that these rules were now in effect and the consequences would be implemented moving forward.

The young girl asked if she lost television given that she just raised her shirt and attempted to touch the mother's breast moments before. The mother looked at the clinician, who gave a head shake, and then told her daughter, "No. They start right now." The girl looked sad, but did not speak. The mother asked Alyssa if she understood or had any questions. The girl crossed her arms and shook her head.

Session 3

Ms. Prentice began this session by noting that Alyssa was discovered to have inserted an object into her vagina over the past week. When asked to describe the situation, the mother said it was during bath time, and she left the room for approximately 90 seconds to change the laundry. When she returned, she found Alyssa had inserted a toy. The mother quickly clarified that she knew the monitoring plan dictated not leaving the girl alone during baths, but since the behavior had not been seen in over 10 days, she thought it was eliminated. The clinician clarified that behavior can be dormant for a period of time and return when the opportunity presents itself, and that 10 days is not a long period. Ms. Prentice apologized and said she regretted leaving her alone and had returned to using the monitoring plan.

The mother then stated that Alyssa continued trying to touch her (the mother's) private areas during hugs and laughed afterward. The clinician asked which consequences were implemented after these inappropriate touching attempts and Ms. Prentice said she never had the opportunity to deliver a consequence, nor did she implement one of the consequences after Alyssa inserted the toy. The clinician, not understanding Ms. Prentice's phrasing of the event, asked for clarification. The mother responded, "After she touched me, I pulled her away and started explaining that such behavior was not acceptable. I reminded her of the rules, but before I could finish, she walked away, laughing." The clinician rehearsed with the mother how to respond in future instances, emphasizing that no further explanation is required, as it has been explained to Alyssa several times that such behavior is inappropriate. The mother was instructed to simply say, "That breaks one of our body rules and now you have lost television for the remainder of the day." Ms. Prentice was noticeably uncomfortable, but understood and practiced the sequence with the clinician. It was also emphasized that Ms. Prentice must follow through when a consequence is delivered and ensure that television is not allowed during the remainder of that day. It was clarified that Alyssa was not allowed to earn it back by improving behavior, as then breaking the rules was irrelevant because consequences could be canceled by later behaviors.

Alyssa joined the session and energetically took her seat. The clinician asked her to recite the "body rules," which she did with little difficulty. This prompted the clinician to say to the mother, "It looks like she knows the rules pretty well, mom." This simple comment was intended to underline the fact that explaining the rules in depth at the moment Alyssa breaks one is not required. Ms. Prentice looked at the clinician and stated, "I guess so." The clinician then proceeded to present to the girl a handful of carefully crafted scenarios, given her young age. The first asked whether it would break a rule if she hugged her mother and squeezed her breast in the process. Alyssa easily stated this would break a rule. The second scenario repeated the first, but changed the behavior to, "Your hand happened to be near mom's private area, but nothing was touched on purpose." The girl correctly responded that it would not break a rule. A similar scene was described in the bathtub where a toy was intentionally inserted, with the next scenario only mentioning that a toy was floating near her vagina. The girl correctly answered both of these situations and Ms. Prentice provided consistent praise. The clinician reinforced for the mother that Alyssa appeared to accurately understand the rules and the goal now was for her (the mother) to consistently enforce them.

Session 4

Ms. Prentice arrived to this final session of the phase reporting improvement in Alyssa's behaviors. No new incidents of inserting objects were observed over the past week and touching her mother's private areas occurred only twice. The clinician asked Ms. Prentice to review her responses to these two incidents. Both times she stated that she immediately cut off contact and informed her daughter that the television was off limits for the remainder of the day. Alyssa responded both times by laughing and walking away, but later threw a tantrum when the mother prohibited her from turning on the television. Both of these incidents occurred earlier in the week and no inappropriate touching had occurred over the past 3 days. The clinician praised the mother for following through on the implementation of consequences.

Noting that the last intrusive behavior incident was a few days in the past, the clinician asked, "But, you have hugged your daughter in the past 3 days, right?" Ms. Prentice smiled and said, "Of course, a handful of times every day." This led the clinician to ask the mother how often she was praising her daughter for following the rules when these hugs did not include inappropriate touching (as discussed in the second session). Ms. Prentice appeared surprised and thought for a moment. "I'm not sure that I have," she answered, before continuing, "I should do that more." The clinician agreed and encouraged her to also do the same for bath times that do not involve inserting objects. The clinician reminded the mother that the goal is to provide significant positive attention and reinforcement for abiding by the rules to complement the delivery of consequences when she breaks the rules. The mother agreed to make a concerted effort to increase positive feedback.

Alyssa joined the session for the remainder of the time. The clinician noted that her mother reported significant improvement adhering to the "body rules" over the prior week and lavished praise on the girl. She smiled and said, "Yeah, I've been good." The clinician allowed her to pick a sticker out of a bin and to select games she wished to play during session. The clinician spent the remainder of the time building rapport with Alyssa and modeling praise and other forms of positive feedback for the mother.

Phase 2

Session 1

Given previous discussions with Ms. Prentice, the clinician anticipated that the mother would be very open to discussing sex and sexuality with her daughter. However, the mother previously demonstrated a limited knowledge of developmental expectations and how to approach topics in an effective way with such a young child. To open this session, the clinician restated what was previously learned through sessions, including that Ms. Prentice was open with sexual topics, did not want her daughter to be ashamed of her body, and hoped to instill a view that sex is a natural part of life. This led to the clinician's first question, "What limits, if any, do you think should be placed around sexual behavior?" Ms. Prentice was stumped and struggled to respond. Reflecting her previous laxity with sexual modeling in the home, it quickly became clear that Ms. Prentice was focused so intently on not shaming or hiding sexual behavior that she failed to consider what boundaries were healthy.

Ms. Prentice eventually questioned the clinician, "I mean, I believe there should be some boundaries, but like you said before, she probably won't understand them. So, what do I say?" The clinician reviewed some of the content that the mother previously shared with Alyssa, including descriptions of sexual intercourse. "Let's start there. It seems like she did understand what you told her about how intercourse occurs. I'm wondering if you told her when you believe intercourse is acceptable." Ms. Prentice leaned back and her eyes shifted from side to side, as if deep in thought. After a few moments, she quietly concluded, "No, I don't think that I did." The clinician used this opening to describe the purpose of the current phase: "That's okay. That's our goal here. We'll think through these types of things to give her some more information to make sure she knows what is healthy and safe." Ms. Prentice agreed, though she continued to display a look of regret or, possibly, disappointment that she had omitted such information previously.

The clinician continued to follow this line of discussion, "So, when do you and your family view sexual behavior as acceptable?" Ms. Prentice hesitated and then softly said, "Well, when you're consenting adults. I don't believe you need to be married or anything, but you should be consenting adults." The clinician wrote this down and reflected her statement, "Consenting adults. Okay. Does that require any kind of relationship commitment, like dating, or is it only consenting adults?" The mother then shifted to display a reserved, almost embarrassed expression. "Well, I mean, I had one-night stands and I don't want to be a hypocrite. You probably think that's bad, right?" The clinician replied, "Not at all. People have all kinds of values and beliefs when it comes to sex. My job is to help you teach your values to your daughter. So, we'll leave it at consenting adults." Ms. Prentice appeared relieved.

Over the course of the remainder of the session, Ms. Prentice identified several items for inclusion on the "Should Know" list, but repeatedly struggled to identify topics for the "Should Not Know" list. Her approach was well-intentioned, but often lacked a consideration of her daughter's level of cognitive development. The clinician presented topics that seemed clearly beyond the level of a 4-year-old child, hoping to gain quick agreement, only to see Ms. Prentice hedge on her answer. For instance, the clinician asked, "Do you think Alyssa needs to know about fetishes, like bondage or role playing?" The mother delivered a standard answer to such questions, "Well, if she asks or the conversation goes there, I don't see the harm." Throughout this conversation, Ms. Prentice's responses largely appeared driven by an openness to answer her daughter's questions as opposed to intentionally presenting information too advanced for the child to understand. Even when the clinician asked clarifying questions, such as, "Do you think a 4-year-old would ask about something like bondage?" the mother's response was typically some version of "I don't know. Maybe." By the end of the session, only a few items appeared in the Should Not Know category.

Session 2

The clinician came into session with several fact sheets and other psychoeducation materials, as it was apparent that Ms. Prentice was generally unaware of developmental capacities for a preschooler. These materials included information on sexual development, as well as cognitive and social development. The clinician started by presenting the handouts that traced the development of sexual knowledge and behavior over the childhood years, pointing out that preschool children typically ask questions about body parts or the origins of babies, attempt to look at people undressing, and occasionally touch their own private areas. Ms. Prentice nodded in agreement, seemingly acknowledging that she already possessed this information. However, when the clinician transitioned into discussing typical behaviors of school-age children (e.g., interest in sexual body parts of others, greater interest in sexual behavior) and adolescents (e.g., sexual attraction, deliberate self-stimulation), Ms. Prentice's demeanor changed. The clinician highlighted that some of the topics the mother previously discussed with her daughter, such as orgasms and condoms, were not typically considered by school-aged children, let alone preschool-aged children, and were more commonly topics of conversation for preteens or teenagers.

Seeing that Ms. Prentice was actively looking through the materials and seeming engaged, the clinician transitioned to a discussion of cognitive development and used the example of how preschool children learn math to help the mother understand the concept: "Think about how children Alyssa's age learn math. One apple plus one apple equals two apples. This is very concrete. They can see them, they can hold them, they can point to them and count. Things that are too abstract and not easily experienced are very difficult to learn." Ms. Prentice recognized the point from the previous conversation, "So, you're saying that she can't understand things like orgasms or arousal." The clinician agreed but emphasized that it is true for most preschool-aged children, not just Alyssa. Further, it was emphasized that the concept of an orgasm that Ms. Prentice previously tried to teach her daughter is not the same thing as a pleasurable sensation that is derived from stimulating the genital area. Indeed, even young children may obtain a "funny feeling" when the genitals are stimulated, but this is not the same thing as having an orgasm. Ms. Prentice reflected this last point and asked, "Is that why little kids can't keep their hands out of their pants?" The clinician smiled and said, "That's probably true for some of them."

With the mother having a greater sense of her daughter's cognitive abilities and typical sexual development, the clinician revisited the concept of healthy sexuality. Ms. Prentice looked at the list and identified several topics from the Should Know side that she now believed should be listed under the Should Not Know category. As these were being moved over, she asked, "But what if she asks about these?" The clinician explored that topic with her, highlighting Ms. Prentice's clear desire to not lie to her daughter. The topic was presented as one of recognizing the information that her daughter can understand that would advance the goal of her being healthy. For instance, if Alyssa were to ask why someone might have sex, the mother can refer to the purpose of reproduction. While it is true that people may have sex for other reasons, those reasons are more abstract and difficult to understand. However, producing a baby is a simple, concrete answer that should satisfy her daughter's curiosity. In brief, being honest and providing helpful information does not require telling the child everything the parent knows about the topic. Ms. Prentice felt relieved after this discussion.

The clinician presented the mother with a psychoeducational storybook designed for preschool-aged children and they reviewed the pages together. Ms. Prentice was surprised to see the relatively limited information shared in the book, which prompted the clinician to ask, "What information is missing?" The mother hesitated, searching for an answer that conformed with the previous discussion about developmental appropriateness: "I'm not sure. Yeah, I guess they don't really talk about arousal or romantic relationships or anything like that." The clinician nodded and reframed the mother's comment. "You're right. This is very biological, but that's easy for the child to understand. This will be the most unsexy discussion of sex you've ever had." That comment drew a smile from Ms. Prentice.

The clinician concluded the session by allowing Ms. Prentice to role play her presentation of the book, with the clinician taking on the role of Alyssa. Given that the young girl was talkative in previous sessions, the clinician made a point of presenting several questions to the mother, as well as interrupting her while she read. Ms. Prentice did an excellent job of remaining focused and on only one occasion began drifting into an overly advanced answer to a question. The clinician stopped her and processed how Alyssa was likely to receive the answer. The mother quickly realized the information was beyond her daughter's ability to comprehend and rehearsed a more suitable answer. The clinician ended the session by reviewing a few signals that Ms. Prentice could provide if she needed help, as well as one the clinician might use if the speed of the presentation was too fast.

Session 3

Given the child's age, Session 3 was omitted.

Session 4

When Ms. Prentice and Alyssa entered the session, it was noticeable that the girl was in a bad mood. Her mother noted that she had several tantrums that morning. Hearing this, the girl sternly commented, "No, I didn't!" The clinician chose to ignore the child's comment and continued to greet Ms. Prentice. As everyone took their seats, Alyssa crossed her arms and put her head down. The clinician thanked everyone for coming and noted that discussion was encouraged, emphasizing that Alyssa would not be in trouble for any honest questions she asked during the session. Ms. Prentice quickly seconded that statement. Alyssa looked sternly at her mother, who then looked at the clinician and used one of the prearranged signals for help. The clinician motioned for her to ignore the child's behavior and begin reading the book.

After the first few pages, Alyssa used an irritated tone to state, "This is dumb." Again, the mother looked at the clinician, and, again, the clinician indicated that Ms. Prentice should ignore the girl's negativity. As the mother continued to read, the book opened to the first page that provided cartoon drawings of male and female genitals, including internal organs such as the uterus and ovaries. Hearing the word "vagina," Alyssa looked up and said, "I know. Why are you saying that?" Thankfully, this was one of the situations the clinician presented during the prior session while role-playing. The mother delivered an excellent answer, "Well, because I've learned there are a few other things I should teach you to make sure you stay healthy." The girl continued with the stern look and leaned back in her chair.

The mother proceeded with the book and occasionally stopped to ask Alyssa whether she had questions. At each instance, the girl shook her head to indicate, "No." Her body language clearly conveyed her intention to not speak. When the mother presented information about how sensitive genital areas are and the need to treat them delicately, Alyssa again engaged in a negative manner: "I do. You don't need to say that." Sensing the mother was unsure of how to proceed, the clinician interceded.

CLINICIAN: What's it been now? Four, 5 weeks since she hurt herself in the bathtub?

MS. PRENTICE: It's been 5 weeks. She hasn't tried that in 5 weeks.

CLINICIAN: Wow, 5 weeks. That's awesome!

MS. PRENTICE: Umm, yes, it is awesome. I'm very proud of her!

CLINICIAN: You should be. She's doing great. You should be proud of yourself too, mom.

The clinician's initial comment served the purpose of modeling for the mother the ignoring of the child's negativity, but also resulted in providing an opportunity to praise the girl. Ms. Prentice effectively reflected the clinician's comment to also praise the girl. Upon hearing this, Alyssa ceased protesting and leaned back in her chair.

The mother proceeded with the book, effectively covering the names of sexual body parts, conception, and the conditions under which sexual behavior is allowed (i.e., consenting adults). Alyssa did not ask any questions, but did make comments several times that demonstrated her understanding of the topic. For instance, when the mother mentioned that sexual behavior was only allowed among consenting adults, Alyssa snapped, "Well, I'm not doing that." The mother implemented the previously rehearsed response, "It's okay to feel that way. And, if it changes when you get older, that's okay, too." The young girl was obviously not prepared for that answer, as she furrowed her eyebrows and looked at her mother in a state of surprise.

To end the session, the clinician emphasized that this was meant only to be the first discussion of these topics and that Alyssa was free to ask questions as she developed them. Alyssa snapped, "I don't want to. This is gross." The clinician empathized with her answer and thanked her for participating in the session. Interestingly, Ms. Prentice called the clinician a few days after this session and said that Alyssa had come to her asking, "Is my vagina still hurt? When I put the doll in?" This seemed to be an extension of the conversation about treating private areas delicately that occurred during the conjoint session. Ms. Prentice appropriately told Alyssa, "No, the doctor said everything is okay. But, if you hurt yourself again, there is always a chance that you can hurt those parts inside really bad." The clinician praised the mother for not overreacting and not providing information beyond the girl's ability to understand.

Phase 3

Session 1

Given Alyssa's young age, the clinician brought both her and Ms. Prentice into session together. Alyssa's mood was significantly improved compared to the previous session and she was back to being a talkative child. The clinician decided to teach the girl impulse control skills by making the initial demonstration into a game. The clinician placed a trash can on the floor and told Alyssa to hold her hand over it. Then, the clinician placed two ice cubes in her hand, asked her to close the hand around them, and started a stopwatch. The goal was described as seeing how long she could hold the ice cubes without dropping them into the trash can. Alyssa said the task was not difficult and she could hold them as long as she wanted. However, within 15 seconds, the girl started to show signs of discomfort, as she began giggling and squirming in her chair. When the stopwatch showed 20 seconds, Alyssa started laughing and saying it was too cold and dropped them shortly after. The clinician then took out several stickers and showed them to her. The deal was made that if Alyssa learned some skills during the session and used them to beat her score of 27 seconds, she could take home five stickers. The girl's eyes grew large and she enthusiastically agreed.

The clinician then proceeded to teach her controlled breathing skills, by creating a contest to see who could blow the largest bubble. The girl took the wand out of a bottle of bubbles and quickly blew, spraying the soapy mixture across the table. The clinician then took a controlled breath and slowly let the air out, creating a bubble ever increasing in size. At one point, the girl looked at the size of the bubble and exclaimed, "Wow!" Once it finally popped, the clinician offered to teach Alyssa how to blow such a bubble and she eagerly reloaded her bubble wand in preparation. After a few tries, the girl was able to blow a bubble of sufficient size, impressing both herself and her mother. The game then transferred to Alyssa and Ms. Prentice, with the daughter winning the bubble contest. The clinician removed the bubbles and asked Alyssa to continue breathing in a similar manner, which demonstrated the possibility of using the breathing technique even when bubbles were not available.

The clinician then shifted the session back to the ice cube challenge. However, the clinician instructed Alyssa to close her eyes and focus on her "bubble breathing" as a tool to help prolong her ability to hold the ice. She agreed and the clinician repeated the procedure. After approximately 30 seconds of ice holding and bubble breathing the girl asked the clinician, "Did I do it?" The clinician said, "I'm not going to tell you. Just go until you feel like you can't any longer." The girl dropped the ice cubes after 40 seconds. When the clinician revealed her time, the girl laughed and said, "HA! Now I get the stickers!" The clinician agreed and allowed the girl to choose her stickers.

The clinician then translated the ice cube challenge to other times in Alyssa's life when it seemed her body was trying to send her a message or a thought popped in her head. The girl appeared confused and the clinician revisited the rules previously developed in Phase 1, "For example, when you start getting that urge or feeling to touch mom's private areas, you can do your bubble breathing to help you not do that." Alyssa nodded her head and said, "I don't do that anymore." The mother jumped in to praise her daughter, noting that it had been almost 3 weeks since she tried to touch her mother inappropriately. The clinician reflected this praise and clarified that the techniques can be used anytime she has a thought or feeling that should be controlled. As the session ended, the clinician encouraged the mother to help Alyssa identify times in the coming week where using her new skills might be helpful.

Session 2

Given how well the structure worked in the prior session, both Alyssa and her mother entered session together. The clinician started by asking Alyssa if she used her bubble breathing in the prior week. She said she had, but that her mother refused to let her use the bubbles. Ms. Prentice clarified that Alyssa liked to play with the bubbles and frequently created a mess because she was not using them for the purposes of controlled breathing. The clinician reflected her statement and then said, “How about if I teach you another skill today? Then you have a few different ones to use.” Alyssa eagerly agreed and asked if it involved bubbles too. The clinician presented the young girl with paper and crayons and said, “No, but it does involve these.” Alyssa smiled and began rifling through the crayons.

The clinician presented the technique as the “happy story” exercise and asked Alyssa to think of a time when she felt really happy. She thought for a moment and then answered, “My birthday party!” The clinician asked the girl to color a picture that showed what happened at her party. She quickly went to work, ferociously coloring a picture in red and blue that later included some details in green. Once completed, the clinician asked Alyssa to describe what was happening in the picture. The girl discussed the details of the cake, the games that were played, the friends and family that attended, and the presents she received. After she finished, the clinician asked her how she felt recounting the story of her party. “Really happy,” she replied.

The clinician then provided a basic introduction to the concept of the cognitive triangle, but considering her age, omitted any significant schematic drawings or hypothetical examples. Instead, the clinician said, “You were thinking about happy things and that made you feel happy. When we feel happy, we act in certain ways. Like, I can see you smiling.” Alyssa continued to smile and said, “I get it.” The clinician then continued the basic discussion: “But if you think about angry things, it makes you angry.” The girl then interjected, “And then you do angry things?” The clinician responded, “Yes, exactly. Wow, you’re a smart cookie. You picked that up quickly.” Alyssa calmly replied, “I know.”

The clinician clarified for Alyssa and her mother that, sometimes, when feeling in a bad mood, it can help to draw or talk about a happy memory. Again, the girl picked up on the suggestion, “So, when I’m mad, I draw a picture of my birthday party?” The clinician agreed that this was one idea, or she could pick a different happy memory. The girl volunteered her ideas, “Like dancing and singing?” The clinician confirmed that this was an excellent idea before adding that the happy story tool can even be used when a thought or feeling was leading her to possibly break one of the body rules. As in the session before, the girl snapped that she had not broken the rules in a long time and, again, her mother praised her.

Alyssa announced to the room that she had an idea. Since the session before, she was able to hold ice cubes in her hand longer when doing the bubble breathing, she wanted to see if she could hold them even longer if she used her new happy story technique. However, she quickly added that doing so successfully should result in earning five additional stickers. The clinician agreed to her terms and left the room to retrieve ice cubes. As they prepared for the challenge, the clinician added a twist. "If you can use both the happy story and bubble breathing techniques together, and beat your score, I'll give you seven stickers." The girl violently nodded her head in agreement. She sat at the table with one hand over the trash can, the other hand holding a crayon with a blank sheet of paper, and began her controlled breathing as the clinician placed an ice cube into her hand. The girl succeeded, holding the ice cube for a full minute. The clinician and Ms. Prentice praised her effort and she began picking out her stickers.

Session 3

Only Ms. Prentice came back into the treatment room to begin this session. Given the mother's prior concern that someone had sexually abused her daughter, the clinician used this perspective to highlight the importance of keeping an open line of communication with Alyssa regarding sexual topics. Ms. Prentice agreed and the clinician transitioned into a discussion of who was allowed around her daughter unsupervised. She identified grandparents and a trusted family friend who babysat on occasion. The clinician then discussed the difference between secrets and surprises and how this created a useful way of distinguishing between safe and unsafe actions. Ms. Prentice immediately grabbed on to that concept and said she should teach that to Alyssa. The clinician agreed and stated this could occur later in the session; the two then role played how to present that information.

The clinician also discussed with Ms. Prentice how she can monitor her environment for any potential modeling or safety issues that may present in the future. For instance, the clinician suggested that, every few months, the mother may wish to note for Alyssa that she continued to follow the body rules, provide praise, and then ask if she has noticed anyone not following those rules. The mother also liked this idea and suggested she should ask her daughter this question more frequently, perhaps once per week. The clinician cautioned the mother against broaching the topic too often, as it may inadvertently give the perception that she is expecting a "yes" response from her daughter. Ms. Prentice understood this and agreed to only ask every few months, unless some incident occurred that prompted it being asked sooner.

Lastly, the clinician reviewed the importance of teaching Alyssa the steps to take in the event someone does attempt sexually inappropriate behavior. Ms. Prentice developed a list of individuals that her daughter could tell, and agreed to give the girl permission to leave a situation where she felt uncomfortable. The clinician role played these particular skills with the mother before bringing Alyssa into session.

Ms. Prentice began the conversation by praising Alyssa for continuing to follow the body rules the family put in place. She then asked her daughter whether she had seen anyone else break these rules. The girl responded, "Yeah." This brief statement elicited a look of shock and concern from Ms. Prentice, who immediately asked, "Who?" Alyssa started naming several people in the family and it became clear she was referencing the displays of nudity in the home prior to beginning treatment. Ms. Prentice clarified her question, noting that everyone is now abiding by the body rules in the family and asked if anyone has broken those rules since they were put in place. The girl denied any such violations.

Ms. Prentice transitioned into the next part of the lesson, "If anyone tried to break the body rules, whether it was someone in our family or someone else, then you need to tell them to stop. Let's practice this." The girl looked confused by the phrasing of the instruction. Ms. Prentice then demonstrated by raising her voice and firmly stating, "Stop!" The girl took the cue. She stood up in the room and started repeatedly yelling, "Stop!" This then progressed to her stomping around the room as she repeatedly screamed the word. Ms. Prentice apologized to the clinician, seemingly embarrassed. The clinician smiled and said, "No need. I think she gets it." The mother praised her daughter and told her, "But, there's more." The girl then sat back down and Ms. Prentice described other situations that might create an uncomfortable feeling, such as someone tickling or rubbing her back when she did not want them to. The mother did an exceptional job describing to the girl her rights over her own body and how to firmly request that the other individual stop the touching.

Once these points were made, the mother discussed a list of people that Alyssa should tell if someone broke the body rules or did not stop touching her in an uncomfortable way. The list included parents, grandparents, teachers, the family doctor, and police officers. Alyssa looked confused. When asked by her mother if she understood the directions, the girl asked, "Do I need to tell all those people?" Ms. Prentice quickly clarified that the girl only needed to tell one person. The clinician then interrupted the mother, "Yes, you only need to tell one person, as long as that person believes you and gets help." The mother agreed with the clinician and Alyssa nodded her head.

Session 4

Ms. Prentice attended this session alone, as Alyssa was not feeling well. The clinician started by reviewing with the mother the importance of monitoring a child's peer groups to prevent exposure to undesired information. She understood, but also noted that Alyssa's primary interactions with peers occurred either at preschool or in her gymnastics class. The clinician conceded that the task is actually quite easy at this point in time, but may become more difficult as her daughter aged. The clinician recommended some online resources that could help with promoting positive peer relationships.

Ms. Prentice took a few moments to complete the original assessment measures. She did not endorse any critical items on the ASB-C and the score of 10 fell in the *Typical/Expected* range, indicating no significant ongoing concerns related to PSB. However, she continued to report significant emotional and behavioral concerns on the SDQ. This result, combined with the observations made during treatment sessions, led the clinician to recommend referral to a focused behavioral caregiver training program. The mother asked several questions about the recommended program and what would happen if the PSB returned. The clinician described how the skills learned in that program might benefit Ms. Prentice as they could be used to further address PSB in the event of a recurrence. In addition, the caregiver training program was available within the same clinic, although with a different clinician. This left open the opportunity of consulting with the current clinician if PSB was observed. Ms. Prentice agreed with the referral and thanked the clinician for helping improve Alyssa's behaviors. The clinician praised the mother's efforts and noted that her dedication to her daughter made the difference.

CONCLUSION

The case of Alyssa P. demonstrates the applicability of PBT with caregivers that display overly permissive attitudes toward sex and sexuality within the home. The mother was not ill-meaning, but clearly did not have a firm understanding of typical sexual or cognitive development for preschool-aged children. It also included a fairly common situation where a parent assumed a child with PSB was sexually abused. The clinician in this case handled all of these aspects with empathy and by providing guidance and support to the mother. Rapport with the caregiver proved vital to building parenting efficacy. The girl's behavioral challenges added another layer to this case, but teaching the mother some basic behavior management skills (e.g., ignoring negative attention seeking, praising desired behavior, implementing consequences for breaking rules) proved successful, even with her initial hesitancy to employ them. In short, the clinician's nonjudgmental and supportive approach fostered trust with an opinionated caregiver, which allowed for the teaching of parenting skills and psychoeducation on child development that yielded a successful outcome.

8 ALVI L.

A School-Aged Child Watching Internet Pornography

ASSESSMENT

The case of Alvi L. discusses a topic of contemporary concern, a school-aged child willfully and repeatedly displaying concerning electronic and online sexual behavior. In addition, the clinician contends with a child who is initially hesitant to discuss sexual topics. Shortly into treatment, the clinician learns that the mother has a sexual abuse history and this experience results in unhelpful thoughts about her son and impacts her view of what her son should know about sex.

Background

Alvi L. entered treatment at 9 years of age after his mother, Mrs. Laakso, walked into a room and discovered him watching pornography on a tablet. When she examined the search history on the browser, she learned the boy had accessed multiple internet pornography sites over the past several weeks. The sites ranged from sexually explicit videos with humans to Japanese anime

https://doi.org/10.1037/0000516-009
Children With Problematic Sexual Behavior: Theory, Research, and Evidence-Based Practice, by B. Allen

cartoons depicting sexual acts. When she asked Alvi why he was watching these types of videos, he shrugged his shoulders and said, "I like it." Mrs. Laakso lectured the boy about the inappropriateness of the sites, took away the tablet, restricted him from playing video games, and grounded him to the house. The mother then stated she tried several times since to ask Alvi how he first came to find these sites and why he continued to visit them. The boy remained quiet and refused to engage. She called her pediatrician asking for help, which resulted in the referral to treatment. During the assessment, Alvi sat quietly and refused to speak with the clinician.

Assessment Data

Mrs. Laakso completed the Assessment of Sexual Behavior-Child version (ASB-C). Although she did not endorse any critical items, the total score of 23 clearly suggested problematic behaviors. Reviewing the individual items, four were endorsed as occurring with the highest possible frequency over the past month (i.e., more than 10 times), and all of these items were related in some way to viewing internet pornography (e.g., *uses the internet to seek out information on sexual topics, looks at pictures or videos that show nudity or sexual acts*). Once these items were removed, the total score fell to 7, which is within normal limits for a 9-year-old. This suggested that the problematic sexual behavior (PSB) was clearly limited to Alvi's internet activities. There were no clinically significant concerns noted on the Strengths and Difficulties Questionnaire (SDQ), no trauma history was present on the Child and Adolescent Trauma Screen (CATS), and the mother did not identify any significant stress on the Parenting Stress Index–Short Form (PSI-SF) or the Patient Health Questionnaire-9 (PHQ-9). Mrs. Laakso did complete the ESS, which suggested some exposure to nudity in the home and on television, but no known overt exposure to sexual activity.

Conceptualization

Alvi's case represented a sort of mystery in terms of conceptualization at the beginning of treatment. The lack of any known trauma history ruled out a traumatic sexualization understanding, and he appeared to be well regulated, which argued against employing a developmental psychopathology lens. There was some evidence of exposure to sexual content in the home, making social modeling a possibility. However, there was a disconnect on this point, as Mrs. Laakso reported only exposure to nudity while Alvi's internet searches included graphic sexual acts. With this in mind, the clinician proceeded using the standard phase-based treatment for PSB (PBT) model without any preconceived ideas of specialized techniques or considerations that might need to be integrated, such as might occur in cases of posttraumatic stress, sexual abuse, significant self-dysregulation, or repeated modeling of sexual behavior in the home.

PHASE-BASED TREATMENT

The assessment provided relatively little information to inform treatment delivery other than that the PSB was primarily occurring via electronic and online means. Alvi's mother appeared cooperative, the boy's behavior was generally positive, and social modeling of sexual behavior was limited, leaving it unclear how the PSB developed. The clinician remained attuned throughout treatment to any such factors that might be considered important for the purposes of treatment.

Phase 1

Session 1

Mrs. Laakso attended session eager to talk about her son's behavior. She believed him to be a sexual deviant and was concerned that it was only a matter of time before he either propositioned a peer to engage in a sexual relationship or perpetrated on another child. The clinician tried to put her at ease by discussing the relative frequency with which children access internet pornography. The fact that Alvi searched for and watched sexual topics did not suggest he was likely to become a sexual perpetrator. The mother pushed back that he repeatedly performed this behavior over several weeks and stated that he "liked it." The clinician acknowledged her concerns but replied that this was also something reported by many children as the images can create a sort of excited feeling inside the child, even if they do not fully understand why they are experiencing this sensation.

The clinician then transitioned into a discussion of Mrs. Laakso's answers on the ESS and inquired about the types of nudity to which Alvi was exposed. The mother reported that there were times one person in the family darted from one room to another with breasts or genitals exposed, such as retrieving clothes from a laundry room after a shower. Alvi had witnessed some of these moments. There were also several times that a movie the family was watching briefly showed breasts, but she did not recall any sexual displays in those movies or that Alvi witnessed any sexual behaviors in the home.

She noted her son did not talk much about school and she is unsure what he was exposed to in that setting. The clinician stressed the importance of reducing modeling in the home, even though it seemed limited, to help reinforce the rules shortly to be developed. The mother agreed and said she would discuss this with her husband.

The clinician then turned to developing an ABC chain with Mrs. Laakso. The behavior was easily defined from the ASB-C and her report: watching internet pornography. The antecedent also was easily identified, as the behavior only occurred when Alvi was left alone with the tablet. He never watched sexually explicit material when in the vicinity of other members of the family. However, when it came to identifying the consequence of this behavior, Mrs. Laakso struggled. She identified removing the tablet, and the other punishments discussed above, but when the clinician pointed out that the behavior was ongoing for several weeks and surely there was a consequence that followed all of those prior behaviors, Mrs. Laakso was at a loss for words. The clinician rephrased the question to ask, "What was Alvi getting out of watching pornography that made him keep doing it?" The mother leaned back in the chair and said, "You mean, he enjoyed it." The clinician acknowledged her statement and presented this diagram:

Left alone with tablet (A)

↓

Watches internet pornography (B)

↓

Feels excited, enjoys it (C)

After she agreed with the sequence, Mrs. Laakso quickly retorted, "But how do we stop it?" The clinician used this question to begin a conversation about a monitoring plan.

On the one hand, Mrs. Laakso's response to Alvi's behavior effectively served as a monitoring plan, as he was no longer allowed to access the tablet. On the other hand, this was only a temporary solution, as the boy was required to complete homework assignments and other schoolwork on an electronic device. After removing the tablet, the mother notified Alvi's teacher that they were restricting his access to the internet because of "concerning behaviors," choosing not to disclose his viewing of pornography. In response, the teacher provided Alvi with paper copies of all assignments. When the clinician asked if this was a permanent change to his schooling plan, Ms. Laakso was slow to respond. She admitted that it cannot be permanent because, surely, he would be required at some point to write papers and complete assignments electronically, but she had not considered how to transition to a return to using the tablet.

The clinician spent several minutes discussing this topic with the mother, emphasizing the part of the ABC chain that showed he only accessed sexually explicit material when left unsupervised with the tablet. Mrs. Laakso acknowledged that his use of the tablet around her or her husband probably would not result in pornography viewing but then expressed concern that he might revert to his problematic behavior during short windows when left alone, for instance, if she used the restroom. The discussion then focused on how to restrict access during such moments, even if only for a brief period of time. Mrs. Laakso believed the plan was feasible and agreed to try reinstating access to the tablet under the specified conditions.

Session 2

The mother began session by saying that Alvi was allowed access to the tablet over the past week when in the presence of her or her husband, and no inappropriate behaviors were observed. The clinician presented Ms. Laakso with five potential wordings for the rules and asked her to consider how best to define them for her son. None of the rules explicitly identified viewing sexual content on the internet and she questioned how any of them were relevant. The clinician explained that the rules were meant to be broader in their application, meaning they applied both to online, as well as offline, behaviors. The clinician continued that it would be specified for Alvi that the rules were applicable to online activities. The mother agreed with the presentation and proceeded to discuss the different rules and the ones that best served her goals for treatment. The rules defined for Alvi included the following:

1. It is not OK to look at other people's private areas.
2. It is not OK to touch other people's private areas or for them to touch mine.
3. If people ask me to look at their private areas, I tell mom or dad.

Note that a rule related to watching other people perform sexual acts was unnecessary as it is subsumed under the rule about looking at the private areas of others. The mother considered various consequences that might be implemented in response to her son's behaviors. This included removing his tablet again, as well as restricting his access to video games and certain toys.

When Alvi was brought into session, the clinician provided an orientation to the boy, including a disclaimer that some topics were going to be reviewed with the goal of helping him learn boundaries and helpful information. He nodded his head but did not engage further. Mrs. Laakso explained each rule to Alvi as planned and provided several examples, which included both online and offline behaviors (e.g., looking at someone in the shower). When asked, Alvi continued with nonverbal head movements to indicate he understood, but he declined to ask any questions or to speak. The mother looked at the clinician and asked whether Alvi's quiet stance was typical. The clinician acknowledged that it can happen in some cases, but that children do learn nonetheless. Mrs. Laakso agreed to implement the rules and consequences at home over the coming week.

Session 3

Alvi and his mother attended session conjointly and the clinician brought in several scenarios that were prepared specifically to discuss the rules implemented and the behaviors displayed by Alvi. As in the previous sessions, the boy sat quietly and shrugged his shoulders when asked to recite the rules. The mother worriedly looked at the clinician and said she tried to practice the rules with him over the prior week, but he refused to engage during those moments. The clinician reassured the mother and explained to Alvi that correct answers to the upcoming scenarios may be rewarded with candy (note that the mother previously approved this). The boy motioned as if in agreement and the clinician proceeded to the exercise.

The first scenario was rather easy and simply asked whether a rule would be broken if Alvi watched a video with a friend that showed nudity. Using a head nod, he agreed that it would break a rule and he was rewarded with candy. The second scenario presented a situation where the family doctor inspected Alvi's genitals because of a medical concern. The boy denied this would break a rule, using a head shake. After four scenarios with clear answers, the clinician presented the first "gray area" example. In this instance, Alvi was asked whether it would break a rule if he walked into the restroom at school, another boy was standing in the common area with his pants down, and Alvi saw the boy's penis. Alvi's eyes enlarged and began shifting from side to side. It was clear he did not know how to answer. The clinician pointed out the facial responses and suggested that Alvi talk it out. The young boy continued to look confused and the clinician acknowledged it was a difficult situation and, perhaps, two pieces of candy might be rewarded for a correct answer. Still, he refused to comment and stared at his mother, as if asking for help. The clinician provided an empathic comment that this was a difficult question and emphasized that it is acceptable to get it wrong as this is designed to test his understanding. After approximately 30 seconds, Alvi finally said, "It's not [against the rules] if I didn't want to see it but is [against the rules] if that's why I went in there." The clinician praised Alvi's verbalization and agreed with his conclusion.

After this initial comment, Alvi seemed more comfortable speaking, but still primarily communicated through nonverbal means. Sensing that Alvi spoke more with the "gray area" questions, the clinician constructed a few additional ones during session. For instance, one question asked whether it would break a rule if Alvi was using someone else's computer and an advertisement featuring a naked woman appeared on the screen. Alvi again provided a multistep answer: "If I didn't know it would do that, then no I didn't break a rule. I mean, I didn't mean to see it. But if I knew the computer had those types of things on it, then yeah, that would break a rule. Right?" Mrs. Laakso was surprised at the level of consideration that Alvi put into his answer. She agreed with him and then said she was amazed how well he thought through the possible responses. The clinician seconded her comments and Alvi smiled as the pieces of candy were provided.

The clinician made a point of noting that, although Alvi did not engage with Mrs. Laakso over the prior week, he obviously learned the rules. Not only that, he seemed particularly adept at applying them to a host of different situations. The mother agreed and stated again that she was surprised at how well he processed the questions and derived a coherent response. It then led her to question why he accessed online pornography in the first place as, surely, he knew it was not appropriate. The clinician cautioned that such knowledge cannot be assumed if it was never stated prior to the behavior occurring, but also that it is unclear what Alvi's motivation was for viewing online pornography.

Session 4

The clinician decided to continue fostering Alvi's conversational nature in this last session of the phase. Several new scenarios were written, the candy supply was replenished, and the clinician continued the conversation with Alvi and his mother. Indeed, the boy appeared more talkative and the clinician made a point of discussing nonsexual topics, such as video games and school. Throughout the conversation, the clinician periodically brought the topic back to something of a sexual nature. The goal was to present the sexual discussions as no more embarrassing or shaming than any other conversation. Alvi appeared to welcome this tactic, as he was more talkative throughout and gave verbal responses for clear yes or no answers to the questions about breaking the "sexual behavior rules."

To build on this burgeoning rapport, the clinician allowed Alvi to pick the activities for the final minutes of the session. He chose to play a game and to show the clinician his favorite musician by listening to a song on the clinician's computer. At the end of session, Alvi left the room for a few moments while the clinician reviewed the events of sessions with Ms. Laakso. She expressed concern that the rules and consequences were only superficial and did not address the deeper reasons for Alvi's behavior and she was skeptical of his answers to the scenarios. She stressed that he can provide the correct responses to an exercise in session, but this may have little bearing on his actual behavior. The clinician acknowledged her concern and stressed that there were other parts of treatment still to come. But, at that point, the rules and expectations were clearly specified for Alvi and he cannot claim ignorance in the future, including during future sessions.

Phase 2

Session 1

When the session began, the clinician asked the mother what information related to sex, if any, she previously shared with Alvi. She was taken aback by the question and was unsure how to answer. The clinician rephrased the question, "Given that Alvi is 9 years old, it's probably safe to say that he knows some things, right? I'm just wondering what he might have learned from you." The mother continued with her surprised look and finally stated, "Why would he know things? He's only 9." The clinician reflected the comment and reassured the mother that her sentiment is shared by many other parents. It was pointed out for the mother that, certainly, Alvi was aware of anatomical differences between males and females and had learned something about sexual activity from the videos he watched. The mother agreed but continued to show a disconcerted look. Mrs. Laakso eventually stated she had not taught Alvi anything because she did not think it was necessary to teach a 9-year-old about sex.

The clinician pointed out that the topic appeared to be one that created significant discomfort for Mrs. Laakso. The mother hesitated before answering that she does not like talking about sex because it is associated with unpleasant memories. She went on to describe her own sexual abuse experience as a child, and this event created significant confusion for her around sex as she moved into her teenage years. She became tearful and the clinician handed her tissues while providing supportive comments. Mrs. Laakso continued that she did not understand why children would be so interested in sex, partially because it had such a negative connotation for her, and this was why she viewed Alvi's behaviors as suggesting something was wrong with him internally. She did not expect sexual interests to emerge for her son until his teenage years and, as such, she had avoided any direct discussion on the topic. The clinician again empathized with her statement and reassured her that other parents have made similar comments. The clinician foresaw the potential for the mother blaming herself and decided to shift focus.

Given Mrs. Laakso's distress, the clinician framed the phase as one where the mother could teach her son the lessons she wanted him to learn. She nodded her head and said, "So, I need to teach him appropriate behavior?" The clinician agreed and discussed the goal of this part of treatment as opening a conversation with Alvi where his questions could be answered in a nonjudgmental way. The clinician then asked the mother what she wanted her son to know. She composed herself and began listing off several criteria for engaging in sexual relationships, including being an adult and making sure the other person gave consent and that it did not involve children. The clinician wrote down these points under a "Should Know" heading. The mother was then at a loss and unsure what else to include. The clinician flipped the question and asked, "What should Alvi not know about sex?" The mother quickly opined, "That it can hurt people." Before the clinician could comment, Mrs. Laakso caught herself and decided this information should be placed in the Should Know category.

Refocusing the conversation on the "Should Not Know" elements, the mother identified several aspects of sexual behavior that, indeed, typically are not reviewed with a child of Alvi's age, such as oral sex and lingerie. However, Mrs. Laakso knew for a fact that her son had watched videos that included these topics. As such, she accurately surmised that they should be included in future discussions and placed them in the Should Know category. Other topics were identified for the Should Not Know column, including sex toys, fetishes, and anal sex. By the end of the session, Mrs. Laakso developed a fairly accurate and useful list of topics for a future discussion with her son. There was one important topic, however, that was missing from the list, the fact that Alvi reported liking the pornography and presumably experienced a level of arousal or excitement while watching the videos. Given the level of emotion in this session, the clinician decided to defer that discussion to the next meeting.

Session 2

The clinician reviewed the events of the prior session with Mrs. Laakso and she thanked the clinician for helping her talk through her concerns related to Alvi and how his sexual behavior caused her such distress. The clinician acknowledged her concerns and then presented her with a few handouts that described the typical sexual development of children. The clinician emphasized that it is not uncommon for children Alvi's age to ask questions and be curious about sexual topics. For instance, by the end of elementary school, most children understand that conception requires a contribution from both a penis and a vagina, even if they are unsure of the exact process required. This can lead to questions and, increasingly, it is being observed that children are turning to internet searches to answer such questions.

The clinician then turned to the previously completed lists of topics that should or should not be included in a future conversation with Alvi. Comparing the columns to the new information presented, the clinician praised the mother for developing lists that are both accurate and helpful. The clinician then broached the topic of Alvi's likely arousal in relation to the pornography: "There is one topic that seems to be missing. You've mentioned a few times that Alvi reported liking the videos he watched." Before the clinician could begin the next sentence, the mother interrupted: "Oh geez. We have to talk about sexual feelings, don't we?" The clinician agreed that it would be a rather significant omission to not discuss the feelings he likely experienced while watching the videos. Mrs. Laakso agreed, but began shaking her head and said, "How do you discuss that with a child?" The clinician assured her there are ways and she could choose the one that worked best for her.

Mrs. Laakso then flipped through three different books the clinician brought into session to identify the one she felt most comfortable using in a conversation with Alvi. She settled on a book that reviewed various body parts, as well as internal and external sexual organs, and that discussed the process of reproduction. The clinician then helped the mother consider the points in the book at which each of the items listed under the Should Know list might be discussed. Some of the points were already included within the text of the book, but the issue of sexual arousal was not. The clinician explained to Mrs. Laakso that there are several different explanations caregivers have given to children for why the body experiences sexual arousal, and she was free to select a reason that best suited her values. She was unable to identify any options herself and the clinician provided several: Sexual arousal creates a motivation to engage in sex, which allows for propagation of the species (evolution), sexual arousal allows one the opportunity to take pleasure in their own body, and God created the body in this way so a husband and wife could share a special and pleasurable experience with one another. Mrs. Laakso decided that she felt most comfortable with the more evolutionary perspective and the clinician helped her consider where this might be discussed within the context of the selected book.

Once the plan was developed, the clinician role played the conjoint session with the mother, allowing her to test out her ability to discuss these topics.

She did exceptionally well reading the book and stopping to review topics such as consent, but understandably struggled when trying to discuss sexual arousal. After working through that point, she again had difficulty clearly articulating the reasons that someone might engage in oral sex or wear lingerie. The clinician suggested connecting all three of these difficult topics. First, the topic of sexual arousal was reconceptualized as a positive aspect of human experience as it ensures the continuity of humanity. Second, sexual arousal is merely a biological response of the body and can be activated by various stimuli, including oral stimulation, people wearing lingerie, or even by watching videos of others. The mother liked this last point as she suggested that connecting so many of these different aspects to one issue (i.e., arousal) allows for reviewing the rules and how they apply to a variety of sexual topics. The clinician agreed and helped the mother practice the presentation again.

Session 3

The clinician invited Alvi back into session and allowed him to pick a game for the two to play while they talked. As they sat down and began playing, Alvi was relatively talkative and made several comments about school and the musician he previously showed the clinician in session. After a few minutes, the clinician transitioned to reminding Alvi about the reasons for treatment, specifically his watching sexual videos online. The boy became quieter and told the clinician, "I don't want to talk about that." The clinician reflected his statement and said, "I heard in your voice that you got quieter. I'm guessing this is difficult to talk about." Alvi nodded his head in agreement. The clinician tried to reassure the boy: "I know, you got in a lot of trouble over those videos. It doesn't sound like that was a very fun experience." Alvi agreed and said that his mom "lost it." The clinician then asked whether his mother or father ever talked to him about the things in the video. He shook his head and asked, "Are we done talking about this?" The clinician smiled and tried to reframe the discussion. "I know, this brings up some bad feelings. What if I told you that mom believes she should have taught you more about sexual things and she wants to try and do that now?" Alvi looked up and said, "My mom wouldn't say that. She won't talk about these things."

The clinician reviewed with Alvi that the past few sessions had been spent helping his mother think through how best to teach him healthy information about sex and explain some of the things he saw in the videos. The boy looked confused and asked, "Why would she want to do that?" The clinician answered, "Because she wants to make sure you get good information and answers to your questions." The boy quickly blurted out, "I don't have questions. The videos answered them." The clinician reframed the boy's statement and asked whether he watched the videos to answer questions. Alvi then told how he heard various terms at school and on the bus, such as "blowjob" and "boning," and performed internet searches to find out what they meant. Several of the first links took him to videos where he watched graphic sexual acts. He reported being confused and feeling strange while watching the videos and, after a few seconds, left the websites. Within a few days, however, he began to wonder why people would engage in such behavior and decided to watch the videos a second time. After a few instances of visiting these websites, he reported having unusual feelings in his body and that he found the videos exciting. The clinician asked, "Why do you think your body responded this way?" Alvi could not answer and looked ashamed with his head hanging. "Well," the clinician continued, "I'll make sure we get you some answers for that." Alvi slowly nodded his head and then asked to finish the game.

After the clinician walked Alvi out of the treatment room, Mrs. Laakso anxiously sat down. "Well?" she asked. "What did he say?" The clinician proceeded to explain to the mother that her son's behavior stemmed from curiosity, particularly related to terms he heard at school and on the bus. The internet searches then spiraled as he was exposed to the videos and he began finding them exciting for unknown reasons. The mother started asking questions about why children would make such comments and why the school did not address such behaviors. The clinician reflected her comments, and clarified that sexual comments are known to happen with some frequency in school settings and, oftentimes, school staff are unaware unless a child says something. Mrs. Laakso again argued that children should not be interested in such topics and wondered who was teaching these things to children. The clinician refocused her on the discussion with Alvi. In particular, her son did not provide any questions that were not already planned as part of the conjoint session. The remainder of the session was spent allowing Mrs. Laakso to practice her presentation of the information and preparing for the conjoint discussion.

Session 4

Alvi and his mother came into session with Mrs. Laakso noticeably anxious. The clinician took her aside and asked if she felt prepared to have the conjoint discussion. She took a deep breath and said, "Yes. I just might need you to help me." The clinician provided reassurance and agreed to help as needed. The two returned to the table and sat down with Alvi. The clinician provided an overview of the session and emphasized to Alvi that nothing he said, respectfully, would be cause for discipline. He nodded his head and looked toward his mother. Mrs. Laakso again took a deep breath and began reading the book.

Alvi looked at the pictures with interest and seemed to listen to his mother. At a few early points, Mrs. Laakso's voice broke and the clinician decided to interject: "Let me pause for a second there, mom. Alvi, have you ever seen pictures like this before?" The question was designed to give the mother a moment to collect herself and to elicit a simple answer from the boy. Alvi nodded his head and quietly whispered, "Yeah." The clinician, looking at the mother, then said, "Mom, you're doing great. Alvi is listening." Alvi, perhaps sensing his mother's level of anxiety, agreed with the clinician, "Yeah, you're doing good, Mom." The mother's eyebrows raised as she looked at her son and then at the clinician. The mother then proceeded to the section of the book that discussed sperm and eggs and that the union of the two resulted in the conception of a baby. Alvi's face scrunched up and he leaned in to look closer at the book. The mother glanced at the clinician who provided a slight head nod to indicate that this was a positive development. Alvi then abruptly stated, "Oh, and that happens when the penis is put in the vagina, right?" The mother appeared shocked by Alvi's conclusion, and she quickly confirmed the boy's statement. The clinician then prompted the mother, "And that action of putting a penis in a vagina has a name." The mother took the prompt and replied, "Yes, that is called sex."

After a few more pages, the point arrived to discuss the topic of sexual arousal. Mrs. Laakso's voice again began to break. Looking at Alvi, the clinician interjected, "So, this is the part where we're going to talk about that strange, excited feeling you told me you got when you watched the videos." The mother again looked at the clinician, seemingly surprised by the matter-of-fact bluntness of the comment. Alvi, clearly understanding the clinician's comment, looked wearily at the clinician and simply said, "Okay." The mother seemed also immediately more relaxed and acted as though Alvi's comment gave her permission to approach the topic. She quietly, but effectively, discussed sexual arousal as a way of promoting reproduction so that humans will continue to live on the planet.

Alvi followed his mother's explanation and then asked, "But, why did I get excited watching movies? I wasn't trying to have a baby." His question halted Mrs. Laakso's presentation and preempted her plan to discuss the topic a short while later. The mother was seemingly lost in thought for a moment and the clinician commented, "That's a good question, mom. If arousal is meant to encourage reproduction, then why might it happen from watching movies, or maybe from some other types of activities?" The clinician's comment was designed to give the mother a moment to collect her thoughts and jump ahead to a later part of the discussion. The mother understood the signal and said, "Well, the arousal is just a process in your body and lots of things can cause it to happen, like watching movies. It's like how your body gets excited in a different way when you watch a movie with big explosions. You don't really want to be near a big explosion, but your body still responds." (This was a previously identified example given Mrs. Laakso's knowledge of her son's movie preferences.) Mrs. Laakso's explanation and example resonated with Alvi, as he leaned back in his chair and said, "Ohhhhh."

The clinician subtly reminded Ms. Laakso of the other two pieces of this specific topic. She then explained that sometimes other things can cause a sexual response, including seeing people wear lingerie or "use their mouth instead of a vagina." Alvi did not say anything but nodded his head as if understanding her explanation. He then sat quietly and looked down as if starting to withdraw from the discussion, which seemed odd given how well the session was progressing. The clinician made a motion to Mrs. Laakso, encouraging her to make a comment about her son's posture. She looked at him and asked, "Alvi, you got quiet. Is something wrong?" Without looking up, the boy quietly stated, "You'll probably get mad." The mother shot a look at the clinician who again motioned for her to engage the boy. She responded, "No, my dear, you can ask anything you like. I'll give you a real answer." Continuing with his head down, Alvi softly asked, "If this is supposed to be a good feeling, why do some women scream?" Mrs. Laakso was at a loss for words; she had no idea how to respond. The clinician spoke up: "That's a good question Alvi. I'm guessing you saw that in some of the videos?" The boy nodded. The clinician continued, "Well, mom, I guess maybe we can talk about how different people respond in different ways." The mother took the hint and told her son, "Yes, sometimes, people are really quiet when having sex and sometimes people are really loud. People act in all kinds of ways." Alvi looked up and asked, "Like when people cry even though they're happy?" The mother agreed with her son, "Yes, my dear, that is a great example."

As the session neared completion, Alvi had one last question for his mother. "Mom, do you and Dad do sex?" The clinician had previously prepared the mother for this question, given that it occurs with some regularity. The mother responded in a controlled and effective manner, "Well, Alvi, you are here, so yeah, Dad and I had to have sex to have you." Alvi nodded his head and then asked a follow-up question, "No, I mean now. Do you and Dad do sex now?" The mother effectively delivered the previously prepared response that emphasized the values she taught her son earlier in the session: "Dad and I are consenting adults in a committed relationship, and we are free to have sex if we like. And that's where we'll leave it." Alvi seemed satisfied with that answer. The clinician praised Mrs. Laakso and Alvi for their ability to discuss these topics and emphasized that this was only the beginning of the conversation. Again, in a prepared statement, Mrs. Laakso told her son, "Yes, Alvi. If you have any questions in the future, you can ask me and you won't be in trouble. I promise." Alvi nodded his head and said, "Okay." As they walked out of session, Mrs. Laakso looked at the clinician with a smile, and the clinician responded with a thumbs-up to praise the mother.

Phase 3

Session 1

Given that Alvi did not display any significant concerns with impulse control skills, the clinician made the procedure more cognitively based. Although the clinician explained the concept of urges or impulses and taught relaxation skills, as done with other cases discussed in this book, the clinician emphasized the cognitive aspects of impulse control. This primarily involved teaching him to utilize the "Stop, Think, Go" technique. The clinician initially asked Alvi to think about a situation that did not involve sexual topics by presenting him with the example of a classmate at school that stole candy from the teacher and wanted to share it with him. Alvi admitted it would be tempting to take the candy but also acknowledged it would be wrong because it was stolen. After mentally picturing a stop sign, which the clinician allowed him to draw and color, Alvi was asked to consider options that might be more appropriate in the situation. He developed several options, including telling the peer "No, thank you," and notifying the teacher of the theft. The clinician encouraged him to think through these options to their conclusions. He reported the possibility of an ongoing negative feeling if he simply declined and did not report the stealing. However, reporting the stealing might result in his friend being angry with him. In the end, Alvi decided the best option would be to convince his friend to return the candy, even if he did so without notifying the teacher that it was ever stolen. The final step was simply to then enact the plan.

The clinician then applied this same process to a situation where Alvi was on a device and developed the thought of searching for and watching sexually explicit videos online. Alvi went through the same process, picturing the imaginary stop sign, employing relaxation skills, and developing alternative solutions. In this case, he identified possible options as talking to his mother or father, putting away the device, or playing video games as a distraction. The clinician helped him think of the consequences that might come with each of these options. Alvi agreed that closing the device was unlikely to occur and worried that his mother might ask too many questions (although he was not concerned about her being upset). He decided the best option in this instance was to trade his tablet for his video game console.

After Alvi successfully demonstrated this Stop, Think, Go process, Mrs. Laakso joined the session and the boy taught these techniques to his mother. She listened attentively as Alvi first described the situation with a peer in the classroom and then transitioned to discussing the use of the techniques to prevent watching inappropriate videos. The mother sought to reassure her son that, if he came to her in this situation, she would not ask questions but rather praise his efforts and join him in playing a game or discussing another topic. Alvi looked at the clinician and said, "Okay, maybe I need to change my answer then." He went on to say he would rather approach his mother in these moments if this was her response, as opposed to the previous decision to play video games. The clinician encouraged Mrs. Laakso to continue with her efforts to support her son and to talk about these topics freely.

Session 2

Similar to the previous session, teaching Alvi cognitive coping skills was relatively straightforward. He quickly learned the elements of the cognitive triangle and correctly used it to derive more helpful thoughts about ambiguous situations, including being pushed by another child at school and finding out that he failed a test. When the clinician applied the cognitive triangle to a sexual situation, it was notable that Alvi's answers required significantly more time and thought than in the previous examples. The clinician asked Alvi what his first thought would be in a situation where a movie on television, which he was watching with a peer, unexpectedly showed nudity. He replied, "Why is this in the movie?" The clinician asked why he would have this thought, to which Alvi replied he would not intentionally watch a movie that he knew displayed nudity. As such, the sudden appearance of such content would be surprising. Indeed, the feeling he identified was surprised and he was unsure of how he would respond.

When asked for alternative thoughts to the movie example, Alvi struggled. Talking through the situation with the clinician, Alvi noted the peer pressure that surely would accompany any overt behavioral responses. The clinician empathized with the boy and agreed that getting up to leave or actively protesting could elicit a negative reaction from the peer. The clinician then demonstrated for Alvi that this is actually a complex thought process. At the same time he is thinking the peer would judge his response, he is also thinking that the content of the movie was inappropriate and he should not be watching it. As such, two different thoughts might co-occur and leave him feeling confused or conflicted as to his response. Alvi then reverted to the impulse control technique learned in the previous session and concluded that his best response may be to simply close his eyes, which would prevent him from seeing the inappropriate content and also prevent any negative peer consequences. He developed the idea of saying something to the friend that would not necessarily result in a negative response, such as, "Umm . . . I didn't know this was in the movie." In this way it conveys his displeasure without upsetting his friend and may serve as a distraction from the content itself.

Alvi was also asked to consider his own thoughts about his previous accessing of the explicit videos online. His initial thought was that he should not have done this and that thinking of it made him feel sad and ashamed, which resulted in a noticeable facial reaction and slumping of the shoulders. The clinician then asked him to consider any other thoughts he might have about those earlier behaviors. He was unsure how to respond and was unable to immediately identify alternative thoughts. The clinician revisited a previous comment Alvi made regarding curiosity being the motivation of his initial web searches. Once Alvi agreed to this statement, the clinician asked if curiosity is a bad thing. Alvi, of course, replied that it was not, but quickly retorted that he should not have searched for those topics. The clinician reflected his statement and then asked, "But how would you have known not to search for those topics if you didn't know what those words meant?" That question puzzled the boy. After thinking for a few moments, he said he was unsure how to answer. The clinician then asked another question of Alvi: "Have you ever searched for any other topic online that was not sexual?" Alvi readily admitted that he had searched for various topics over the past few years, allowing the clinician to ask what was different in his mind about searching for these particular sexual words. Alvi admitted there were no real differences and then concluded that an alternative thought was "I didn't know what the words meant and didn't look up those topics on purpose." The feelings and behaviors associated with this thought were neutral and Alvi concluded he both liked this explanation better and that it more accurately described his experience.

Alvi did an exceptional job teaching the cognitive triangle to his mother. He emphasized the last exercise in explaining that his initial searches were not done for inappropriate purposes and that he felt better thinking of it in terms of an accident or an innocent mistake. Mrs. Laakso accepted this explanation but asserted that she would still have preferred he came to her with questions. Alvi nodded his head, but qualified that he did not know the terms were sexual and, even after he discovered the sexual videos, he did not feel comfortable approaching his mother. She understood his thoughts and redirected her comments to emphasize that going forward, they can be more open about discussing anything Alvi wishes, including sexual topics. The young boy nodded his head and said, "I know." The mother praised her son's efforts and thanked him for sharing his thoughts and feelings with her.

Session 3

Reviewing sexual abuse prevention skills with Mrs. Laakso proved relatively straightforward, as she quickly identified those placed in caregiving roles of her son and agreed with several recommendations for improving safety. The clinician stressed the importance of teaching Alvi internet literacy skills, particularly when it comes to his consumption of online content. This aspect of safety skills left her more uncertain. She did not know how to effectively approach the topic with her son or what information was the most helpful to include. The clinician provided her with a handout that reviewed topics such as how to avoid internet pornography, how to safely engage on social media, and the dangers of sexting. This topic turned into a sustained discussion as she asked several questions about the most common forms of technology usage for children Alvi's age. The clinician restructured the conversation to focus not just on the present moment but also on the coming years as Alvi would become an adolescent, when he would begin using a cell phone and social media. This approach of taking a longer view of the issue helped Mrs. Laakso understand that these conversations must be ongoing as development progresses and does not end with the termination of treatment.

The clinician and mother spent time considering how best to explain these topics to Alvi. Mrs. Laakso had the idea of using her own social media account to discuss the posting of pictures, as well as demonstrating how easy it was to text pictures to other people. She suggested that this activity may demonstrate the ease with which anything posted or shared through electronic means can be saved by another person or continue to reside on the internet. With the help of the clinician, she constructed demonstrations by taking pictures within the treatment room and then called her husband to plan a back-and-forth text chain that would include the pictures. Also, she planned to have her husband post the picture on social media so that she could then access the post in session and show Alvi how easy it was to create a screenshot and keep the picture.

After this plan was established, Alvi joined the discussion. Mrs. Laakso reviewed basic sexual abuse prevention skills with her son, as discussed in prior cases in this book, and proceeded to her demonstration of how social media and texting can create everlasting pictures. She texted her husband, who quickly replied with the picture she took of the treatment room. Alvi looked confused at first, given that his father had never visited the room. The mother then explained that she had sent the picture to his father a few minutes earlier, but the father saved the picture and just texted it back. She used this as a demonstration that pictures, or videos, could be shared to a countless number of people and explained that he could have sent the picture to any other individual. The mother then opened the father's page on social media and showed Alvi that the picture was posted there too. The boy soon understood the point; anyone in his father's social media network could be looking at that picture. The mother used this demonstration as the beginning of a larger discussion that anything Alvi said or posted online, or texted to someone, might be spread to others and Alvi loses all control of the message. It was an effective exercise as Alvi quickly noted, "So, even something that might be bad or embarrassing could be on there." The mother agreed and stressed the importance of not sharing such information via electronic means, especially sexual pictures and messages.

Session 4

The session began with the clinician discussing with Alvi recent events at school. One of Alvi's friends was in trouble for teasing a peer and he was upset about what his friend did. The clinician listened to the boy express his frustrations and then transitioned into asking Alvi what he liked about his friend. He mentioned that the boy was funny, good at sports, and was usually nice during their interactions. After establishing these positive traits, the clinician asked what qualities Alvi did not like about his friend. Alvi responded by saying that his friend typically wants to control whatever games they are playing and gets upset when he loses. The clinician asked whether other friends also responded this way and Alvi said, "Not the same way. No one likes to lose, but he [the friend] gets really mad. I don't like playing with him when he does that." The clinician empathized with his comment, agreeing that it did not sound like much fun to have a friend act in that way.

The clinician made a list of qualities Alvi identified as positive and negative about his friend and then presented it to him. The boy then discussed a few other peers and identified various traits for both columns. What Alvi found most appealing in his peers were the traits of liking sports and games, and he was most turned off by people being unkind. The clinician presented several different hypothetical questions attempting to identify any potential social pressures (e.g., "Do you ever feel like your friends try to get you to do things you don't want to do?"). Alvi denied most of these influences but did reference one time he stopped associating with a friend because that individual threatened to spread rumors about him. In short, there were no apparent social pressures negatively influencing Alvi's behaviors. Before finishing the discussion, the clinician asked about the peers who made the comments about sexual acts that first resulted in Alvi's curiosity about those topics. He stated they were older children on his bus and not really friends. In other words, they were comments heard in passing.

The clinician then shared this information with Mrs. Laakso. She was not particularly surprised, as she stated Alvi had a positive friend group, many of whom were frequently at their home. Most of these friends lived in the neighborhood and Mrs. Laakso was on good terms with their parents. This allowed for effective communication among the parents and supervision of the children typically was an easy task. Alvi played on multiple sports teams, but again, the coaches and parents were typically present for practices and games, and no significant concerns were reported. The clinician encouraged Mrs. Laakso to remain vigilant and to occasionally discuss peer groups with Alvi. In addition, the clinician encouraged the mother to sporadically broach the topic of whether Alvi had seen or heard any sexually based content, either online or offline, and to do so in a nonjudgmental manner. The goal moving forward was to maintain an open line of communication where Alvi felt comfortable and supported in approaching his mother with any concerns or questions about sexual topics.

Mrs. Laakso completed the ASB-C and reported a score of 6, indicating developmentally typical or expected behavior, and did not endorse any critical items. She also reported feeling more confident talking with her son about sex and sexuality and believed she was better equipped to monitor his behavior in the coming years. Given the lack of any ongoing emotional or behavioral concerns, it was decided that treatment was complete. Nonetheless, one additional session was held to say goodbye and conduct graduation activities.

CONCLUSION

The case of Alvi L. discusses the use of PBT with cases of internet pornography, a growing concern for many within society and an increasingly common presentation in mental health clinics. In this instance, the behavior was driven by curiosity that combined with the child's perception that such topics were off limits for discussion with the caregivers. Children are taught early in the school-age years, if not earlier, how to conduct web searches and Alvi merely conducted a search to answer his questions. Unfortunately, searching for sexual topics often results in children finding sexually explicit media and the problem can spiral, as it did for Alvi. Establishing clear rules, monitoring internet usage, and demystifying sexual topics through open dialogue, effectively addressed this concern. This case also added the complicating factor of the mother having her own sexual abuse history and, subsequently, displaying significant anxiety regarding sexual topics. The clinician provided additional support throughout Phase 2 to help her discuss sexual topics and manage her anxiety. By doing so, the clinician effectively engaged the mother in becoming her son's primary source for answering sexual questions.

9 JAMAR W.

A Preteen Child Interested in Sexual Relationships

ASSESSMENT

The case of Jamar W. is unique in that the behaviors he displayed were considered problematic, not because they were coercive or potentially injurious, but because they were advanced for his age and offered the potential for negative consequences. His behaviors were complicated by a strained relationship with his father, and his father was both frustrated and unsure how to manage his son's behaviors.

Background

Jamar W. was a 12-year-old child who arrived to the assessment session with his father, Mr. Williams. The tension between the two was apparent from the beginning, as Jamar said he would not speak with the clinician with his father present. Each member of the dyad was interviewed separately. Mr. Williams reported that his son had left the home repeatedly after curfew to meet up

https://doi.org/10.1037/0000516-010
Children With Problematic Sexual Behavior: Theory, Research, and Evidence-Based Practice, by B. Allen

with his girlfriend, who was 13 years of age. The father said he installed a security system at the home to notify him in the event that Jamar attempted to leave again, but no new incidents had occurred since that time. Jamar frequently made sexual comments around the home and, according to Mr. Williams, Jamar believed he was "a player" and claimed to be sexually experienced. During the interview with Jamar, the boy attempted to provide the same picture, as he frequently mentioned various sexual acts that he said he performed with multiple partners. However, his comments often suggested superficial ideas that led the clinician to doubt whether Jamar actually engaged in any of the acts he described. Nonetheless, the father was concerned that Jamar may become sexually active relatively soon if, indeed, he was not already.

Assessment Data

Mr. Williams completed the Assessment of Sexual Behavior-Child version (ASB-C) and most of the items he endorsed related to interest in sexual topics. He endorsed relatively few overt sexual acts, as he had no proof these occurred. Nonetheless, his total score of 11 was in the *problematic* range for the measure. There was no known trauma history or posttraumatic stress symptoms on the Child and Adolescent Trauma Screen (CATS), although it was reported that Jamar's mother died when the boy was only 3 years old. On the Strengths and Difficulties Questionnaire (SDQ), Mr. Williams noted his son displayed significant behavioral problems, which then resulted in a discussion of Jamar's disciplinary history at school. He was suspended three times in the prior 2 years for fighting and bullying another student, but nothing sexual was known to have occurred. Mr. Williams did not report any significant concerns related to his own personal distress, nor did he report any modeling of sexual behavior on the Exposure to Sexuality Scale (ESS). Jamar completed the self-report versions of the CATS and SDQ and did not report any significant concerns. When asked about the suspensions from school, he described the incidents as forms of self-defense and that he was being treated unfairly.

Conceptualization

Jamar's case was one of a preteen child, who may or may not have entered puberty, displaying significant interest in sexual topics. If he was not already sexually active, there were noted concerns that he may experience his sexual debut shortly. Although there was no known exposure in the home to sexual behavior, it was safe to conclude that a child in seventh grade, as Jamar was, likely had been exposed to sexual topics in some way through popular culture, school, and/or peers. Considering his noted behavioral problems that were severe enough to result in multiple suspensions from school, it appeared that a combined developmental psychopathology and social learning conceptualization was appropriate. In other words, Jamar developed relatively poor behavior regulation skills and the perception he developed regarding sexual behavior was unhealthy.

PHASE-BASED TREATMENT

Given the conceptualization, the clinician was attuned to the parenting skills employed by Mr. Williams to address his son's behavioral challenges and the cognitive perceptions Jamar held regarding sexual behavior. The strain in the caregiver–child relationship was pronounced and required the clinician to consider how best to approach conjoint sessions.

Phase 1

Session 1

Mr. Williams sat down in the first session and quickly stated, "Alright, Doc, let's fix my kid." The clinician was surprised at the father's statement but praised the father's enthusiasm for treatment. In addition, the clinician focused on the idea that it was a collaborative effort that would require the father's active participation. The father continued to seem eager to participate, and the clinician transitioned into a review of the ESS. Although the father did not endorse any items as occurring in the home, the clinician stressed monitoring other settings as well, such as social media. Mr. Williams clarified that his son did not have a cell phone or access to social media. This prompted the clinician to ask how he made plans to meet up with a girlfriend after curfew and the father said he did not know. However, he felt certain his son did not have access to a cell phone because they lived in a small apartment and doors to bedrooms were required to be left open.

The clinician turned to the items the father endorsed on the ASB-C. Most of the endorsed behaviors were the use of sexual words, viewing nonsexual topics in a sexual way, and talking about private parts in an inappropriate way. The clinician asked for examples, and the father had many ready to provide. Jamar was known to frequently discuss "banging girls," made lewd comments regarding oral sex, and on several occasions made references to the size of his penis. About 2 weeks prior to session, Mr. Williams was on a work-related call discussing a project with a female coworker and, from another room, Jamar yelled, "When you gonna bang that girl?" Mr. Williams said he was so concerned his coworker heard the comment that he stepped out in the hallway of the apartment building to finish the call.

The clinician asked Mr. Williams how he responded in these moments when Jamar made inappropriate comments. He paused for a moment and then said, "I teach him it isn't right. You don't treat women like that." When asked for clarification on this correction, the father effectively said the discussion is no more than one or two sentences and that the father is often angry during those talks. In other words, his typical response was usually to yell at his son, but no consequences followed any of the behaviors and no conversations occurred when both were in a calm emotional state. The clinician asked Mr. Williams to identify moments during the day when these comments occurred and he was unable to identify specific situations. Sometimes, they occurred when watching television, other times in the car, and at other times while eating dinner. There did not seem to be a particular setting or activity that predicted these comments.

The clinician compiled Mr. Williams's comments into the following diagram and turned it toward him to evaluate its accuracy:

Anytime (A)

↓

Makes inappropriate comments (B)

↓

Father yells at him (C)

Mr. Williams agreed to the fit, but questioned the antecedent: "There has to be something that's leading him to make these comments, right?" The clinician agreed with the father but stressed that this diagram was meant to display the sequence that occurs immediately before and after the troubling behavior, not necessarily longer standing issues or concerns. The father nodded in agreement, but continued with his questioning: "Yeah, but still, the thought has to enter his head for some reason, right? I mean, does he just go around all day with sex stuff in his head?" The father's comment was insightful and potentially helpful. The clinician revised the antecedent part of the diagram to reflect the father's input:

Sexual thoughts (A)

↓

Makes inappropriate comments (B)

↓

Father yells at him (C)

Mr. Williams agreed to the shape of the ABC chain, but returned to his original question, "But what do we do about it, Doc?"

The clinician took the opportunity to reinforce the father's attempts to monitor his son's movements. Although it is difficult to develop a monitoring plan when no discernible, overt antecedent is identified, the father's implementation of a security system appeared to stop his son from leaving the home at night. The clinician used the ABC chain to suggest, perhaps, his father's yelling was ineffective at stopping Jamar's sexual comments. The father looked confused and then asked, "Am I just supposed to not say anything? That's not teaching him anything." The clinician rephrased the comment to ask the father, "When you yell at him, are you saying anything to him that you haven't said before?" The question perplexed the father. He sat back in his chair and eventually concluded, "No, I guess not." The clinician then provided an alternative idea: "Okay, so yelling isn't going to teach him anything new. But, what if he was saying the sexual things because it got your attention?" The comment caused the father's eyes to enlarge as he started looking around the room. "I don't know, Doc, maybe that's what he's doing." The clinician encouraged the father to ignore the comments, to the best of his ability, in the coming week. The father agreed to try.

Session 2

Mr. Williams again came into session in a positive mood and ready to talk about his son's behavior over the past week. Mr. Williams did not report any new attempts by Jamar to leave the house at night but did mention that his attempts to ignore his son's behavior failed. In describing what occurred, Mr. Williams said that Jamar's behaviors worsened. The boy made sexual comments the evening of the previous session and the father ignored them, as planned. But as the father walked into another room, Jamar followed him and continued to make comments that soon turned into personal attacks on the father. The way Mr. Williams described it, Jamar stated his father was "not a man" because he had not dated in several years. This enraged the father, who then began yelling at his son. The clinician empathized with the father's struggle and suggested that Jamar's response to the ignoring likely suggested the comments were, indeed, attention seeking.

The clinician went on to apologize for not better preparing Mr. Williams for what might occur when he stopped responding to his son's comments. The clinician explained that when a behavior has been reinforced over time, it is common for that behavior to increase in frequency and become more intense when the reinforcement stops. The clinician used the example of getting in a car in the morning only to find that the car battery is dead. The typical person does not try to start the car only once and then stop, but rather continues trying, perhaps swearing or pleading. Eventually, the person will stop the attempts and find another solution, but the repeated experiences of the standard ignition sequence working results in the increased intensity that occurs before reaching that point. Mr. Williams understood the analogy and then asked if the clinician knew any tricks to help him get through Jamar's intense reaction to the ignoring.

The clinician discussed with the father the concept of "selective attention." In short, the father can walk away, insert headphones to listen to music, or engage in some other activity, which not only provides a distraction or is soothing for Mr. Williams but also conveys to Jamar that the father is not listening to him. All the while, however, Mr. Williams is to remain vigilant of Jamar's behavior. When he returns to discussing appropriate topics or stops the antagonistic behavior, the father then provides attention, possibly through engaging in discussion or moving on to a different topic (e.g., dinner plans, homework). In this way, Jamar would receive Mr. Williams's attention when he engages in desired behavior but would not receive his attention when engaged in undesired behavior. The father agreed to try this approach.

After the check-in, which lasted for over half of the session, the clinician presented Mr. Williams with three rules:

1. It is not OK to look at or touch the private areas of others.
2. It is not OK for other people to look at or touch my private areas.
3. It is not OK to make rude comments about private areas.

Mr. Williams agreed the rules were acceptable, but then asked the clinician, "Do you think he doesn't already know these?" The clinician admitted that the boy was probably aware of these rules and asked whether the father had ever discussed them with the boy. He admitted such a conversation never took place, unless it was in the context of yelling after Jamar made inappropriate comments. The clinician then reframed the purpose of the rules as making them explicit, which would allow the father to implement consequences. Also, this conversation would occur in a neutral tone of voice and not in the heat of the moment.

Next, the father was asked to identify appropriate consequences. This was a struggle, as the father mentioned that video games were the only things the boy cared about other than playing the guitar. Mr. Williams stressed that he did not want to remove the guitar from the boy because he supported music in Jamar's life. The clinician agreed with the father and then discussed the possibility of restricting video games. The father agreed and it was determined that sexual comments would result in the boy losing his video game system for 48 hours. The father and clinician also determined that the boy may lose desserts and have an earlier bedtime by 30 minutes. Since Jamar did not attend the session, teaching him these rules was put off until Session 3. Nonetheless, the clinician encouraged Mr. Williams to use the selective attention technique during the coming week.

Session 3

The clinician decided to check in with Mr. Williams at the beginning of the session to ascertain his ability to selectively attend to Jamar's behaviors over the past week. The father stated the boy's behaviors did improve. The first instance when Jamar began making sexual comments, Mr. Williams put in his earphones and walked into another room. When Jamar followed him, making more outlandish comments, the father started singing the song that was playing and continued to turn away from Jamar. His son became more upset and started screaming, which prompted Mr. Williams to walk out into the hallway of the apartment. Jamar did not follow and, after a few minutes, Mr. Williams returned to the apartment. Jamar had stopped yelling and was playing video games. Mr. Williams said there had been several other incidents over the past week, but he now steps into the hallway more quickly and Jamar has yet to follow him.

The clinician reviewed with the father how to teach the three sexual behavior rules to Jamar. Mr. Williams insisted that Jamar probably would not engage in the conversation. The clinician reflected his statement and assured him that this does happen on occasion. Nonetheless, it was imperative to explicitly state the rules and the consequences, so that Jamar understood the change in response that would occur in the home. The clinician also stressed to Mr. Williams that implementation of the consequences is to occur when Jamar breaks one of the rules, regardless of any other event. For instance, Mr. Williams may continue with his current tactic of stepping into the hallway when Jamar uses inappropriate language, but the consequence should still be applied when he returns to the apartment. Mr. Williams understood and Jamar joined the session.

The clinician oriented Jamar to the session and emphasized that the purpose of treatment was to help him stay safe and healthy. The clinician noted there were concerns that some of his behaviors may have an adverse effect on his well-being. Jamar rolled his eyes and said, "I'm good. Just being me." The clinician reflected that Jamar was unbothered by his choices, but that treatment was an opportunity to learn more about those choices and how they might affect him. Jamar nodded his head in a condescending manner. The clinician then mentioned that Mr. Williams developed rules that would be enforced around the house. Jamar sighed, "Oh, great. Here we go." The clinician motioned to the father to ignore Jamar's statement and continue as planned.

Mr. Williams read the three rules to Jamar and reviewed the consequences that would be applied for breaking the rules. Jamar continued to roll his eyes as the father read the rules and became upset when his father discussed the consequences. "You can't take away my games. Those are mine. You can't do that." Mr. Williams insisted that he planned to take away the power cords in the event the rules were broken, and Jamar continued to protest. The clinician planned to begin discussing potential scenarios during the latter portion of the session, but Jamar was not in an emotional state conducive to that exercise. He continued to protest, folded his arms, and repeatedly stated, "This is crap, man." He made vague threats to his father, including, "You take those power cords and see what happens." Jamar willfully stepped out of the session when given the opportunity. The clinician reviewed what transpired with Mr. Williams, who had no concerns about physical violence or destruction from his son. It seemed Jamar's comments were a common response to being upset, but his behavior never spiraled into active aggression. The clinician encouraged the father to implement the rules and consequences as designed, including continuing with the selective attention plan.

Given that Jamar refused to participate in the remainder of the session, the clinician spent time with Mr. Williams discussing the importance of providing positive feedback for Jamar abiding by the rules. The clinician noted there are several moments throughout the day when Jamar is not using sexual language, and these are opportunities to thank him for speaking in appropriate terms. Mr. Williams asked whether he could provide other types of positive consequences, such as a later bedtime. The clinician agreed this is possible, but the terms should be clearly stated to avoid confusion or argument. The father appreciated the clarification and decided to wait until the next session to discuss it with the clinician more but agreed to provide positive verbal feedback.

Session 4

Given the negative attitude from Jamar when his father was in the room, the clinician decided to try a different tactic during this last session of the phase.

Jamar came into session alone and the clinician began with rapport-building activities, including playing a card game with the boy. Jamar sat quietly and rarely responded to the clinician's questions. After a few minutes, the clinician asked, "So, do you not feel like talking today?" Jamar sneered at the clinician and said, "Nope, because you're in it with my dad. You know he took my games? That's your fault." The clinician used this as an opportunity to explore the events of the past week. "Why did he take your games?" the clinician asked. "Because you told him to," the boy replied. The clinician rephrased Jamar's statement and told him that taking away the video games was a consequence his father developed and was only to be implemented for breaking one of the rules. Jamar looked up at the clinician and said, "Well, the rules are stupid." The clinician empathized that the boy was unhappy with having consequences for making sexual comments and having to change his manner of speaking.

The clinician asked Jamar if he would answer a few questions. The boy shrugged his shoulders and said, "It depends on what the question is." The clinician responded, "Fair enough," and began reading out the first scenario. The story involved a child making a sexual comment to a peer and ended with the question of whether it broke one of the rules. Jamar sarcastically replied, "Not if she likes it." The clinician asked the boy to explain how breaking the stated rule was dependent on whether the recipient of the comment liked the comment. Jamar indicated that his language was not a concern because "everyone talks like that." He then reverted to criticizing his father by saying he was "old" and "not cool," and this was the reason he had a problem with sexual language. The clinician recounted the incident where his father was on a work call with a female colleague and asked Jamar how his behavior in that situation related to sexual language being used in everyday conversation. Jamar stared blankly at the clinician, seemingly surprised the clinician knew of the incident, and then shrugged his shoulders again without speaking.

The clinician recited another scenario that discussed the consensual sexual touching of a peer. Again, Jamar stated that it would not break a rule if the peer consented and wanted to engage in that behavior. The clinician asked the boy, "So, you don't really care about the rules your dad set up?" Jamar began shaking his head and bluntly said, "Nope." The clinician then replied that, as long as that was the case, the consequences would probably continue. The boy sighed, rolled his eyes, folded his arms, and leaned back in his chair. Sensing that the child was not going to willfully engage in any further discussion of the rules or scenarios, the clinician decided to shift the conversation: "It sounds like you know a lot about sex. Can you teach me something?" Jamar's eyebrows rose and he looked puzzled for a moment.

He then began to stammer incoherently as if trying to find a response. At last, he murmured, "You're an adult. You should know." The clinician smiled and said it would be great to talk to Jamar about that at some point in the future.

Jamar returned to the waiting room as Mr. Williams joined the session. The father sat down and immediately smiled at the clinician, "It was a good week, Doc." Mr. Williams relayed how he continued ignoring Jamar's comments the night after the previous session and then, when he returned from the hallway, took the power cord to his video game system. The boy became upset and started yelling. Mr. Williams returned to the hallway, listening to music in his earphones. The boy remained in his room the rest of that evening and refused to speak to his father throughout the following day. After 48 hours, the father returned the power cord. This prompted Jamar to make a snide remark warning his father not to take it again. However, the next day Jamar made a sexual comment related to his father's clothing and Mr. Williams again removed the power cord. His son protested, but to no avail. At the time of the session, it had been almost 2 complete days since the power cord was last returned and no additional incidents had occurred.

The clinician praised the father's ability to implement the behavior management plan and recommended that he continue doing so in the weeks to come. When the clinician asked about positive feedback, the father admitted he had not provided much in terms of praising his son's appropriate behavior. The clinician reiterated the father's recent comment that no sexual remarks had been made by Jamar in almost 2 complete days. As such, it seemed possible to praise him for this at any moment, including at the end of the session. The father nodded his head in agreement. The clinician recounted the events of session with Jamar, including his dismissive comments when attempting to discuss scenarios, and his shocked and evasive answer when given the opportunity to discuss sex. The father laughed at this last comment. "You mean you told him to teach you something about sex, and he couldn't come up with anything? That's funny." The clinician reassured the father that this is somewhat common in the preteen ages; the use of sexual language conveys an image or is used to elicit social approval, but many children this age actually know relatively little about sex. When given the opportunity to discuss it, they may demonstrate significant misunderstandings or reveal how little they know. The clinician urged the father to keep this in mind during the coming sessions.

Phase 2

Session 1

This first session of the second phase began by orienting Mr. Williams to the goals of the coming sessions. As the clinician discussed the importance of teaching Jamar healthy information about sex, Mr. Williams interjected, "Do you mean teaching him about things like HIV and condoms?" The clinician clarified for the father that these topics may be part of the session if this is the information he wished to teach his son, but that the discussion can also include more basic information that Jamar may not know. The father retorted that he wanted to teach his son that he is too young to have sex and needs to wait until he is older. The clinician wrote this down on a piece of paper under the heading "Should Know" and asked the father if he also wanted the topics of sexually transmitted infections (STIs) and condoms listed in that column. The father agreed that he did and these were written down accordingly.

The clinician then backed up and asked the father to describe what his values are around the topics of sex and sexuality. The father quickly opined that he does not have a problem with sex but believes 12 years is too young. While agreeing that 12 years is too young, the clinician asked the father the conditions under which sex was allowed. This stumped the father for a moment; although he was opposed to his preteen son engaging in sexual relations, he had not considered when sexual behavior was appropriate. The father thought for a moment and then determined that he believed his son should graduate high school before becoming sexually active. However, while explaining his answer, he stopped himself and said, "But I know teenagers are more sexual these days. Am I wrong on this?" The clinician clarified that the answer to this question is unique to all parents and there is no one right answer. Mr. Williams then revised his thought and said, "Okay, then I'll say 16, but using protection." He added to his response, "And with a girlfriend. You don't go having sex with just anybody." The clinician wrote all of this information under the Should Know column.

The clinician asked Mr. Williams whether he believed Jamar knew the basics of reproduction, including the anatomical names of genital areas. He was certain that his son knew the words "penis" and "vagina" and that intercourse was required for conception but doubted that his son knew more detailed information related to gametes, such as sperm and eggs. He also suspected that his son knew relatively little about the various sexual acts that he frequently referenced in his comments, such as oral sex. The clinician asked Mr. Williams if he would like to include these types of sexual acts on the list. "Sure, why not?" replied the father, and the clinician wrote them down.

The clinician then shifted by asking Mr. Williams the types of information that should not be included in a discussion with his son. This question also perplexed the father, who finally said, "Well, I don't want to hide anything. What types of things should we not talk about?" The clinician used an extreme example to stimulate the father's thought process. "What about things like multiple partners or bondage?" The father was noticeably surprised by that question and then smiled and said, "Yeah, I don't think we need to include that." Operating with this frame of reference, the father then provided several other topics that he believed were not appropriate for his son. The clinician showed the father the two lists of topics and asked whether they accurately captured his idea of "healthy sexuality." The father agreed they did.

Session 2

Mr. Williams began session by stating that Jamar did not use any sexual language around him during the prior week. However, a teacher at school notified him that Jamar was heard making a sexual comment to a female student. This resulted in a 2-day suspension. Mr. Williams removed the power cord from Jamar's video game system as a result, which led Jamar to protest that it was never stated that the consequence would be delivered for behaviors at school. Mr. Williams asked the clinician to weigh in on whether Jamar's point was valid. The clinician told the father that removing the power cord was appropriate and that the rules were designed for use in all settings.

The clinician turned to a discussion of typical sexual development for children entering the adolescent years. This included providing handouts and discussing a few important topics. Given that Mr. Williams already demonstrated a fairly accurate understanding of sexual knowledge among children Jamar's age, the clinician focused on aspects of consent and relevant dynamics of interpersonal relationships, neither of which Mr. Williams included in his previous Should Know list. As for consent, much of the discussion revolved around ways that consent is often misconstrued, such as some people believing consent is implied if a potential sexual partner does not explicitly refuse. The clinician emphasized a focus on ensuring noncoerced, nonpressured agreement from a partner before engaging in sexual behavior. The father quickly agreed and seemed surprised that he had not considered the issue before.

Mr. Williams was more confused by the idea of teaching his son about interpersonal relationships. The father admitted he never thought of such a topic in the past and could not remember his own parents ever discussing dating relationships with him. The clinician qualified that the purpose of the discussion was to provide guidance beyond the already established limits related to sexual partners. Mr. Williams stated his son should be 16, use protection, and be dating the partner. The clinician pointed out that, according to the current definition, sex on the first date was allowed, meaning Jamar could date someone with the intention of having sex and then, after a sexual encounter, break up with that person to date someone else with the intention of having a new sexual partner. Mr. Williams understood the point after this hypothetical situation. He decided to amend his guidance by defining a "serious relationship" as one in which Jamar believed he loved the other person. This qualification allowed Mr. Williams to begin placing additional parameters around the concept of a "serious relationship," including commitment, affection, and the length of time required to develop such a relationship. In effect, Mr. Williams further specified his requirements for engaging in sexual behavior with another person. This information was added to the Should Know column.

The clinician discussed with Mr. Williams different ways of teaching the information in the Should Know column to Jamar. It was decided to use several drawings available on the internet that depict male and female genitalia and the process of reproduction for the purposes of teaching these topics. As it came to relationships and consent, Mr. Williams decided he wanted to use some personal examples from his own life. He believed this would allow him to better relate to his son and make the conversation more a review of "lessons learned" than a parent-dictated lecture. The clinician role played the father's delivery of these different pieces of information and helped him consider responses to different types of questions Jamar might ask. When the father felt comfortable with the material, the clinician encouraged the father to continue implementation of the behavior management plan and praised his efforts.

Session 3

Jamar spoke with the clinician alone to begin the session. The boy continued to display his negative attitude and made a few offhand comments about the clinician's age and likely sexual prowess. The clinician agreed with Jamar about being old and confessed to having a limited sexual vocabulary according to contemporary standards. This surprised Jamar, who clearly had not expected the clinician to respond in this way. Before he had a chance to collect his thoughts, the clinician added, "Maybe you can teach me some things. What's something I probably don't know?" Jamar threw a side-eyed look at the clinician, again unsure how to respond. "No, seriously. Do they still call an erection, 'wood'?" asked the clinician. Jamar smiled and started to laugh. The boy answered, "Nah, I've never heard that. We call it a chubby or a fatty." The clinician nodded, "Okay, so you just taught me something."

The boy was seemingly disarmed by this initial conversation and asked, "So, is this designed to trick me into talking about sex stuff so my dad takes my games again?" The clinician acknowledged the boy's concern and clarified, "Nope. You won't be in trouble for anything you say in here, as long as it's done respectfully." Jamar's forehead wrinkled and his eyes squinted as if in disbelief. "You serious?" he asked. The clinician confirmed that anything could be discussed, and it was hoped Jamar could provide more information about contemporary sexual discussions. The clinician followed this by asking a simple question, "What does it mean to have sex?" Jamar again smiled and looked at the clinician, "You know." The clinician suggested to the boy that people often have different definitions of that word and it was relevant to know what Jamar considered to be "sex."

The boy began reciting a list of euphemisms (e.g., "you do it," "a boy and girl get freaky") to describe his perception of sex, but never actually provided an explicit definition of what the act involved. He then made a reference to oral sex, again in euphemism (e.g., "going down on someone") and, when pressed, clearly stated the act involved placing a mouth on the genitals of another person. The clinician reflected Jamar's statement and asked for the same level of detail about the act of sex itself. Jamar finally provided a description of a boy "putting it in" a girl. When asked where in the girl the boy is supposed to insert his penis, Jamar began to fumble his words. He started answering twice before stopping and reevaluating his response. Finally, Jamar suggested that sex involved a male inserting his penis into the anus of a female. Jamar surmised that this is the process through which babies are conceived and, in keeping with his understanding, suggested that a baby is birthed through the anus. The clinician reflected his statements but provided no indication of the accuracy of his thoughts.

Throughout the remainder of the conversation, Jamar displayed a number of faulty assumptions regarding sex. It quickly became apparent that, in all likelihood, Jamar was not sexually experienced. Nonetheless, he clearly displayed an interest in the topic and was attempting to demonstrate a level of sexual sophistication. The clinician asked Jamar whether he might be interested in discussing the topic with his father. The boy's face dropped as he said, "No. He doesn't like to talk about this stuff. Plus, that's weird." The clinician reflected the boy's statement that it can be difficult to discuss sexual topics with a parent. The clinician stressed, however, that Mr. Williams did want to talk with Jamar about these issues to make sure he has a healthy understanding of sex going forward. The boy nodded his head but did not provide a verbal response.

The clinician walked Jamar to the waiting room and brought Mr. Williams into session. The father listened intently as the clinician summarized the content of the previous discussion with his son. When hearing that his son believed sexual intercourse to involve anal sex, Mr. Williams was shocked. "What?! That's what he thinks? Where did he learn that?" The clinician explained that this is a common belief among preadolescent boys, as they often understand the female body the same as they understand the male body, that is to say that there is one opening for urination and one opening for defecation. Of these two options, sex seems more plausible to occur via the rectum. The father's mouth opened and his head tilted back as he comprehended the logic and then responded by stating, "I get it. Okay, I guess it's not that strange." The clinician then reviewed other pieces of the conversation and revisited with the father the information they previously planned to present to the boy. Before ending, the clinician encouraged the father to pay close attention to his own responses. His surprised look and blunt statement made in response to hearing about Jamar's understanding of sex may have the effect of shutting down the boy if it occurred in front of him. Mr. Williams understood and promised to control his reactions during the conjoint session.

Session 4

Jamar and his father came into session and the clinician provided an overview of the conjoint session, emphasizing to Jamar that the goal was for his father to provide him with helpful information and to stimulate a conversation. Jamar sat quietly but acknowledged the clinician's statement. Mr. Williams began by showing his son the figure drawings and describing the parts of the male anatomy. The only comment uttered by Jamar during this part of the discussion was a quiet, "I know." The father then presented a picture of the female anatomy and began discussing the different parts. After a few moments, the boy stopped his father. "Wait, you're saying there's three openings down there?" The father, in accordance with plans made in the previous session, had labeled the vaginal, urethral, and anal openings, which elicited the boy's response. The father confirmed the boy's understanding and proceeded to discuss the process of conception. The boy, again, looked surprised, as he heard that babies are born through the vaginal canal and not the anus. The clinician cued the father to give Jamar time to respond. Eventually, the boy noted, "That's messed up. Like, how does it . . . Man, that's crazy." The father pointed out the aborted question and asked whether Jamar had questions, but the boy declined.

The father then moved on to discuss STIs and the possibility of the woman becoming pregnant as a result of sex. Jamar questioned his father about STIs, seemingly unaware of the possibility of significant health consequences. The father did an excellent job providing factual information without attempting to scare the boy, and Jamar was surprised to hear how many different infections can be transmitted sexually. The father used this information to transition into the topic of when sex was allowable to his mind. However, Jamar stopped him and went back to the topic of STIs. "So, it's all good if you use your mouth though, right?" he asked. The father, without hesitation, accurately discussed the possibility of transmitting STIs through oral contact as well. Jamar placed his head in hand and began rubbing his hair, as if trying to process this new information. He then looked at his dad and, in a soft tone of voice, asked, "Have you ever used your mouth before?" The clinician looked at the dad, ready to offer assistance, but the father responded without the need for support, "Yeah, I have. But there's rules about doing this stuff. That's what I want to talk about next." The boy looked down as if processing the information and the clinician motioned for the father to inquire as to his thoughts. Mr. Williams asked an unexpected question, "Jamar, have you ever used your mouth before to do this?" The boy looked up at his father and said, "No, but I asked my girl to. She said no, but I didn't know all this." The clinician watched the father, worried about his potential response. But Mr. Williams handled the information well, "Okay, son. Let's talk about when this is acceptable."

The father then proceeded to describe the values he wished to teach his son, as defined in previous sessions. The boy did exceptionally well, asking his father several follow-up questions, and Mr. Williams answered them all with relative ease. When it came to the issue of condoms, the father described how they can reduce the risk of contracting an STI and pregnancy before quickly emphasizing that they are not "100% effective." Seemingly caught up in the moment and having forgotten his previous inhibitions, Jamar asked his father, "How do I know if I'm using it right?" Mr. Williams responded that when Jamar turned 16, was in a relationship, and considering having sex, that he would explain in more detail how to use them correctly. The boy seemed satisfied with this answer and the conversation continued to the final aspects. As the session came to an end, Mr. Williams praised Jamar for talking about the issue so openly, emphasized that he wanted him to be healthy, and told his son that he loved him. Jamar, appearing uncomfortable with his father's display of affection, merely said, "Thanks, Dad."

Phase 3

Session 1

Jamar's first comment entering session was related to the conjoint session that occurred the week before. He wanted to emphasize to the clinician how strange that discussion was and that he did not want to talk about sexual topics anymore in session. The clinician agreed that it can be uncomfortable for a preteen to talk about such topics with adults and told him that, while the coming sessions would not be as focused on sex as the last session, there would still be some discussion of the topic. Jamar sighed and rolled his eyes. The clinician used this moment to review the material discussed during the conjoint session related to sexual arousal and a desire to perform sexual behaviors, with an emphasis on highlighting physiological changes that one often experiences. Jamar looked at the clinician and asked, "You mean like getting a chubby?" The clinician agreed that an erection is one example of physiological arousal, but qualified that there are other sensations as well.

Having engaged Jamar in a discussion of sexual arousal, the clinician allowed him to discuss other feelings and thoughts he had experienced related to the topic. The boy made a point of discussing "fine-looking females" and thoughts of sexual acts that occur when seeing a physically attractive woman. The clinician normalized these experiences and emphasized that the goal is to not act on these thoughts and feelings, which may result in negative consequences. Jamar nodded his head and said he had not attempted anything sexual other than the one incident with a girlfriend. Given his level of self-disclosure, the opportunity presented itself to ask Jamar to identify what mechanisms, skills, or other barriers allowed him to refrain from acting on his sexual thoughts and feelings. He was unsure but did note he knows such behaviors would result in getting in trouble. When asked to consider the topic further, he concluded he did not want to hurt other people or have other people think of him as "crazy or weird." As such, Jamar endorsed some consideration of social perception and pressures as at least partially inhibiting his behavior.

The clinician suggested that it may be easier for Jamar to control his behaviors, including sexual verbalizations, if he learned more effective impulse control skills. The boy agreed, and the clinician taught him various forms of controlled breathing and positive imagery. Jamar engaged in the techniques but appeared to do so half-heartedly. When completed, the clinician asked whether Jamar might consider using the techniques in the future, and the boy responded, "I don't know. We'll see." The clinician asked Jamar if he might demonstrate the skills for his father and discuss those factors that prevent him from engaging in more overt sexual behavior. The boy politely declined, again referencing his desire to not speak any further with his father about these topics.

When Mr. Williams spoke during session, the clinician was amazed to hear the father immediately talk about a discussion he had with Jamar. Assuming the father was still processing the previous conjoint session, the clinician praised Mr. Williams's effort and performance. The father stopped the clinician and clarified that he and his son had a different conversation later in the evening following the prior session. Jamar asked additional questions about relationships, what sex was like, and what people think of those who engage in early sexual behavior. Mr. Williams took this opportunity to speak with Jamar about how some people might develop a negative reputation if they engaged in sexual behavior with multiple people, and those who talk about sex a lot may find themselves ostracized by others who do not view sex as such an important aspect of their lives. Importantly, the father focused on how few 12-year-old peers are interested in sexual relationships, a point to which Jamar conceded that not many people respond in positive ways to his sexual comments. "I couldn't believe it, Doc. I felt like my son actually talked to me for the first time in years," the father said with a grin.

The clinician praised the father's ability to continue with the conversation in a neutral and supportive manner and encouraged him to continue with that effort. Mr. Williams asked if he should broach the topic with his son on a regular basis and suggested scheduling a weekly time. The clinician cautioned against this tactic and highlighted that such regularity may turn his son off to discussing the topic. Instead, the clinician suggested revisiting the topic irregularly, perhaps three or four times per year, unless Jamar initiates the conversation. Mr. Williams agreed with the logic after some consideration and planned to follow up with his son in another week to simply ensure the boy knew the door was open. The clinician ended the session by reviewing with the father the contents of the discussion with Jamar and the techniques he learned.

Session 2

Jamar entered session and began by rhetorically asking, "Are we going to talk about sex again?" The clinician smiled and said, "Yes, but that'll be in a little while. Let's see how far we get." The clinician explained the cognitive triangle to Jamar and gave several nonsexual examples to help him understand the concept. Jamar engaged readily with the concept and, as time began to run out, he stated that he was glad sex did not come up during the session. It was an excellent segue and the clinician responded, "I'm happy to hear you say that. Let's do a sexual example." The boy sighed and laid his head on the table.

The clinician used an example of Jamar making a sexual comment toward a girl that he liked, which was a behavior, and worked backward through the triangle. Jamar mentioned the behavior likely stemmed from a feeling of sexual arousal, which is the consequence of a thought that the girl is attractive. It was a relatively easy exercise for the boy to complete. With some probing, he acknowledged that, in some situations, his initial thought was that "sex is cool, people might laugh," which resulted in a kind of excitement or urge to improve his standing among peers, which led to him making such comments. In this instance, Jamar identified two different thought patterns that may result in his making a sexual comment. The first was out of genuine attraction to another person; the second was a social interpretation that sexual comments might improve his social standing.

To help Jamar with perspective-taking skills, the clinician returned to the initial completed triangle that suggested his sexual comments originally stemmed from an attraction to a girl. However, in this case, Jamar was asked to place himself in the position of the girl who was confronted by a boy who made a sexual comment. His first thought was that the girl would think the boy was interested in her, it would prompt a feeling of arousal or excitement, and result in the behavioral response of making a similar comment or proposition in return. The clinician asked Jamar if this is the common behavior he sees from the girls to whom he makes sexual comments. The boy quickly responded, "Yeah, of course. I mean, look at me," and made a motion showcasing his body and face. However, when asked to provide a specific example of a time that a girl provided such an engaging response to his sexual comments, he was unable to respond. With more discussion, Jamar admitted the far more common response was for girls to give him disgusted looks and make dismissing comments. Starting with these responses (behaviors) and working backward, Jamar identified that the girls likely felt repulsed and unaroused, and these feelings stemmed from negative thoughts about him. "Maybe that's not the best way to tell a girl you like them," the boy reluctantly decided.

Again, Jamar declined to teach the cognitive coping skills to his father. The clinician reviewed the cognitive triangle with Mr. Williams and the father nodded enthusiastically at various points throughout the session. "Can I use this stuff to get him to focus on his homework?" the father asked. The clinician agreed it can be used for various purposes, but the goal was to help Jamar think through his behavioral options in a more deliberate way before he acted, not to hurry him to the desired conclusion. The father asked a few follow-up questions and practiced implementing the technique, with the clinician taking on the role of his son. Mr. Williams eagerly asked for more information. The clinician provided the father with handouts that could help him continue to practice the skill with his son at home.

Session 3

Mr. Williams started session alone with the clinician and the discussion focused on helping the father to identify potential sources of concern within the family's environment. Given that the father and son lived alone and the father had few responsibilities beyond his child, there were not many times the father relied on a babysitter. In those rare situations when Mr. Williams did need to leave his son in the care of another person, it was usually the grandparents. Outside of school and his guitar instructor, Mr. Williams was unable to identify any other adults that might be in an unsupervised situation with Jamar. As such, the discussion on safety turned quickly to discussions of peer relationships.

Mr. Williams was concerned that his son may fall prey to an older woman or a male peer that might in some way convince him to perform sexual acts. Jamar was not particularly assertive and the father's concern about his son's ability to protect himself was notable. The clinician emphasized the importance of maintaining an open line of communication with Jamar and trying to promote his perception of autonomy. The father and clinician designed several different scenarios where an individual attempted to persuade Jamar into various troubling behaviors, such as engaging in sexual acts, watching sexual videos, or making inappropriate comments to another person. The father decided to play the role of the other individual in these situations while the clinician moderated the discussion.

When Jamar joined session, the clinician briefly reviewed the importance of discussing certain situations with an adult when they occur, with a focus on Mr. Williams as a source of support. It was clearly pointed out by the father that these situations included any inappropriate touching or sexual discussions. Jamar rolled his eyes and said, "Great, we're talking about this again?" The clinician qualified that this discussion was different, in that the aim was to see how he would handle different situations. It was explained that his father would play the role of another individual and Jamar was to respond to his father's comments in a way he believed most appropriate.

Mr. Williams began by suggesting he was a 17-year-old girl that Jamar found attractive, and referenced his appearance as being similar to that of a famous singer. Mr. Williams then started making comments meant to convey a sexual interest in Jamar. The boy looked down and said, "I know I'm supposed to say no, but what if I say yes?" The clinician praised Jamar for giving an honest answer and asked him to think through the different consequences that may result. Referring to previous discussions, Jamar easily concluded, "She could get pregnant or I could get a disease." Mr. Williams also jumped in and asked his son to recall the conditions under which he deemed sexual activity acceptable. Jamar remembered his father did not approve until the age of 16, within the confines of a committed relationship, and using protection.

Mr. Williams went to the next scenario and played the role of a same-aged peer who wanted Jamar to make sexual comments to a girl. When Jamar refused, the father started pressuring him, including ridiculing him for not agreeing. The boy started to smile and said he found it funny to see his father acting in such ways. The clinician reflected and agreed with his statement, which made the father smile too. But the question remained for Jamar of how he would respond given such social pressures. He decided the best response would be to make a joke of the situation and tell the peer to do it himself. He went on to make a comment suggesting he was afraid of the girl having a negative image of him if he made sexually suggestive comments. Mr. Williams gave his son a brief round of applause and commented, "You got it, boy. Girls don't like that from guys. Not the girls you want, anyway." This led Jamar to ask his father, "What do you say to girls then?" Given that session was over, the clinician recommended the father and son continue that conversation in the car.

Session 4

To start this final session of the protocol, the clinician informed Jamar that it would involve very little discussion of sexual topics. He was pleased to hear that, but then quickly asked, "Then what are we talking about?" The clinician said he wanted to talk about Jamar's friends and the things he likes to do in his free time. The boy almost immediately started talking about his two closest friends, including how much fun they have together. The clinician asked Jamar to provide examples of activities in which they all participate, but the boy struggled. He discussed previous conversations the boys had at school and some of the comments the peers said that Jamar found humorous, but he was unable to provide any examples of shared interests. The clinician asked the question in a more pointed way, "Tell me what you and your friends have in common. What types of things do you all enjoy doing together?" Other than playing video games, Jamar was unable to identify any hobbies or common experiences he shared with his friends. The clinician asked whether Jamar played video games with his friends, but it appeared he did not.

The clinician shifted into trying to identify potential social influences related to this peer group and whether it influenced his sexual interests and comments. Given that one of the jokes Jamar mentioned the group telling did have a sexual connotation, the clinician asked the boy, "That joke you told me a few minutes ago . . . was that your joke or one that your friends told you?" Jamar, obviously sensing the question was designed to examine the sexually inappropriate nature, responded bluntly, "A friend's." The clinician followed his statement by asking, "Do you all tell a lot of sexual jokes like that?" Jamar just nodded his head before stating that he did not want to get his friends in trouble and wished not to speak of it further.

The clinician shifted the conversation to the positive aspects of his friends, but Jamar was unable to identify many admirable qualities. Although he seemed to believe he was listing several attributes that placed his friends in a positive light, they largely painted a picture of a convenient peer group that was inclusive of Jamar. For instance, when the clinician asked if any of the friends played the guitar (i.e., exploring for a shared interest), Jamar responded, "No, they don't play instruments, but they think it's cool that I do. No one else seems to care." In response to the clinician asking whether the group discusses the video games they play, the boy responded, "Not really. We play different games; we don't play together online." The clinician reflected the boy's comment and then said, "Is there anything that you wish you could change about your friends?" Jamar hesitated and looked around the room. He began rocking in his chair and stated, "I wish they didn't get in trouble so much." The clinician and Jamar continued to talk about friends while playing a game together, before Jamar returned to the waiting room.

Bringing Mr. Williams into session, the clinician reviewed Jamar's answers: "It looks like Jamar doesn't have a lot of friends. Would you say that's accurate?" The father agreed with the statement and mentioned that their apartment complex did not have a lot of children and Jamar did not ask to go to events or participate in activities. The clinician suggested that Jamar was not particularly close with his friend group, including the peers that influence his sexual commentary, but this group may be one of the few that accepted him. Mr. Williams had not considered this possibility before. "I knew his friends at school weren't good, Doc, but I figured the school keeps track of that sort of thing. What can I do?" The clinician helped Mr. Williams think through different options and activities where Jamar might meet peers that would provide a more positive influence. Mr. Williams was focused almost exclusively on sports, given his own background, but Jamar was not particularly athletic. The clinician suggested speaking with Jamar's guitar instructor about the possibility of joining a band or taking group lessons where he could meet other children with musical interests. The father quickly grabbed on to that idea, "Oh, I like that, Doc. Why didn't I think of that?" The clinician also recommended other community activities that the two of them could participate in together, which might provide them with positive father–son experiences and the opportunity for Jamar to meet peers. The clinician suggested a few websites that listed community activities and recommended that he and Jamar sit down and review them together.

Mr. Williams completed the ASB-C and SDQ before finishing session. On the ASB-C, the total score was a 6, which was in the *concerning* range; however, Mr. Williams reported that most of the problems had not been observed in the prior 3 weeks. This suggested a significant improvement in trajectory and Mr. Williams reported significantly improved confidence in his ability to manage his son's sexual comments and behaviors. As evidence, he offered that he had not removed the video game cords in over 3 weeks and he was extremely pleased that his son was willing to talk about these topics with him. On the SDQ, Mr. Williams continued to provide a score for Jamar that suggested significant behavioral problems. The father believed this too was improving and declined referrals for either family therapy or a caregiver training program.

CONCLUSION

The case of Jamar W. presents a different form of problematic sexual behavior. In this case, the child was nearing puberty, if not already in that stage of development, and displayed more mature sexual interests than is typical for preteen children. Nonetheless, it became clear that Jamar's understanding of sex was elementary, as was his ideas about how to approach sexual relationships. His exposure to sexual topics within his peer group, social pressures, and typical developmental progression combined to result in his sexual comments and interests, but there was little corrective information provided by his father. However, Mr. Williams clearly showed an interest in helping his son and was open to discussing practically any issue that might be relevant. He was engaged and did not shy away from discussions or the implementation of behavioral consequences. Indeed, Mr. Williams served as a primary driver of his son's improvement. Nonetheless, he was generally unaware of behavioral mechanisms, typical development, and the social influences impacting his son. The clinician's ability to build rapport with the father allowed for the implementation of treatment techniques that helped Mr. Williams better understand his son, support him in the home, and manage his behavior.

10 SPECIAL APPLICATIONS OF TREATMENT PHASES

The phase-based nature of phase-based treatment for problematic sexual behavior (PBT) allows for several unique applications of the protocol. For instance, one phase of the protocol can be implemented without necessarily requiring that a previous phase occurred first in sequence. In other words, a clinician can choose to implement the techniques within the Healthy Sexuality segment, such as psychoeducation and communication enhancement (Phase 2), without having established rules or discussed modeling of sexuality, as occurs in the Family Sexuality and Response part of treatment (Phase 1). This type of flexibility increases the ability of the clinician to respond to problematic sexual behavior (PSB) when it occurs in cases where PSB is not the primary target of intervention. Also, clinicians are capable of implementing indicated phases in situations where no PSB is identified, but when concerns regarding future behavior are present. This chapter reviews two such situations: integrating PBT with other treatment protocols and using PBT as a secondary prevention model.

https://doi.org/10.1037/0000516-011
Children With Problematic Sexual Behavior: Theory, Research, and Evidence-Based Practice, by B. Allen

INTEGRATING PBT WITH OTHER TREATMENT MODELS

Many times, clinicians determine that a non–PSB-focused intervention is the most suited clinical approach to a case. In these instances, it may still be beneficial to integrate PSB-focused treatment techniques if PSB is a secondary concern. This section reviews two common situations where this occurs and how PBT components can be integrated in a deliberate and effective manner.

Trauma-Focused Interventions

As discussed in Chapter 1, many children with PSB previously experienced trauma, and these events, at least partially, may be etiologically related to the display of PSB. However, in some cases, the PSB is a secondary concern as posttraumatic stress, depression, anxiety, or some other presenting issue is conceptualized as the primary target for treatment. In such situations, clinicians may opt for a trauma-focused treatment as the intervention of choice, but still wish to integrate evidence-based, PSB-focused techniques. Although this treatment plan is appropriate, it does present concerns related to implementing the trauma-focused treatment protocol with fidelity. However, it is possible to integrate PBT into trauma-focused interventions in a thoughtful way that sufficiently addresses this concern. To demonstrate this process, the discussion below outlines the implementation of PBT into trauma-focused cognitive behavior therapy (TF-CBT; Cohen et al., 2017), a well-validated and widely implemented treatment for posttrauma sequelae among children who experienced a wide range of traumatic events (Allen et al., 2012; Dorsey et al., 2017).

TF-CBT is a multistep treatment using techniques summarized by the acronym PRACTICE (see Exhibit 10.1). One of the first techniques of TF-CBT is to teach the caregiver standard behavior management skills. Within the TF-CBT model, as specified by the developers (Cohen et al., 2010; Cohen et al., 2017), these skills may include ABC chains, establishing rules and boundaries, praise, selective attention, utilizing consequences for breaking rules, and contingency reinforcement programs. These same skills are included within the first phase of PBT. However, PBT also includes a focus on developing a monitoring plan and reducing modeling of sexual behavior within the home, two techniques clearly indicated in cases of PSB. When a child presents with significant PSB, but the clinician determines through assessment that TF-CBT is the most suited treatment, it is advisable to begin treatment with Phase 1 of PBT and conceptualize this as the "parenting skills" component of TF-CBT. In this way, the clinician is attending to immediate needs of safety

EXHIBIT 10.1. The PRACTICE Acronym, Trauma-Focused Cognitive Behavior Therapy Components

	Component
P:	Parenting Skills
	Psychoeducation
R:	Relaxation Skills
A:	Affective Expression and Modulation Skills
C:	Cognitive Coping and Processing Skills
T:	Trauma Narrative & Cognitive Processing
I:	In Vivo Exposure
C:	Conjoint Parent-Child Sessions
E:	Enhancing Safety and Developmental Trajectory

(i.e., monitoring plan), eliminating social modeling of sexual behavior, and then establishing rules and appropriate consequences as dictated by TF-CBT. The benefit of this approach for a clinician is the utilization of a protocol designed for the treatment of PSB that encompasses the directives of TF-CBT in a structured manner.

The second component of TF-CBT, psychoeducation, diverges in more noticeable ways from the psychoeducation component of PBT. Within TF-CBT, the goal is often to teach the child and caregiver about trauma and traumatic stress, including specific aspects of the treatment model. In cases of sexual abuse, this psychoeducation often includes teaching the child anatomical names of genitals and a basic definition of the term "sexual abuse." Also, this component is conceptualized as both an opportunity to provide information that normalizes a child's reactions and behaviors, as well as an introduction to gradual exposure, or the process through which the child is desensitized to reminders of the trauma. It is common for the clinician to provide psychoeducation directly to the child during session and, in many cases, for the child to teach the learned information to the caregiver. The clinician supplements the child's efforts by providing additional information to the caregiver. Within TF-CBT, this component of psychoeducation is often delivered in a single session, although multiple sessions are possible depending on the needs of the case.

Within PBT, psychoeducation is designed to correct a child's unhelpful beliefs about sex and sexuality, satisfy curiosity by providing developmentally appropriate information, teach the family's values, and open the line of communication between the child and caregiver related to sexual topics. To accomplish this, the caregiver takes the lead in providing psychoeducation, and the child is encouraged to engage in an open discussion on the topics.

This process unfolds over the course of several sessions, which allows the caregiver time to consider their own perspective, learn about typical sexual development, craft a plan of how to educate their child, and then teach this information to the child in a conjoint session.

Clinical experience suggests an approach that merges these two goals (see Exhibit 10.2). Given that the psychoeducation component is oftentimes the first individual meeting that a clinician has with a child in TF-CBT, sessions usually include some rapport-building activities in addition to providing psychoeducation. These activities proceed in the manner specified within the TF-CBT protocol during the first session. However, when the clinician meets alone with the caregiver in this first session, the focus is on allowing the caregiver to consider their own views on sexual behavior, including how a sexual abuse experience may have impacted the lessons learned by the child, if applicable (PBT Phase 2, Session 1). The second session with the child continues with the process of TF-CBT–related psychoeducation and prepares the child for the conjoint session to occur in the next session. During clinical time with the caregiver, the clinician provides psychoeducation about sexual development and helps the caregiver identify how to teach this information and their values to the child (PBT Phase 2, Session 2).

The third psychoeducation session includes the conjoint session (PBT Phase 2, Session 4), but important considerations are necessary. First, it is advised that the child begin the session by teaching the caregiver what they learned through psychoeducation with the clinician. This results in the session beginning with a discussion of trauma and posttrauma sequelae; in cases of sexual abuse, this will involve a discussion of topics such as the anatomical

EXHIBIT 10.2. Integrating TF-CBT and PBT Psychoeducation Components

Session 1:

With the Caregiver: Review beliefs about sex and sexuality (PBT Phase 2, Session 1)

With the Child: Build rapport, provide psychoeducation on trauma and traumatic stress (TF-CBT)

Session 2:

With the Caregiver: Provide psychoeducation about sexual development, prepare for conjoint session (PBT Phase 2, Session 2)

With the Child: Provide psychoeducation on trauma and traumatic stress, prepare for conjoint session (TF-CBT)

Session 3:

Conjoint Session with Child and Caregiver: Child shares information learned with caregiver (TF-CBT), caregiver provides a healthy view of sex for the child (PBT Phase 2, Session 4).

Note. TF-CBT = trauma-focused cognitive behavior therapy; PBT = phase-based treatment for problematic sexual behavior.

names of genitals and a definition of abuse. Second, these topics offer a natural transition into the topic of sexual behavior. The caregiver can praise and empathize with the child and begin to take the lead to teach the child the function of sexual organs and how they should be treated safely and appropriately. This allows the caregiver to acknowledge the child's experience, impart knowledge, and begin a discussion around sensitive topics. Third, in keeping with the process of TF-CBT, it is important to remember that each session should include some level of gradual exposure; however, in cases of sexual abuse, discussion of sexual topics is generally considered exposure. Fourth, clinicians must be cautious that the caregiver's commentary in the conjoint session does not venture into blaming or shaming the child or discussing details of the sexual abuse experience not yet talked about in treatment (i.e., through a trauma narrative).

The final phase of PBT (Skill Development) is not easily integrated into TF-CBT as a unified treatment package. However, such integration is not necessary. The first two sessions of Phase 3 (i.e., impulse control and cognitive coping skills) are already subsumed under the TF-CBT techniques of relaxation skills, affective expression and modulation skills, and cognitive coping and processing skills. The key consideration for a clinician is that, while implementing these TF-CBT skills as dictated within the protocol, the skills be applied to PSB, as well as the commonly targeted posttrauma concerns (e.g., intrusive thoughts, anxiety). The third and fourth sessions of PBT Phase 3 (i.e., safety skills, peer relations) likewise are easily included within the final component of TF-CBT (Enhancing Safety and Developmental Trajectory). Indeed, the safety skills are practically identical to those typically taught at the end of TF-CBT. Examining the influence of peers is not a standard aspect of delivering TF-CBT but is easily included within the final component. Also, clinicians are encouraged to consider how the different techniques of TF-CBT (e.g., trauma narrative, in vivo exposure) may be leveraged to improve PSB and how the presence of PSB may inform the delivery of these techniques. For a more detailed discussion of this issue, the reader is referred to Allen (2018).

Behavioral Parent Training Interventions

As mentioned in Chapter 1, the strongest correlate of PSB is broader externalizing problems (e.g., oppositional behavior, aggression). The preferred approach to the treatment of general behavioral problems among children is a behavioral parent management training program (Kaminski & Claussen, 2017). Although several different protocols exist, they all share the common techniques of teaching caregivers to provide positive reinforcement for desired behavior (e.g., praise, attention, tangible rewards) and to respond to undesired behavior with appropriate consequences (e.g., ignoring the behavior, removal of privileges, time out). It should also be mentioned that these programs emphasize teaching the caregivers applied skills through coaching and feedback and eschew physical discipline (e.g., spanking). As such, discussing the integration of PBT into one specific protocol is sufficient and can generalize to the integration of PBT with similar protocols. For the demonstration here, parent–child interaction therapy (PCIT; McNeil & Hembree-Kigin, 2010) is used.

PCIT progresses in two stages. In the first stage, child-directed interaction (CDI), children are allowed to lead the activities of session and caregivers provide various forms of positive feedback (e.g., praises, describing the child's behavior) and engage with the child in play. The clinician coaches the caregiver by providing in-the-moment comments, often through the use of a two-way mirror and an earbud speaker, to build the caregiver's skills in applying these techniques with their child. Also, in CDI, caregivers are taught to apply selective attention (i.e., ignoring undesired behavior) and to utilize it in conjunction with positive feedback. In the second stage of PCIT, parent-directed interaction (PDI), caregivers are taught to utilize logical consequences, removal of privileges, and time out to increase compliance with directives. However, the positive attending skills learned in CDI continue and discipline skills are implemented only when the child breaks a defined rule or is noncompliant. Again, in-the-moment coaching is used to help the caregiver learn the skills more effectively.

In situations where PSB presents alongside other forms of behavioral problems, it seems logical to employ a behavioral parent management training program, such as PCIT, but adaptations are required. As mentioned before, concerns of safety and the potential modeling of sexual behavior are omnipresent in cases of PSB and must be addressed at the outset of treatment. In addition, teaching the child appropriate boundaries and implementing consequences for transgressing those boundaries are a necessary part of promoting safety. In many parent-training programs, there is a directive for establishing rules for severe behavior that result in automatic consequences, without any prior warnings or redirections. In PCIT, this technique is referred to as a "house rule" and is commonly employed in cases of severe aggression or unpredictable property destruction. Indeed, there are recommendations that PCIT be adapted in cases of PSB by establishing house rules (i.e., sexual behavior rules) early in treatment, including delivering appropriate consequences when the rules are broken (Shawler et al., 2018).

With this background, when attempting to integrate PBT with PCIT, it is recommended that Phase 1 of PBT be implemented first without modification

(3–4 sessions), followed by the CDI phase of PCIT. Even after beginning PCIT, it is important for the clinician to evaluate the caregiver's implementation of consequences for breaking the established rules and adherence to the monitoring plan. As the caregiver begins and progresses through CDI, the clinician can coach the caregiver on how to use the learned skills for the purposes of promoting adherence to the sexual behavior rules, as well as for improvement of other behavioral problems.

A clinical choice point emerges when CDI is completed. In many instances, the child's broader behavioral problems are significantly improved, but the PSB remains. In these situations, the clinician must determine whether it is in the best interests of the child and caregiver to continue on with PDI or to implement Phase 2 of PBT. If the clinician determines the child's PSB is largely the result of curiosity, unhelpful beliefs regarding sex, or lack of adequate understanding regarding sexual behavior, then Phase 2 of PBT is indicated, and PDI should occur after the completion of the PBT phase. However, if the clinician determines that the PSB is more the result of a caregiver who is struggling to implement behavior management skills, then the coaching and feedback offered through PDI of PCIT is more appropriate, and Phase 2 of PBT should be delivered after the completion of the complete PCIT protocol.

If, however, PSB is no longer observed when the end of CDI is reached, but broader behavioral problems continue, this is a clear indication for continuing with PCIT. In these situations, given the child's history of PSB, the implementation of Phase 2 of PBT is still recommended to occur when PCIT is completed. Phase 3 of PBT is designated as the last component of treatment when PBT and PCIT are integrated, regardless of the clinician's decision following CDI. This ensures the child learns impulse control and safety skills and the caregiver considers the role of peer influences before being discharged from treatment.

PBT AS A PREVENTION MODEL

Children often present for treatment based on the concern of a caregiver or because of exposure to unfortunate events (e.g., sexual abuse, pornography). However, in many of these cases, there is not a discernible clinical problem to treat as children are commonly resilient and suffer no long-term ill effects of these experiences. Nonetheless, there is often a desire to provide some form of service in the hopes of preventing concerns at a later point. PBT can be employed in these instances. Phase 1 can be used to teach a child rules related to sexual body parts without the presumption that the child displays PSB.

Similarly, Phase 2 can be utilized to provide developmentally appropriate information and help the caregiver process how to talk with the child about sexual topics. The content of these two phases may effectively correct any mistaken beliefs the child developed through their experiences. Lastly, Phase 3 teaches coping and safety skills, two competencies generally viewed as positive qualities for all children. In short, PBT can be implemented as a secondary prevention model in the absence of a discernible PSB.

The manner in which PBT is implemented for the purposes of prevention varies and is a decision best left to the clinician. One common mode of delivery is to initiate services at the beginning of Phase 2 by discussing with the caregiver their views of sexual behavior and what they wish to teach the child. Within this context, the rules are then established and integrated into the later conjoint session. As such, the caregiver teaches the child the information and values they wish to impart and establishes rules in tandem as a logical outgrowth of that discussion. In another common prevention method, Phase 2 is provided with an emphasis on teaching the caregiver about typical child development. This is most commonly done when a caregiver is concerned about the sexual behavior of their child, but assessment shows the child's behavior is within normal limits.

CONCLUSIONS

PBT, by virtue of its phase-based structure, is incredibly adaptable. It can be integrated into other treatment approaches when PSB presents alongside comorbid concerns. Indeed, experience suggests that integrating the protocol into trauma-focused interventions and behavioral parent training programs in a thoughtful and deliberate manner can yield positive clinical outcomes for PSB and a host of other presenting problems. Given that many of the techniques of PBT are applicable even in the absence of PSB, the PBT model also makes for a suitable secondary prevention approach.

11 PITFALLS AND FREQUENTLY ASKED QUESTIONS

Certain questions and issues occur across phase-based treatment for problematic sexual behavior (PBT) cases with sufficient frequency that general suggestions on how to respond are available. In addition, various pitfalls are commonly experienced by clinicians and recommendations on how to avoid them, or how to respond when encountered, are warranted. This chapter provides brief discussions on 12 such questions or situations to help clinicians maximize effectiveness of program implementation.

1. *Can I use PBT with a 13-year-old? How about a teenager with an intellectual or developmental disability?*

   This is perhaps the most frequently asked question about PBT. The literature for children with problematic sexual behavior (PSB) and teenagers displaying illegal sexual behavior (ISB) are quite distinct. For instance, there are significant differences in the identified etiological processes, and evidence-supported treatments for teenagers with ISB typically are systemic in nature. PBT has not been tested with teenagers, and there is no compelling evidence to suggest that PBT will be effective

https://doi.org/10.1037/0000516-012
Children With Problematic Sexual Behavior: Theory, Research, and Evidence-Based Practice, by B. Allen

for teenagers with ISB. As for the question regarding a teenager with a cognitive limitation, the answer centers on the extent of the limitation and the conceptualization of the behavior. For instance, a 13-year-old with a mild intellectual disability where the PSB appears to be the result of a lack of knowledge regarding sexual behavior rules and perspective taking may be a candidate for PBT. However, the more significant the impairment, the less suitable PBT is for the problem. In these latter instances, a clinician must determine whether a more focused behavioral intervention is necessary (e.g., applied behavior analysis). Because this is a nuanced issue that requires a significant degree of clinical assessment and decision making, the best advice is to not use PBT for children older than 12 years.

2. *Should I use PBT if the problematic behavior occurred in the past?*

   It is not uncommon for a caregiver to seek treatment because it was discovered that a PSB happened several months (or even years) in the past. Like any mental health intervention, PBT is meant to treat active problems. The challenge becomes defining how far in the past a behavior may have occurred and still be considered "active." There is no definitive rule to provide guidance. It is generally recommended that the PSB occurred within the past 6 months to be considered a clinical problem in need of treatment. However, given that PBT involves establishing rules, providing psychoeducation, and developing applied skills, it can be used in a preventative manner in cases where the PSB was more distant. In other words, there are no known risks to implementing these techniques and they may help improve a child's development, including in cases where no active PSB is identified. The challenge for a clinician in this last instance is to not undermine whatever response appears to have been effective at preventing recurrences of the behavior, and not inadvertently shame or embarrass the child for behaviors that are well in the past.

3. *Can siblings be treated together?*

   A common situation is a child who engaged in PSB with a sibling. As such, it is tempting to treat both children together to minimize the burden on the family and improve efficiency. However, clinicians must be cautious. Sibling relationships often have their own dynamics that can make joint sessions difficult. For instance, one sibling may be the more dominant personality and the weaker one may refuse to ask questions or engage in session if the stronger child does not. As another example, one sibling may take the material seriously while the other makes jokes or displays negative attention-seeking behavior. Even if such dynamics are minimal, children may still display negative emotions given the topics of discussion and these emotions may be stronger in the presence of a sibling. For these reasons, it is generally not recommended to see siblings together. Seeing children separately also allows each child time to ask their own questions, it gives the clinician or caregiver the opportunity to explain topics in a way tailored to the child, and the psychoeducation materials may change to be considerate of developmental differences. Nonetheless, the clinician may not need to repeat some sessions that involve only caregivers. For example, clarifying family beliefs about sexuality (Phase 2, Session 1) usually only needs to occur once as the results generalize to multiple children. Similarly, the family rules defined for one sibling (Phase 1, Session 2) may apply to everyone in the family, including multiple siblings.

4. *Should each sibling have their own clinician?*

   A child may have thoughts and/or feelings about a sibling that are difficult to share with a clinician who also treats that sibling. As such, it is generally a good idea for each child to have their own clinician. However, some clinical settings simply do not have the staffing that allows for this option. Given that PBT is primarily caregiver focused, it can be implemented by a single clinician serving multiple siblings. It is the responsibility of the clinician in these situations to prevent, to the extent possible, work with one sibling negatively affecting work with another sibling.

5. *Are there any recommendations on how to reunite siblings separated as a result of the PSB?*

   Reuniting siblings that were separated due to safety concerns must not be a hurried process. Several steps should be completed before this occurs, including completing PBT treatment for the initiating child, completing whatever treatment was indicated for the sibling, developing monitoring and safety plans within the home, the initiating child making amends for their behavior, jointly reviewing the safety rules in the home to ensure clarity for all family members, and gradually reintroducing of the siblings. Lipovsky et al. (1998) discussed a more defined procedure for a similar process that centered on a physically abusive caregiver reuniting with their child, what they termed the "clarification process." Many clinicians who work with children displaying PSB have adopted and modified this process to accomplish the goals stated earlier. However, this process is itself subject to several lessons learned and it is best for clinicians to consult with a clinician experienced in this procedure before implementing it.

6. *When should caregivers discontinue monitoring plans?*

   Monitoring plans often cause disruption to the caregiver's schedule and the home environment. However, they are critical for preventing the recurrence of the sexual behavior and for maintaining safety. It is recommended that the monitoring plan remain in place until the end of PBT treatment. At that point, it is common practice that the child or family wean off of the monitoring plan in controllable doses. For instance, the parent may find opportunities to leave two children alone (e.g., siblings) for a brief period of time, perhaps 1 to 2 minutes (e.g., walk into another room to perform a chore). This brief trial may last 1 to 2 weeks. After that time, the length of unsupervised time may increase to 5 to 10 minutes. This process continues until the monitoring plan is completely removed. The exact timing of the separations and the length of the trials is a decision best left to the clinician and family. However, this process should be viewed as requiring weeks to months to complete, and not days. If any concerning behavior is noted, the monitoring plan is reinstituted. It is important to be clear with caregivers on the function and long-term nature of the monitoring plan during the first session of PBT when it is designed.

7. *Should schools be involved in the treatment process? Are there any special considerations when working with schools?*

   The answer is an equivocal one. If the PSB is not occurring in school and there are no noted concerns regarding safety in the school setting, then there may be little to gain by involving the school. Also, caregivers are typically hesitant to disclose PSB to those outside of the immediate family. However, if the PSB is occurring in the school setting or the child is engaging peers in the behavior, which creates concerns about safety, then coordinating with the school is indicated. In these situations, the clinician is advised to obtain consent from the caregiver to speak with school personnel. The nature of collaborations with schools, however, varies widely. Schools have differing levels of resources, policies regarding how to address PSB may be more or less punitive (e.g., suspension, "zero tolerance"), and personnel often have limited time available for consultation. Nonetheless, clinicians are encouraged to attempt such coordination with school personnel to the best of their abilities, when indicated. Caregivers must be involved in all plans developed with the school. An example of this is provided in the case of Maria C., discussed in Chapters 4, 5, and 6.

8. *What should I do in cases where the caregivers are divorced or otherwise separated and only one agrees to attend sessions? What about when the attending caregiver blames the nonattending caregiver for the PSB?*

   These situations provide a delicate challenge for the clinician to navigate. Of course, it is preferable for all caregivers of a child to agree on rules, consequences, monitoring plans, and so on. Consistency across settings is generally considered beneficial for creating behavior change. However, when the caregivers are living in separate homes, it can be difficult to achieve cross-setting consistency. Nonetheless, clinicians can make good faith efforts to engage both caregivers for the benefit of the child. For example, the clinician may work with one caregiver in session and talk with the other on the telephone at a different time to review the contents of session. However, clinicians must accept that it is not always possible to engage all caregivers in treatment.

   When one caregiver actively blames another for the development of a child's PSB, it can be difficult for the clinician to focus that caregiver on behavior change. This is because one caregiver commonly wants to focus on changing the circumstances at the other caregiver's home or may dismiss the effectiveness of treatment in the absence of such change. In some circumstances, one caregiver may attempt to enlist the clinician in legal action against the other caregiver. It is recommended that the clinician remain focused on what can be changed and implemented with the attending caregiver. This may require the use of motivational enhancement or therapeutic confrontation techniques. In short, the clinician is advised to focus the caregiver on acknowledging that they can only control the environment within their own home and the information they impart to the child. With this, it is possible to conduct PBT, but it may not be possible to make changes within the nonattending caregiver's home.

9. *How do you handle a parent who is overly negative and actively shames the child?*

   Caregivers who display a negativistic approach to their child or to treatment often hold counterproductive cognitions related to the child or their future prospects. For instance, caregivers may view the child's behavior as suggesting an internal moral failing (e.g., perverted) or that the child is a budding sex offender. It is also common that caregivers experience negative reactions because the child's PSB reminds them of an unpleasant experience from their past, such as a cheating spouse or a sexual abuse experience (see the case of Alvi L. in Chapter 8). However, these views often convey a lack of understanding child development and attribute to the child qualities that are not defensible. Psychoeducation and cognitive change techniques can help address these perceptions (see case of Alex J. in Chapter 4). The clinician must remember that the development of rapport with the caregiver is of the utmost importance in PBT and these maladaptive cognitions must be challenged in a respectful and supportive manner. In rare circumstances, it may be necessary to refer a caregiver for their own mental health treatment.

10. *How do you handle value-laden topics, such as masturbation or same-sex relationships?*

    Perhaps more than any other, this issue creates significant discomfort for clinicians. Most mental health professions view social justice as an aspirational goal, and clinicians are taught in graduate school to work toward equality for minority groups. When a caregiver or family presents for treatment with cultural beliefs that conflict with a clinician's beliefs or ethics, it can create a difficult situation. The concepts of sexual orientation and gender identity are prominently discussed in contemporary society and, on occasion, caregivers present with strong feelings on these topics. It is important for a clinician to maintain a focus on treating the child's PSB and recognize that changing perceived discriminatory beliefs will not occur in the span of a few clinical sessions. After all, these beliefs likely developed over the course of several decades in the caregiver's own development. Attempting to change the caregiver's views or declining to integrate their beliefs into treatment risks damaging the therapeutic rapport and/or premature termination of treatment. In these circumstances, the clinician's ability to treat the child's PSB is compromised.

    A related concern is the possibility that caregiver beliefs may result in undue shame or confusion for the child. For instance, a caregiver who wants to emphasize that only heterosexual relationships are acceptable or that masturbation is sinful may prompt negative emotions for a child who is a sexual minority or finds it extremely difficult to refrain from self-stimulating behavior. Again, however, it is not practical to change these beliefs in a span of a few sessions. Clinicians may find a resolution by reviewing with the caregiver the impact such beliefs may have on the child. For instance, the masturbation conundrum has been successfully handled many times by highlighting for the caregiver the inability to observe this behavior if the child performs it at nighttime or in the shower. In other words, if the caregiver cannot see it and no obvious problem related to the behavior requires intervention (e.g., self-harm), there is a clear potential for shame in discussing this point without any discernible benefit. In many cases, the issue of heterosexual relationships can similarly be skirted. As demonstrated throughout several of the case studies in the earlier chapters, psychoeducation for the child often focuses on reproduction and the conditions under which sexual behavior is acceptable. It is often possible to define these limits without referencing heterosexual or same-sex relationships.

11. *What if I can't complete the protocol in 12 sessions?*

    The 12-session protocol specified in this volume is used in clinical trials of PBT and clinicians in those trials take great strides to adhere closely to the protocol during sessions. This is for the purpose of improving the internal validity of the trial. However, there is no rule that PBT must be implemented in this manner in general clinical practice. It is recognized that crises occur and, sometimes, session time must be spent on activities outside of those prescribed by PBT. Similarly, some caregivers or children may be particularly difficult or require more time to grasp the concepts of treatment. In these situations, it is understandable for the clinician to implement more sessions than designed within the protocol. However, a word of caution is warranted. There is a noted concern in the treatment literature that some clinicians insert various forms of nonprescribed treatment techniques into protocols or believe certain benchmarks for treatment progress must be met before continuing on to the next stage of treatment. These types of modifications are not a part of PBT and are discouraged. For instance, an acceptable alteration of the protocol may be taking five or six sessions in Phase 1, instead of four, because the caregiver needs a great deal of help modifying behavior management or monitoring plans. However, extending Phase 1 by an additional two sessions for the purposes of integrating nonprescribed techniques is ill advised. In this latter situation, the clinician may be prohibiting the delivery of more effective techniques or breaking the flow of the prescribed techniques with no evidence that integrating such techniques will improve outcome.

12. *After completing treatment, can I notify the court or school that the child is no longer a risk to other children? What should I say, if anything, about the child's risk?*

    As reviewed in Chapter 1, the risk of a preteen child with intrusive or interpersonal sexual behavior committing a future sexual offense is exceptionally low, perhaps no more than 10% of such cases (see Carpentier et al., 2006). Risk assessment generally implies that the factors which increase the likelihood of an individual displaying a certain behavior in the future (a) are known and (b) can be reliably assessed. As it relates to preteen children with PSB, sufficient data is not available to guide clinical assessment for the purposes of determining such risk. While it is true that effective treatment appears to reduce risk for future offenses, it is also true that no intervention is successful in every case and having completed PBT is not a guarantee that future behavior will not occur. In brief, the risk of a future sexual offense for a child with PSB is low and the current data does not provide directions to clinicians as to what factors should be assessed to determine future risk. Current best practice is that clinicians refrain from making statements to courts, schools, or other organizations regarding the risk of a given child.

Appendix A

RESOURCES

The resources identified here are a small sample of the larger body of websites, books, and materials that are available. Clinicians are not limited to using only the resources listed here; they are encouraged to seek out helpful materials and may utilize those with which they are already familiar. See Clinical Tip 5.3 (Chapter 5) for more guidance.

WEBSITES

The following websites offer helpful handouts, fact sheets, videos, recommendations, and other resources that the clinician may find helpful.

Phase-Based Treatment (PBT) Resource Site: https://med.psu.edu/pbt
National Center on the Sexual Behavior of Youth (NCSBY): https://www.ncsby.org/
National Child Traumatic Stress Network (NCTSN): https://www.nctsn.org/
Amaze: https://amaze.org/

FACT SHEETS/HANDOUTS/PAMPHLETS/GAMES

The PBT Resource Site (see under Websites) includes informational sheets for caregivers on the process of PBT, tables that clearly explain typical sexual development, and other helpful handouts.

"Sexual Development and Behavior in Children: Information for Parents and Caregivers" by the National Child Traumatic Stress Network (https://

www.nctsn.org/resources/sexual-development-and-behavior-children-information-parents-and-caregivers)

"Understanding and Coping With Sexual Behavior Problems: Information for Parents and Caregivers" by the National Child Traumatic Stress Network (https://www.nctsn.org/resources/understanding-and-coping-sexual-behavior-problems-children-information-parents-and)

"Staying Safe While Staying Connected: Facts and Tips for Teens" by the National Child Traumatic Stress Network (https://www.nctsn.org/resources/staying-safe-while-staying-connected-facts-and-tips-teens)

Johnson, T. C. (2016). *Helping children with sexual behavior problems: A guidebook for professionals and caregivers* (5th ed.). This pamphlet is available for purchase from the author at https://www.tcavjohn.com/

"What Do You Know?" A card game available for purchase from the CARES Institute at Rowan University (https://centers.rowanmedicine.com/cares/)

BOOKS

Typical Sexual Development

Cole, J. (2009). *Asking about sex & growing up: A question-and-answer book for kids*. Harper Collins.

Dunham, K. (2015). *The boy's body book* (3rd ed.). Applesauce Press.

Hancock, L., & Rayne, K. (2023). *Sex ed for the stroller set: How to have honest conversations with young children*. American Psychological Association.

Harris, R. H. (2006). *It's not the stork: A book about girls, boys, babies, bodies, families, and friends*. Candlewick Press.

Harris, R. H., & Emberley, M. (2014). *It's perfectly normal: Changing bodies, growing up, sex, and sexual health*. Candlewick Press.

Natterson, C. (2018). *The care and keeping of you 2: The body book for older girls*. American Girl Publishing.

Saltz, G. (2005). *Amazing you! Getting smart about your private parts*. Puffin Books.

Saltz, G. (2007). *Changing you! A guide to body changes and sexuality*. Puffin Books.

Schaefer, V. L. (2012). *The care and keeping of you 1: The body book for younger girls*. American Girl Publishing.

Safety Skills/Assertiveness

Aboff, M. (1996). *Uncle Willy's tickles: A child's right to say no*. Magination Press.
King, Z., & King, K. (2020). *I said no! A kid-to-kid guide to keeping private parts private*. Boulden Publishing.
Sanders, J. (2018). *Let's talk about body boundaries, consent, & respect*. Educate2 Empower Publishing.
Spelman, C. (1997). *Your body belongs to you*. Albert Whitman & Company.

Appendix B

THE ASSESSMENT OF SEXUAL BEHAVIOR-CHILD VERSION (ASB-C)

The items below describe various types of behaviors. Some items refer to behaviors involving private parts (such as penis, vagina, or rectum) or sexual acts. Please report how often your child has shown the following behaviors in the **PAST MONTH** using the scale provided.

	Never	1 time (Once)	2-4 times	5-10 times	More than 10 times
1. Stands or sits too close to others.	0	1	2	3	4
2. Hugs people they do not know well.	0	1	2	3	4
3. Kisses people they do not know well.	0	1	2	3	4
4. Touches or tries to touch the breasts of others.	0	1	2	3	4
5. Asks questions about private parts and/or sexual acts to a trusted adult (such as a parent or teacher).	0	1	2	3	4

(continues)

	Never	1 time (Once)	2–4 times	5–10 times	More than 10 times
6. Asks questions about private parts and/or sexual acts to people other than a trusted adult.	0	1	2	3	4
7. Views nonsexual things or topics in a sexual way.	0	1	2	3	4
8. Uses the internet to seek out information on sexual topics.	0	1	2	3	4
9. Talks about private parts, sexual topics, or toileting behaviors at inappropriate times.	0	1	2	3	4
10. Uses sexual words in an insulting, disrespectful, and/or suggestive way.	0	1	2	3	4
11. Plays with toys in a sexual way; draws pictures or writes about private parts or sexual topics.	0	1	2	3	4
12. Moves, dances, or makes hand gestures that are sexually suggestive.	0	1	2	3	4
13. Looks at or tries to look at others who are nude, undressing, and/or toileting.	0	1	2	3	4
14. Looks at or tries to look at people engaged in sexual acts.	0	1	2	3	4
15. Looks at pictures or videos that show nudity or sexual acts.	0	1	2	3	4
16. Looks at pictures or videos of violent, aggressive, and/or extreme sex acts.	0	1	2	3	4
17. Touches or rubs own private parts when ***alone***.	0	1	2	3	4
18. Touches or rubs private parts when around ***other people***.	0	1	2	3	4
19. Rubs private parts on or with an object (such as furniture, toy, blanket, remote control).	0	1	2	3	4
20. Inserts or tries to insert objects inside ***own*** private parts.	0	1	2	3	4

		Never	1 time (Once)	2-4 times	5-10 times	More than 10 times
21.	Shows own private parts to others.	0	1	2	3	4
22.	Shows picture(s) of their own or other people's private parts to others.	0	1	2	3	4
23.	Asks others to show their private parts or engage in sexual acts while talking ***in-person***.	0	1	2	3	4
24.	Sends sexual messages, pictures, and/or videos to others (such as through email, texts, social media).	0	1	2	3	4
25.	Asks others to send them pictures or videos showing nudity or sexual acts (such as through email, texts, social media).	0	1	2	3	4
26.	Coerces others to send sexual pictures or videos. (Note: "coerces" means using force, threats, pressure, bribery, and/or trickery)	0	1	2	3	4
27.	Threatens to share sexual pictures or videos of others.	0	1	2	3	4
28.	Strokes, massages, or caresses the bodies of others.	0	1	2	3	4
29.	Rubs private parts on other people.	0	1	2	3	4
30.	Slaps or pokes the buttocks of others.	0	1	2	3	4
31.	Touches or tries to touch the private parts of others.	0	1	2	3	4
32.	Puts mouth on the breasts or private parts of others.	0	1	2	3	4
33.	Inserts or tries to insert objects in ***another child's*** private parts.	0	1	2	3	4
34.	Tries to undress others against their will.	0	1	2	3	4

(continues)

	Never	1 time (Once)	2-4 times	5-10 times	More than 10 times
35. Plans to get others to engage in sexual behavior.	0	1	2	3	4
36. Coerces others to engage in sexual behavior. (Note: "coerces" means using force, threats, pressure, bribery, and/or trickery)	0	1	2	3	4
37. Performs sexual behaviors with an animal.	0	1	2	3	4
38. Continues to engage in sexual behavior after being told to stop.	0	1	2	3	4

***Please tell us of any other sexual behaviors your child has displayed that were not mentioned above:

____

____

***The questions below are to help us better understand the behaviors you described above.

Note: *If you answered "0" (Never) to all the questions above, you do not need to complete the section below.*

A. With whom did your child engage in any of the behaviors above? (check all that apply):

- ☐ Children who live in the same home (such as siblings)
- ☐ Strangers or people they do not know well
- ☐ Children who do not live in the same home (such as cousins)
- ☐ Neighbor(s)
- ☐ Children at school (such as schoolmates)
- ☐ Adult(s)
- ☐ Children with developmental delays or disabilities
- ☐ Children who are younger
- ☐ Children with another vulnerability (please describe):

____

B. Where did the behaviors you reported above occur? (check all that apply):

☐ Home
☐ Neighbor's house
☐ Public setting (such as stores)
☐ School/preschool/school bus
☐ Childcare provider
☐ Outside (such as a playground)
☐ Other (please describe):

____

C. During any of the behaviors you reported above, did your child use coercion, such as force, threats, pressure, bribery, and/or trickery?

☐ No ☐ Yes (please describe):

____

ASB-C SCORE FORM

Step 1: Critical Items

Check each item below with a non-0 response (i.e., 1, 2, 3, 4).

16. _____
20. _____
22. _____
23. _____
24. _____
25. _____
26. _____
27. _____
29. _____
31. _____
32. _____
33. _____
34. _____
35. _____
36. _____
37. _____
38. _____

Step 2: Total Scale Score

Sum all item scores (#1–#38).

Total Score = ______________

Step 3: Total Score Interpretation

Circle the appropriate answer based on the child's age and total scale score

Age Group	*Typical/Expected*	*Concerning*	*Problematic*
3–5 years	0–10	11	12–152
6–9 years	0–6	7–10	11–152
10–12 years	0–5	6–9	10–152

Step 4: Final Interpretation

a. If any critical items are checked in Step 1, the child's behavior is considered *Problematic* and clinical services are likely indicated. (Interpretation of the Total Scale score may be helpful, but is not necessary to classify behavior as "problematic.")

b. In Step 3, a score in the *Concerning* range indicates the child's pattern of behavior is more likely to occur among clinical samples of children with problematic behavior. Further assessment is advised.

c. In Step 3, a score in the *Problematic* range indicates the score is among the highest 5% in the normative population. Clinical services are likely indicated.

Appendix C

THE EXPOSURE TO SEXUALITY SCALE (ESS)

Please indicate whether each of the items below happened in the past six (6) months.

1.	My child saw other people using the bathroom.	YES	NO
2.	My child bathed or showered with another individual (for example, a sibling, a parent).	YES	NO
3.	My child saw people naked around the home.	YES	NO
4.	My child saw people naked in settings other than the home (for example, preschool, locker rooms).	YES	NO
5.	People were watching TV shows, movies, or online material that showed naked people and my child saw this.	YES	NO
6.	There are printed materials in the home that show naked people (for example, pictures, magazines).	YES	NO
7.	A person touched their own genitals in a sexual manner in a common area of the home (for example, living room, kitchen). **Note:** This item refers to touching over or under clothing.	YES	NO
8.	A person touched the genitals or breasts of another person in a common area of the home (for example, living room, kitchen). **Note:** This item refers to touching over or under clothing.	YES	NO
9.	My child saw a person touching their own genitals in a sexual way, or touching the genitals or breasts of another person, in a private area of the home (for example, bedroom, bathroom).	YES	NO
10.	One or more people discussed sexual topics or sexual behaviors, or made sexual comments, in a common area of the home (for example, living room, kitchen).	YES	NO
11.	My child heard a person discussing sexual topics or sexual behaviors, or making sexual comments, in a private area of the home (for example, bedroom, bathroom).	YES	NO
12.	One or more people engaged in sexual acts in a common area of the home (for example, living room, kitchen).	YES	NO

(continues)

13. My child saw one or more people engaged in sexual acts in a private area of the home (for example, bedroom, bathroom).	YES	NO
14. My child received pictures or videos from others (for example, on smartphones, social media).	YES	NO
15. My child mentioned hearing sexual comments or topics discussed in a setting other than home (for example, school, locker rooms).	YES	NO

Appendix D

SAMPLE SEXUAL BEHAVIOR RULES

1. It's not OK to touch other people's private parts.
2. It's not OK to make inappropriate sounds or use inappropriate words.
3. It's not OK to look at other people's private parts.
4. It's not OK to show other people my private parts.
5. It's not OK for other people to touch my private parts.
6. If someone touches my private parts, I tell my parents, a teacher, or a doctor.
7. It's not OK to take my clothes off around other people.
8. It's not OK to put things into my body.
9. It's not OK to touch my private parts around other people.

Appendix E

SAMPLE SCENARIOS

1. You watch a TV show and start making moaning sounds when people kiss on the show.
2. You ask mom or dad about something you heard at school that involved private parts.
3. A girl at school is standing next to you laughing and you smack her on the butt.
4. You have a sore spot on your private parts and you ask dad to look at it.
5. You hear a funny joke involving private parts, so you tell it to other kids at school.
6. You are at the doctor's office and he asks you to take your pants off so he can look at your private parts.
7. You and another girl at school are cleaning up after an activity and she is reaching over you to put something away and her chest touches your arm.
8. A teacher at school asks you to take off your pants so he can see your private parts.
9. You know that mom is in the shower, so you decide to walk into the bathroom to see her naked.
10. You are trying to make your friend laugh in the bathroom and pull down your pants and stick your butt out at him.

References

Abel, G. G., Becker, J. V., Mittelman, M., Cunningham-Rathner, J., Rouleau, J. L., & Murphy, W. D. (1987). Self-reported sex crimes of nonincarcerated paraphiliacs. *Journal of Interpersonal Violence, 2*(1), 3–25. https://doi.org/10.1177/088626087002001001

Abidin, R. R. (2012). *Parenting stress index* (4th ed.). Psychological Assessment Resources.

Achenbach, T. M., & Rescorla, L. A. (2001). *Manual for the ASEBA school-age forms & profiles: Child Behavior Checklist for ages 6–18, teacher's report form, & youth self-report*. University of Vermont, Research Center for Children, Youth & Families.

Adam Walsh Child Protection and Safety Act of 2006, Pub. L. No. 109-248, 120 Stat. 587 (2006). https://www.govinfo.gov/app/details/PLAW-109publ248

Aldridge, N. C. (1998). Strengths and limitations of forensic child sexual abuse interviews with anatomical dolls: An empirical review. *Journal of Psychopathology and Behavioral Assessment, 20*(1), 1–41. https://doi.org/10.1023/a:1023084525733

Allen, B. (2017). Children with sexual behavior problems: Clinical characteristics and relationship to child maltreatment. *Child Psychiatry and Human Development, 48*(2), 189–199. https://doi.org/10.1007/s10578-016-0633-8

Allen, B. (2018). Implementing trauma-focused cognitive-behavioral therapy (TF-CBT) with preteen children displaying problematic sexual behavior. *Cognitive and Behavioral Practice, 25*(2), 240–249. https://doi.org/10.1016/j.cbpra.2017.07.001

Allen, B. (2023a). Etiological pathways to the emergence of preteen problematic sexual behavior: An exploratory mediational model. *Sexual Abuse, 35*(4), 488–502. https://doi.org/10.1177/10790632221128313

Allen, B. (2023b). Etiological perspectives on problematic sexual behavior of preteen children: Implications for treatment. *Clinical Child and Family Psychology Review, 26*(1), 50–64. https://doi.org/10.1007/s10567-022-00412-5

Allen, B. (2025). Childhood sexual behavior as a mediator of the relationship between sexual abuse and early sexual debut: A prospective analysis. *Archives of Sexual Behavior, 54*(7), 2463–2473. https://doi.org/10.1007/s10508-025-03228-w

Allen, B., & Armstrong, N. E. (2014). Burden of proof: The evidence clinicians require before implementing an intervention. *Child and Adolescent Mental Health, 19*(1), 52–56. https://doi.org/10.1111/camh.12005

Allen, B., & Berliner, L. (2015). Evidence-informed, individual treatment of a child with sexual behavior problems: A case study. *Archives of Sexual Behavior, 44*(8), 2323–2331. https://doi.org/10.1007/s10508-014-0460-6

Allen, B., Berliner, L., & Ferrer Pistone, L. (2025). Phase-based treatment for problematic sexual behavior of preteen children: Clinical outcomes from community implementation trials. *Evidence-Based Practice in Child and Adolescent Mental Health*. Advance online publication. https://doi.org/10.1080/23794925.2025.2534941

Allen, B., Berliner, L., Shenk, C. E., Bendixsen, B., Zellhoefer, A., Dickmann, C. R., Arnold, B., & Chen, M. J. (2018). Development and pilot testing of a phase-based treatment for preteen children with problematic sexual behavior. *Evidence-Based Practice in Child and Adolescent Mental Health, 3*(4), 274–285. https://doi.org/10.1080/23794925.2018.1515580

Allen, B., & Ferrer Pistone, L. (2023). Psychometric evaluation of a single-item screening tool for the presence of problematic sexual behavior among preteen children. *Child Abuse & Neglect, 143*, 106327. https://doi.org/10.1016/j.chiabu.2023.106327

Allen, B., & Ferrer Pistone, L. (2025). A meta-analysis of the association between posttraumatic stress symptoms and problematic sexual behavior among preteen children. *Journal of Traumatic Stress, 38*(6), 895–903. https://doi.org/10.1002/jts.23186

Allen, B., Gharagozloo, L., & Johnson, J. C. (2012). Clinician knowledge and utilization of empirically-supported treatments for maltreated children. *Child Maltreatment, 17*(1), 11–21. https://doi.org/10.1177/1077559511426333

Allen, B., & Hoskowitz, N. A. (2017). Structured trauma-focused CBT and unstructured play/experiential techniques in the treatment of sexually abused children: A field study with practicing clinicians. *Child Maltreatment, 22*(2), 112–120. https://doi.org/10.1177/1077559516681866

Allen, B., Silovsky, J. F., Berliner, L., Kolko, D. J., & Wamser, R. (2026). *The assessment of sexual behavior-child version: A manual for administration, scoring, and interpretation*. Penn State College of Medicine.

Allen, B., Silovsky, J. F., Ferrer Pistone, L., Crowell, K. R., Wamser, R., Kolko, D. J., & Berliner, L. (2025). *Electronic and online sexual behavior among preadolescent children: A nationally representative survey* [Unpublished manuscript]. The Pennsylvania State University.

Allen, B., Silovsky, J. F., Kolko, D. J., Berliner, L., & Wamser, R. (2026). The development and psychometric validation of the Assessment of Sexual Behavior–Child version (ASB-C). *Psychological Assessment.* Advance online publication. https://doi.org/10.1037/pas0001461

Allen, B., Tellez, A., Wevodau, A., Woods, C. L., & Percosky, A. (2014). The impact of sexual abuse committed by a child on mental health in adulthood. *Journal of Interpersonal Violence, 29*(12), 2257–2272. https://doi.org/10.1177/0886260513517550

Allen, B., Thorn, B. L., & Gully, K. J. (2015). A comparison of self-reported emotional and trauma-related concerns among sexually abused children with and without sexual behavior problems. *Child Maltreatment, 20*(2), 136–140. https://doi.org/10.1177/1077559514566864

Allen, B., Timmer, S. G., & Urquiza, A. J. (2016). Parent–child interaction therapy for sexual concerns of maltreated children: A preliminary investigation. *Child Abuse & Neglect, 56*, 80–88. https://doi.org/10.1016/j.chiabu.2016.04.008

Allen, B., & Tussey, C. (2012). Can projective drawings detect if a child experienced sexual or physical abuse? A systematic review of the controlled research. *Trauma, Violence & Abuse, 13*(2), 97–111. https://doi.org/10.1177/1524838012440339

Allen, B., & Wamser, R. (2025). Child sexual and physical abuse, self-regulation, and problematic sexual behavior: A prospective mediational model. *Developmental Psychology, 61*(11), 2097–2105. https://doi.org/10.1037/dev0002046

Allen, B., Wamser, R., Ferrer Pistone, L., & Campbell, C. L. (2025). Problematic sexual behavior among children: A meta-analysis of demographic and clinical correlates. *Research on Child and Adolescent Psychopathology, 53*(6), 831–847. https://doi.org/10.1007/s10802-025-01300-6

American Psychiatric Association. (2013). *Diagnostic and statistical manual of mental disorders* (5th ed.). https://doi.org/10.1176/appi.books.9780890425596

Astle, S., Anders, K. M., McAllister, P., Hanna-Walker, V., & Yelland, E. (2025). The conceptualization and measurement of sexual self-concept and sexual self-schema: A systematic literature review. *Journal of Sex Research, 62*(1), 95–106. https://doi.org/10.1080/00224499.2023.2244937

Astle, S., Leonhardt, N., & Willoughby, B. (2020). Home base: Family of origin factors and the debut of vaginal sex, anal sex, oral sex, masturbation, and pornography use in a national sample of adolescents. *Journal of Sex Research, 57*(9), 1089–1099. https://doi.org/10.1080/00224499.2019.1691140

Baker, A. J. L., Gries, L., Schneiderman, M., Parker, R., Archer, M., & Friedrich, B. (2008). Children with problematic sexualized behaviors in the child welfare system. *Child Welfare, 87*(1), 5–27.

Bandura, A., Ross, D., & Ross, S. A. (1961). Transmission of aggression through imitation of aggressive models. *Journal of Abnormal and Social Psychology, 63*(3), 575–582. https://doi.org/10.1037/h0045925

Beauchaine, T. P. (2015). Future directions in emotion dysregulation and youth psychopathology. *Journal of Clinical Child and Adolescent Psychology, 44*(5), 875–896. https://doi.org/10.1080/15374416.2015.1038827

Berliner, L., & Saunders, B. E. (1996). Treating fear and anxiety in sexually abused children: Results of a controlled 2-year follow-up study. *Child Maltreatment, 1*(4), 294–309. https://doi.org/10.1177/1077559596001004002

Berry, J. O., & Jones, W. H. (1995). The parental stress scale: Initial psychometric evidence. *Journal of Social and Personal Relationships, 12*(3), 463–472. https://doi.org/10.1177/0265407595123009

Bonner, B. L., Walker, C. E., & Berliner, L. (1999). *Children with sexual behavior problems: Assessment and treatment-final report* (Grant No. 90-CA-1469). U.S. Department of Health and Human Services, National Clearinghouse on Child Abuse and Neglect.

Briere, J. (2005). *The Trauma Symptom Checklist for Young Children: Professional manual*. Psychological Assessment Resources, Inc.

Brilleslijper-Kater, S. N., & Baartman, H. E. M. (2000). What do young children know about sex? Research on the sexual knowledge of children between the ages of 2 and 6 years. *Child Abuse Review, 9*(3), 166–182. https://doi.org/10.1002/1099-0852(200005/06)9:3<166::aid-car588>3.0.co;2-3

Cale, J., & Lussier, P. (2017). Sexual behaviour in preschool children in the context of intra-parental violence and sexual coercion. *Criminal Behaviour and Mental Health, 27*(2), 176–190. https://doi.org/10.1002/cbm.1996

Calzo, J. P., Antonucci, T. C., Mays, V. M., & Cochran, S. D. (2011). Retrospective recall of sexual orientation identity development among gay, lesbian, and bisexual adults. *Developmental Psychology, 47*(6), 1658–1673. https://doi.org/10.1037/a0025508

Campbell, B. C. (2011). Adrenarche and middle childhood. *Human Nature, 22*(3), 327–349. https://doi.org/10.1007/s12110-011-9120-x

Campbell, C. L., & Wamser, R. A. (2024). Children with sexual behavior problems: Ties to child maltreatment, family functioning, and help-seeking. *Journal of Traumatic Stress, 37*(1), 35–46. https://doi.org/10.1002/jts.22978

Carpentier, M. Y., Silovsky, J. F., & Chaffin, M. (2006). Randomized trial of treatment for children with sexual behavior problems: Ten-year follow-up. *Journal of Consulting and Clinical Psychology, 74*(3), 482–488. https://doi.org/10.1037/0022-006x.74.3.482

Chaffin, M. (2008). Our minds are made up—don't confuse us with the facts: Commentary on policies concerning children with sexual behavior problems and juvenile sex offenders. *Child Maltreatment, 13*(2), 110–121. https://doi.org/10.1177/1077559508314510

Chaffin, M., Berliner, L., Block, R., Johnson, T. C., Friedrich, W. N., Louis, D. G., Lyon, T. D., Page, I. J., Prescott, D. S., Silovsky, J. F., & Madden, C. (2008). Report of the ATSA task force on children with sexual behavior problems. *Child Maltreatment, 13*(2), 199–218. https://doi.org/10.1177/1077559507306718

Chaffin, M., & Bonner, B. (1998). "Don't shoot, we're your children": Have we gone too far in our response to adolescent sexual abusers and children with sexual behavior problems? *Child Maltreatment, 3*(4), 314–316. https://doi.org/10.1177/1077559598003004003

Choi, J. Y., & Song, D. H. (2022). Psychometric properties of the Korean version of the Child Sexual Behavior Inventory. *Journal of Child Sexual Abuse, 31*(7), 805–816. https://doi.org/10.1080/10538712.2022.2142183

Chouinard-Thivierge, S., Lussier, P., & Daignault, I. V. (2022). A longitudinal examination of developmental covariates of sexual behavior problems among youth referred to child protection services. *Sexual Abuse, 34*(5), 537–567. https://doi.org/10.1177/10790632211047184

Cicchetti, D., & Rogosch, F. A. (1996). Equifinality and multifinality in developmental psychopathology. *Development and Psychopathology, 8*(4), 597–600. https://doi.org/10.1017/s0954579400007318

Cicchetti, D., & Toth, S. L. (1995). A developmental psychopathology perspective on child abuse and neglect. *Journal of the American Academy of Child and Adolescent Psychiatry, 34*(5), 541–565. https://doi.org/10.1097/00004583-199505000-00008

Cohen, J. A., Berliner, L., & Mannarino, A. (2010). Trauma focused CBT for children with co-occurring trauma and behavior problems. *Child Abuse & Neglect, 34*(4), 215–224. https://doi.org/10.1016/j.chiabu.2009.12.003

Cohen, J. A., Deblinger, E., Mannarino, A. P., & Steer, R. A. (2004). A multisite, randomized controlled trial for children with sexual abuse-related PTSD symptoms. *Journal of the American Academy of Child and Adolescent Psychiatry, 43*(4), 393–402. https://doi.org/10.1097/00004583-200404000-00005

Cohen, J. A., & Mannarino, A. P. (1998). Interventions for sexually abused children: Initial treatment outcome findings. *Child Maltreatment, 3*(1), 17–26. https://doi.org/10.1177/1077559598003001002

Cohen, J. A., Mannarino, A. P., & Deblinger, E. (2017). *Treating trauma and traumatic grief in children and adolescents* (2nd ed.). Guilford Press.

Cortoni, F., Babchishin, K. M., & Rat, C. (2017). The proportion of sexual offenders who are female is higher than thought. *Criminal Justice and Behavior, 44*(2), 145–162. https://doi.org/10.1177/0093854816658923

Darby, R. J., Taylor, E. P., & Cadavid, M. S. (2023). Phase-based psychological interventions for complex post-traumatic stress disorder: A systematic review. *Journal of Affective Disorders Reports, 14*, 100628. https://doi.org/10.1016/j.jadr.2023.100628

Davies, C., & Robinson, K. (2010). Hatching babies and stork deliveries: Risk and regulation in the construction of children's sexual knowledge. *Contemporary Issues in Early Childhood, 11*(3), 249–262. https://doi.org/10.2304/ciec.2010.11.3.249

Davies, S. L., Glaser, D., & Kossoff, R. (2000). Children's sexual play and behavior in pre-school settings: Staff's perceptions, reports, and responses. *Child Abuse & Neglect, 24*(10), 1329–1343. https://doi.org/10.1016/s0145-2134(00)00184-8

Davis, T. N., Machalicek, W., Scalzo, R., Kobylecky, A., Campbell, V., Pinkelman, S., Chan, J. M., & Sigafoos, J. (2016). A review and treatment selection model for individuals with developmental disabilities who engage in inappropriate sexual behavior. *Behavior Analysis in Practice, 9*(4), 389–402. https://doi.org/10.1007/s40617-015-0062-3

de Haan, A. M., Boon, A. E., de Jong, J. T. V. M., Hoeve, M., & Vermeiren, R. R. J. M. (2013). A meta-analytic review on treatment dropout in child and adolescent outpatient mental health care. *Clinical Psychology Review, 33*(5), 698–711. https://doi.org/10.1016/j.cpr.2013.04.005

de Waal, F. B. M. (2007). *Chimpanzee politics: Power and sex among apes* (25th ed.). Johns Hopkins University Press.

Deblinger, E., Stauffer, L. B., & Steer, R. A. (2001). Comparative efficacies of supportive and cognitive behavioral group therapies for young children who have been sexually abused and their nonoffending mothers. *Child Maltreatment, 6*(4), 332–343. https://doi.org/10.1177/1077559501006004006

DeLago, C., Schroeder, C. M., Cooper, B., Deblinger, E., Dudek, E., Yu, R., & Finkel, M. A. (2020). Children who engaged in interpersonal problematic sexual behaviors. *Child Abuse & Neglect, 105*, 104260. https://doi.org/10.1016/j.chiabu.2019.104260

Department of Defense, Office of Inspector General. (2020). *Evaluation of the Department of Defense and Department of Defense Education Activity responses to incidents of serious juvenile-on-juvenile misconduct on military installations* (DODIG-2020-127). U.S. Department of Defense. https://www.dodig.mil/reports.html/Article/2340558/evaluation-of-the-department-of-defense-and-department-of-defense-education-act/

Dickmann, C. R., Zellhoefer, A., Arnold, B., & Allen, B. (2018). Implementing a phase-based treatment for preteen children with problematic sexual behavior: Case examples. *Evidence-based Practice in Child and Adolescent Mental Health, 3*(4), 286–293. https://doi.org/10.1080/23794925.2018.1515581

Dopp, A. R., Mundey, P., Silovsky, J. F., Hunter, M., & Slemaker, A. (2020). Economic value of community-based services for problematic sexual behaviors in youth: A mixed-method cost-effectiveness analysis. *Child Abuse & Neglect, 105*, 104043. https://doi.org/10.1016/j.chiabu.2019.104043

Dorsey, S., McLaughlin, K. A., Kerns, S. E. U., Harrison, J. P., Lambert, H. K., Briggs, E. C., Revillion Cox, J., & Amaya-Jackson, L. (2017). Evidence base update for psychosocial treatments for children and adolescents exposed to traumatic events. *Journal of Clinical Child and Adolescent Psychology, 46*(3), 303–330. https://doi.org/10.1080/15374416.2016.1220309

Drach, K. M., Wientzen, J., & Ricci, L. R. (2001). The diagnostic utility of sexual behavior problems in diagnosing sexual abuse in a forensic child abuse evaluation clinic. *Child Abuse & Neglect, 25*(4), 489–503. https://doi.org/10.1016/s0145-2134(01)00222-8

Elkovitch, N., Latzman, R. D., Hansen, D. J., & Flood, M. F. (2009). Understanding child sexual behavior problems: A developmental psychopathology framework. *Clinical Psychology Review, 29*(7), 586–598. https://doi.org/10.1016/j.cpr.2009.06.006

Ensink, K., Borelli, J. L., Normandin, L., Target, M., & Fonagy, P. (2020). Childhood sexual abuse and attachment insecurity: Associations with child psychological difficulties. *The American Journal of Orthopsychiatry*, *90*(1), 115–124. https://doi.org/10.1037/ort0000407

Ensink, K., Godbout, N., Bigras, N., Lampron, J., Sabourin, S., & Normandin, L. (2018). Persistent and transitory sexualized behavior problems in children. *Child Psychiatry and Human Development*, *49*(4), 621–631. https://doi.org/10.1007/s10578-017-0778-0

Feinstein, B. A., van der Star, A., Dorrell, K. D., & Blashill, A. J. (2024). Sexual orientation and mental health in a US cohort of children: A longitudinal mediation study. *Journal of Child Psychology and Psychiatry, and Allied Disciplines*, *65*(2), 188–198. https://doi.org/10.1111/jcpp.13873

Finkelhor, D., & Browne, A. (1985). The traumatic impact of child sexual abuse: A conceptualization. *The American Journal of Orthopsychiatry*, *55*(4), 530–541. https://doi.org/10.1111/j.1939-0025.1985.tb02703.x

Foa, E. B., Asnaani, A., Zang, Y., Capaldi, S., & Yeh, R. (2018). Psychometrics of the Child PTSD Symptom Scale for *DSM-5* for trauma-exposed children and adolescents. *Journal of Clinical Child and Adolescent Psychology*, *47*(1), 38–46. https://doi.org/10.1080/15374416.2017.1350962

Frayser, S. G. (2003). Cultural dimensions of childhood sexuality in the United States. In J. Bancroft (Ed.), *Sexual development in childhood* (pp. 255–273). Indiana University Press.

Freud, S. (1966). *Introductory lectures on psychoanalysis*. Liveright. (Original work published 1920)

Friedrich, W. N. (1997). *Child Sexual Behavior Inventory: Professional manual*. Psychological Assessment Resources, Inc.

Friedrich, W. N. (2003). Studies of sexuality in non-abused children. In J. Bancroft (Ed.), *Sexual development in childhood* (pp. 107–120). Indiana University Press.

Friedrich, W. N. (2007). *Children with sexual behavior problems: Family-based attachment-focused therapy*. W. W. Norton.

Friedrich, W. N., Davies, W. H., Feher, E., & Wright, J. (2003). Sexual behavior problems in preteen children: Developmental, ecological, and behavioral correlates. *Annals of the New York Academy of Sciences*, *989*(1), 95–153. https://doi.org/10.1111/j.1749-6632.2003.tb07296.x

Friedrich, W. N., Fisher, J. L., Dittner, C. A., Acton, R., Berliner, L., Butler, J., Damon, L., Davies, W. H., Gray, A., & Wright, J. (2001). Child Sexual Behavior Inventory: Normative, psychiatric, and sexual abuse comparisons. *Child Maltreatment*, *6*(1), 37–49. https://doi.org/10.1177/1077559501006001004

Friedrich, W. N., Luecke, W. J., Beilke, R. L., & Place, V. (1992). Psychotherapy outcome of sexually abused boys. *Journal of Interpersonal Violence*, *7*(3), 396–409. https://doi.org/10.1177/088626092007003008

Friedrich, W. N., Sandfort, T. G. M., Oostveen, J., & Cohen-Kettenis, P. T. (2000). Cultural differences in sexual behavior: 2–6-year-old Dutch and American children. *Journal of Psychology and Human Sexuality, 12*(2), 117–129. https://doi.org/10.1300/j056v12n01_08

Friedrich, W. N., & Trane, S. T. (2002). Sexual behavior in children across multiple settings. *Child Abuse & Neglect, 26*(3), 243–245. https://doi.org/10.1016/s0145-2134(01)00322-2

Gershoff, E. T., Goodman, G. S., Miller-Perrin, C. L., Holden, G. W., Jackson, Y., & Kazdin, A. E. (2018). The strength of the causal evidence against physical punishment of children and its implications for parents, psychologists, and policymakers. *The American Psychologist, 73*(5), 626–638. https://doi.org/10.1037/amp0000327

Gershoff, E. T., & Grogan-Kaylor, A. (2016). Spanking and child outcomes: Old controversies and new meta-analyses. *Journal of Family Psychology, 30*(4), 453–469.

Goodman, R. (1997). The Strengths and Difficulties Questionnaire: A research note. *Journal of Child Psychology and Psychiatry, and Allied Disciplines, 38*(5), 581–586. https://doi.org/10.1111/j.1469-7610.1997.tb01545.x

Goodman, S. H., Simon, H. F. M., Shamblaw, A. L., & Kim, C. Y. (2020). Correction to: Parenting as a mediator of associations between depression in mothers and children's functioning: A systematic review and meta-analysis. *Clinical Child and Family Psychology Review, 23*(4), 461. https://doi.org/10.1007/s10567-020-00325-1

Gray, A., Busconi, A., Houchens, P., & Pithers, W. D. (1997). Children with sexual behavior problems and their caregivers: Demographics, functioning, and clinical patterns. *Sexual Abuse, 9*(4), 267–290. https://doi.org/10.1177/107906329700900402

Hackett, S. (2014). *Research in practice: Children and young people with harmful sexual behaviours*. Dartington.

Hall, D. K., Mathews, F., & Pearce, J. (1998). Factors associated with sexual behavior problems in young sexually abused children. *Child Abuse & Neglect, 22*(10), 1045–1063. https://doi.org/10.1016/s0145-2134(98)00078-7

Hall, D. K., Mathews, F., & Pearce, J. (2002). Sexual behavior problems in sexually abused children: A preliminary typology. *Child Abuse & Neglect, 26*(3), 289–312. https://doi.org/10.1016/s0145-2134(01)00326-x

Harris, M., Lanni, D., & Svendsen, S. (2023). A conceptual analysis of system responses to the issue of problematic sexual behaviors in children and recommendations for future work in children's advocacy center multidisciplinary teams. *Frontiers in Psychiatry, 14*, 1266463. https://doi.org/10.3389/fpsyt.2023.1266463

Hashimoto, C., & Furuichi, T. (1994). Social role and development of noncopulatory sexual behavior of wild bonobos. In R. W. Wrangham, W. C. McGrew, F. B. M. de Waal, & P. G. Heltne (Eds.), *Chimpanzee cultures* (pp. 155–168). Harvard University Press.

Heiman, J. R., Verhulst, J., & Heard-Davison, A. R. (2003). Childhood sexuality and adult sexual relationships: How are they connected by data and by theory? In J. Bancroft (Ed.), *Sexual development in childhood* (pp. 404–420). Indiana University Press.

Herdt, G., & McClintock, M. (2000). The magical age of 10. *Archives of Sexual Behavior, 29*(6), 587–606. https://doi.org/10.1023/a:1002006521067

Hong, S. W., Suh, Y. S., & Kim, D. H. (2018). The risk factors of sexual behavior among middle school students in South Korea. *International Journal of Sexual Health, 30*(1), 72–80. https://doi.org/10.1080/19317611.2018.1429513

Hukkelberg, S., Tømmerås, T., & Ogden, T. (2019). Parent training: Effects beyond conduct problems. *Children and Youth Services Review, 100*, 405–414. https://doi.org/10.1016/j.childyouth.2019.03.009

Jonkman, C. S., Verlinden, E., Punt, D.-J., & Lamers-Winkelman, F. (2019). The Child Sexual Behavior Inventory: Reliability and validity in a Dutch normative and clinical sample. *Child Abuse & Neglect, 98*, 104176. https://doi.org/10.1016/j.chiabu.2019.104176

Kaminski, J. W., & Claussen, A. H. (2017). Evidence base update for psychosocial treatments for disruptive behaviors in children. *Journal of Clinical Child and Adolescent Psychology, 46*(4), 477–499. https://doi.org/10.1080/15374416.2017.1310044

Kaplow, J. B., Rolon-Arroyo, B., Layne, C. M., Rooney, E., Oosterhoff, B., Hill, R., Steinberg, A. M., Lotterman, J., Gallagher, K. A. S., & Pynoos, R. S. (2020). Validation of the UCLA PTSD Reaction Index for DSM-5: A developmentally informed assessment tool for youth. *Journal of the American Academy of Child and Adolescent Psychiatry, 59*(1), 186–194. https://doi.org/10.1016/j.jaac.2018.10.019

Kenny, M. C., & Wurtele, S. K. (2013). Child Sexual Behavior Inventory: A comparison between Latino and normative samples of preschoolers. *Journal of Sex Research, 50*(5), 449–457. https://doi.org/10.1080/00224499.2011.652265

Kroenke, K., & Spitzer, R. L. (2002). The PHQ-9: A new depression diagnostic and severity measure. *Psychiatric Annals, 32*(9), 509–515. https://doi.org/10.3928/0048-5713-20020901-06

Kuhle, B. X., Melzer, D. K., Cooper, C. A., Merkle, A. J., Pepe, N. A., Ribanovic, A., Verdesco, A. L., & Wettstein, T. L. (2015). The "birds and the bees" differ for boys and girls: Sex differences in the nature of sex talks. *Evolutionary Behavioral Sciences, 9*(2), 107–115. https://doi.org/10.1037/ebs0000012

Labella, M. H., & Masten, A. S. (2018). Family influences on the development of aggression and violence. *Current Opinion in Psychology, 19*, 11–16. https://doi.org/10.1016/j.copsyc.2017.03.028

Långström, N., Grann, M., & Lichtenstein, P. (2002). Genetic and environmental influences on problematic masturbatory behavior in children: A study of same-sex twins. *Archives of Sexual Behavior, 31*(4), 343–350. https://doi.org/10.1023/a:1016224326301

Larsson, I., & Svedin, C. G. (2002). Teachers' and parents' reports on 3- to 6-year-old children's sexual behavior—A comparison. *Child Abuse & Neglect, 26*(3), 247–266. https://doi.org/10.1016/s0145-2134(01)00323-4

Larsson, I., Svedin, C.-G., & Friedrich, W. N. (2000). Differences and similarities in sexual behaviour among pre-schoolers in Sweden and USA. *Nordic Journal of Psychiatry, 54*(4), 251–257. https://doi.org/10.1080/15024725.2000.12462233

Latzman, N. E., & Latzman, R. D. (2015). Exploring the link between child sexual abuse and sexually intrusive behaviors: The moderating role of caregiver discipline strategy. *Journal of Child and Family Studies, 24*(2), 480–490. https://doi.org/10.1007/s10826-013-9860-9

Lengua, L. J., Sadowski, C. A., Friedrich, W. N., & Fisher, J. (2001). Rationally and empirically derived dimensions of children's symptomatology: Expert ratings and confirmatory factor analyses of the CBCL. *Journal of Consulting and Clinical Psychology, 69*(4), 683–698. https://doi.org/10.1037//0022-006x.69.4.683

Lepage, J., Tourigny, M., Pauzé, R., McDuff, P., & Cyr, M. (2010). Sexual behavior problems in children in Quebec youth protection services: Associated factors. *Sexologies, 19*(2), 87–91. https://doi.org/10.1016/j.sexol.2009.05.002

Lévesque, M., Bigras, M., & Pauzé, R. (2010). Externalizing problems and problematic sexual behaviors: Same etiology? *Aggressive Behavior, 36*(6), 358–370. https://doi.org/10.1002/ab.20362

Lévesque, M., Bigras, M., & Pauzé, R. (2012). Persistence of problematic sexual behaviors in children. *Journal of Clinical Child and Adolescent Psychology, 41*(2), 239–245. https://doi.org/10.1080/15374416.2012.651991

Lindblad, F., Gustafsson, P. A., Larsson, I., & Lundin, B. (1995). Preschoolers' sexual behavior at daycare centers: An epidemiological study. *Child Abuse & Neglect, 19*(5), 569–577. https://doi.org/10.1016/0145-2134(95)00016-2

Lipovsky, J. A., Swenson, C. C., Ralston, M. E., & Saunders, B. E. (1998). The abuse clarification process in the treatment of intrafamilial child abuse. *Child Abuse & Neglect, 22*(7), 729–741. https://doi.org/10.1016/s0145-2134(98)00051-9

Luby, J. L., Barch, D. M., Whalen, D., Tillman, R., & Freedland, K. E. (2018). A randomized controlled trial of parent–child psychotherapy targeting emotion development for early childhood depression. *The American Journal of Psychiatry, 175*(11), 1102–1110. https://doi.org/10.1176/appi.ajp.2018.18030321

Lussier, P., Chouinard-Thivierge, S., McCuish, E., Nadeau, D., & Lacerte, D. (2019). Early life adversities and polyvictimization in young persons with sexual behavior problems: A longitudinal study of child protective service referrals. *Child Abuse & Neglect, 88*, 37–50. https://doi.org/10.1016/j.chiabu.2018.10.017

Lussier, P., McCuish, E., Mathesius, J., Corrado, R., & Nadeau, D. (2018). Developmental trajectories of child sexual behaviors on the path of sexual behavioral problems: Evidence from a prospective longitudinal study. *Sexual Abuse, 30*(6), 622–658. https://doi.org/10.1177/1079063217691963

MacKenzie, M. J., Nicklas, E., Brooks-Gunn, J., & Waldfogel, J. (2011). Who spanks infants and toddlers? Evidence from the Fragile Families and Child

Well-Being Study. *Children and Youth Services Review, 33*(8), 1364–1373. https://doi.org/10.1016/j.childyouth.2011.04.007

Marshall, W. L., Barbaree, H. E., & Eccles, A. (1991). Early onset and deviant sexuality in child molesters. *Journal of Interpersonal Violence, 6*(3), 323–335. https://doi.org/10.1177/088626091006003005

Martin, K. A., & Luke, K. (2010). Gender differences in the ABC's of the birds and the bees: What mothers teach young children about sexuality and reproduction. *Sex Roles, 62*(3–4), 278–291. https://doi.org/10.1007/s11199-009-9731-4

McLay, L., Carnett, A., Tyler-Merrick, G., & van der Meer, L. (2015). A systematic review of interventions for inappropriate sexual behavior of children and adolescents with developmental disabilities. *Review Journal of Autism and Developmental Disorders, 2*(4), 357–373. https://doi.org/10.1007/s40489-015-0058-5

McNeil, C. B., & Hembree-Kigin, T. L. (2010). *Parent–child interaction therapy* (2nd ed.). Springer.

Menting, A. T. A., Orobio de Castro, B., & Matthys, W. (2013). Effectiveness of the Incredible Years parent training to modify disruptive and prosocial child behavior: A meta-analytic review. *Clinical Psychology Review, 33*(8), 901–913. https://doi.org/10.1016/j.cpr.2013.07.006

Merrick, M. T., Litrownik, A. J., Everson, M. D., & Cox, C. E. (2008). Beyond sexual abuse: The impact of other maltreatment experiences on sexualized behaviors. *Child Maltreatment, 13*(2), 122–132. https://doi.org/10.1177/1077559507306715

Merrick, M. T., Litrownik, A. J., Margolis, B., Wiley, T. R. A., Everson, M. D., Dubowitz, H., & English, D. (2015). Sexualized behaviors partially mediate the link between maltreatment and delinquent behaviors. *Journal of Child and Family Studies, 24*(8), 2217–2228. https://doi.org/10.1007/s10826-014-0024-3

Meyer-Bahlburg, H. F. L., Dolezal, C., & Sandberg, D. E. (2000). The association of sexual behavior with externalizing behaviors in a community sample of prepubertal children. *Journal of Psychology & Human Sexuality, 12*(1–2), 61–79. https://doi.org/10.1300/j056v12n01_05

Morawska, A., Dittman, C. K., & Rusby, J. C. (2019). Promoting self-regulation in young children: The role of parenting interventions. *Clinical Child and Family Psychology Review, 22*(1), 43–51. https://doi.org/10.1007/s10567-019-00281-5

Mori, C., Park, J., Racine, N., Ganshorn, H., Hartwick, C., & Madigan, S. (2023). Exposure to sexual content and problematic sexual behaviors in children and adolescents: A systematic review and meta-analysis. *Child Abuse & Neglect, 143*, 106255. https://doi.org/10.1016/j.chiabu.2023.106255

Mundey, P., Slemaker, A., Dopp, A. R., Beasley, L. O., & Silovsky, J. F. (2021). Sustaining treatment for youth with problematic sexual behavior: Administrator and stakeholder perspectives following implementation. *The Journal of Behavioral Health Services & Research, 48*(3), 410–426. https://doi.org/10.1007/s11414-020-09726-0

National Children's Alliance. (2017). *Where we begin: CACs and youth with problematic sexual behaviors*. https://www.nationalchildrensalliance.org/wp-content/uploads/2018/03/2017-PSB-Fact-Sheet-CACs-2.pdf

Negriff, S. (2018). Developmental pathways from maltreatment to risk behavior: Sexual behavior as a catalyst. *Development and Psychopathology, 30*(2), 683–693. https://doi.org/10.1017/s0954579417001201

Nieto, J. A. (2004). Children and adolescents as sexual beings: Cross-cultural perspectives. *Child and Adolescent Psychiatric Clinics of North America, 13*(3), 461–477. https://doi.org/10.1016/j.chc.2004.02.001

Nigg, J. T. (2017). Annual research review: On the relations among self-regulation, self-control, executive functioning, effortful control, cognitive control, impulsivity, risk-taking, and inhibition for developmental psychopathology. *Journal of Child Psychology and Psychiatry, and Allied Disciplines, 58*(4), 361–383. https://doi.org/10.1111/jcpp.12675

Nolen-Hoeksema, S., Wisco, B. E., & Lyubomirsky, S. (2008). Rethinking rumination. *Perspectives on Psychological Science, 3*(5), 400–424. https://doi.org/10.1111/j.1745-6924.2008.00088.x

Noll, J. G., Haralson, K. J., Butler, E. M., & Shenk, C. E. (2011). Childhood maltreatment, psychological dysregulation, and risky sexual behaviors in female adolescents. *Journal of Pediatric Psychology, 36*(7), 743–752. https://doi.org/10.1093/jpepsy/jsr003

Oginni, O. A., Alanko, K., Jern, P., & Rijsdijk, F. V. (2024). Genetic and environmental influences on sexual orientation: Moderation by childhood gender nonconformity and early-life adversity. *Archives of Sexual Behavior, 53*(5), 1763–1776. https://doi.org/10.1007/s10508-023-02761-w

Okami, P., Olmstead, R., & Abramson, P. R. (1997). Sexual experiences in early childhood: 18-year longitudinal data from the UCLA Family Lifestyles project. *The Journal of Sex Research, 34*(4), 339–347. https://doi.org/10.1080/00224499709551902

Okami, P., Olmstead, R., Abramson, P. R., & Pendleton, L. (1998). Early childhood exposure to parental nudity and scenes of parental sexuality ("primal scenes"): An 18-year longitudinal study of outcome. *Archives of Sexual Behavior, 27*(4), 361–384. https://doi.org/10.1023/a:1018736109563

Pickett, M., Satifka, E., Shah, R. S., & Wiener, V. (2020). *Labeled for life: A review of youth sex offender registration laws*. Juvenile Law Center. https://jlc.org/resources/labeled-life-review-youth-sex-offender-registration-laws

Pithers, W. D., Gray, A., Busconi, A., & Houchens, P. (1998). Caregivers of children with sexual behavior problems: Psychological and familial functioning. *Child Abuse & Neglect, 22*(2), 129–141. https://doi.org/10.1016/s0145-2134(97)00123-3

Prescott, A. T., Sargent, J. D., & Hull, J. G. (2018). Meta-analysis of the relationship between violent video game play and physical aggression over time. *Proceedings of the National Academy of Sciences of the United States of America, 115*(40), 9882–9888. https://doi.org/10.1073/pnas.1611617114

Pulkki-Råback, L., Barnes, J. D., Elovainio, M., Hakulinen, C., Sourander, A., Tremblay, M. S., & Guerrero, M. D. (2022). Parental psychological problems were associated with higher screen time and the use of mature-rated media in children. *Acta Paediatrica, 111*(4), 825–833. https://doi.org/10.1111/apa.16253

Racz, S. J., & McMahon, R. J. (2011). The relationship between parental knowledge and monitoring and child and adolescent conduct problems: A 10-year update. *Clinical Child and Family Psychology Review, 14*(4), 377–398. https://doi.org/10.1007/s10567-011-0099-y

Reid, R., Trout, A. L., & Schartz, M. (2005). Self-regulation interventions for children with attention deficit/hyperactivity disorder. *Exceptional Children, 71*(4), 361–377.

Remer, T., Boye, K. R., Hartmann, M. F., & Wudy, S. A. (2005). Urinary markers of adrenarche: Reference values in healthy subjects, aged 3–18 years. *The Journal of Clinical Endocrinology and Metabolism, 90*(4), 2015–2021. https://doi.org/10.1210/jc.2004-1571

Reynolds, C. R., & Kamphaus, R. W. (2015). *Behavior assessment system for children–Third edition* (BASC-3). Pearson.

Robson, D. A., Allen, M. S., & Howard, S. J. (2020). Self-regulation in childhood as a predictor of future outcomes: A meta-analytic review. *Psychological Bulletin, 146*(4), 324–354. https://doi.org/10.1037/bul0000227

Romero, S., Swan, F., Barton, N., Bautista, R., Lopez, K., Simmons, J., & Silovsky, J. F. (2025, February 26). *What role does re-experiencing symptoms of PTSD have on PSB expression*? [Poster session]. National Symposium on the Sexual Behavior of Youth, Norman, OK, United States.

Sachser, C., Berliner, L., Holt, T., Jensen, T. K., Jungbluth, N., Risch, E., Rosner, R., & Goldbeck, L. (2017). International development and psychometric properties of the Child and Adolescent Trauma Screen (CATS). *Journal of Affective Disorders, 210*, 189–195. https://doi.org/10.1016/j.jad.2016.12.040

Sandnabba, N. K., Santtila, P., Wannäs, M., & Krook, K. (2003). Age and gender specific sexual behaviors in children. *Child Abuse & Neglect, 27*(6), 579–605. https://doi.org/10.1016/s0145-2134(03)00102-9

Schoentjes, E., Deboutte, D., & Friedrich, W. (1999). Child Sexual Behavior Inventory: A Dutch-speaking normative sample. *Pediatrics, 104*(4 Pt. 1), 885–893. https://doi.org/10.1542/peds.104.4.885

Schulte, J. A., Boone, M. K., Aronson, K. R., & Perkins, D. F. (2023). A non-clinical referral tool to help identify problematic child sexual behavior: Development, training, and initial user feedback. *Journal of Child Sexual Abuse, 32*(8), 1016–1035. https://doi.org/10.1080/10538712.2023.2276289

Shawler, P. M., Elizabeth Bard, M., Taylor, E. K., Wilsie, C., Funderburk, B., & Silovsky, J. F. (2018). Parent–child interaction therapy and young children with problematic sexual behavior: A conceptual overview and treatment considerations. *Children and Youth Services Review, 84*, 206–214. https://doi.org/10.1016/j.childyouth.2017.12.006

Shenk, C. E., Allen, B., Dreschel, N. A., Wang, M., Felt, J. M., Brown, M. P., Bucher, A. M., Chen, M. J., & Olson, A. E. (2022). Respiratory sinus arrhythmia change during trauma-focused cognitive-behavioral therapy: Results from a randomized controlled feasibility trial. *Research on Child and Adolescent Psychopathology, 50*(11), 1487–1499. https://doi.org/10.1007/s10802-022-00946-w

Silovsky, J. F., & Niec, L. (2002). Characteristics of young children with sexual behavior problems: A pilot study. *Child Maltreatment, 7*(3), 187–197. https://doi.org/10.1177/1077559502007003002

Silovsky, J. F., Niec, L., Bard, D., & Hecht, D. B. (2007). Treatment for preschool children with interpersonal sexual behavior problems: A pilot study. *Journal of Clinical Child and Adolescent Psychology, 36*(3), 378–391. https://doi.org/10.1080/15374410701444330

Simon, V. A., & Feiring, C. (2008). Sexual anxiety and eroticism predict the development of sexual problems in youth with a history of sexual abuse. *Child Maltreatment, 13*(2), 167–181. https://doi.org/10.1177/1077559508315602

Smith, C., Allardyce, S., Hackett, S., Bradbury-Jones, C., Lazenbatt, A., & Taylor, J. (2014). Practice and policy in the UK with children and young people who display harmful sexual behaviours: An analysis and critical review. *Journal of Sexual Aggression, 20*(3), 267–280. https://doi.org/10.1080/13552600.2014.927010

Smith, T. J., Lindsey, R. A., Bohora, S., & Silovsky, J. F. (2019). Predictors of intrusive sexual behaviors in preschool-aged children. *Journal of Sex Research, 56*(2), 229–238. https://doi.org/10.1080/00224499.2018.1447639

Southam-Gerow, M. A. (2013). *Emotion regulation in children and adolescents: A practitioner's guide*. Guilford Press.

St. Amand, A., Bard, D. E., & Silovsky, J. F. (2008). Meta-analysis of treatment for child sexual behavior problems: Practice elements and outcomes. *Child Maltreatment, 13*(2), 145–166. https://doi.org/10.1177/1077559508315353

Stone, L. L., Otten, R., Engels, R. C. M. E., Vermulst, A. A., & Janssens, J. M. A. M. (2010). Psychometric properties of the parent and teacher versions of the strengths and Difficulties Questionnaire for 4- to 12-year-olds: A review. *Clinical Child and Family Psychology Review, 13*(3), 254–274. https://doi.org/10.1007/s10567-010-0071-2

Tarren-Sweeney, M. (2008). Predictors of problematic sexual behavior among children with complex maltreatment histories. *Child Maltreatment, 13*(2), 182–198. https://doi.org/10.1177/1077559508316043

Thigpen, J., & Fortenberry, J. D. (2009). Understanding variation in normative childhood sexual behavior: The significance of family context. *Social Service Review, 83*(4), 611–631. https://doi.org/10.1086/650401

Thigpen, J. W. (2009). Early sexual behavior in a sample of low-income, African American children. *Journal of Sex Research, 46*(1), 67–79. https://doi.org/10.1080/00224490802645286

Tremblay, M.-J., Daignault, I. V., Fontaine, N. M. G., Boisvert, I., & Tourigny, M. (2020). School-aged children with sexual behavior problems: Untangling the relationship between externalizing behavior problems and non-sexual victimization on the variety and severity of sexual behaviors. *Child Abuse & Neglect, 107*, 104490. https://doi.org/10.1016/j.chiabu.2020.104490

van Duin, E. M., Verlinden, E., Vrolijk-Bosschaart, T. F., Diehle, J., Verhoeff, A. P., Brilleslijper-Kater, S. N., & Lindauer, R. J. L. (2018). Sexual abuse in very young children: A psychological assessment in the Amsterdam sexual abuse case study. *European Journal of Psychotraumatology, 9*(1), 1503524. https://doi.org/10.1080/20008198.2018.1503524

Wamser-Nanney, R., & Campbell, C. L. (2019). Children's sexual behavior problems: An ecological model using the LONGSCAN data. *Child Abuse & Neglect, 96*, 104085. https://doi.org/10.1016/j.chiabu.2019.104085

Wamser-Nanney, R., & Campbell, C. L. (2020). Childhood sexual abuse characteristics, abuse stress, and PTSS: Ties to sexual behavior problems. *Child Abuse & Neglect, 105*, 104290. https://doi.org/10.1016/j.chiabu.2019.104290

Wamser-Nanney, R., & Campbell, C. L. (2022). Sexual behavior problems among sexually abused children: Associations with co-occurring symptoms. *Child Maltreatment, 27*(1), 78–87. https://doi.org/10.1177/1077559520971362

Wamser-Nanney, R., Sager, J. C., & Campbell, C. L. (2019). Maternal support as a predictor of children's sexualized behaviors following childhood sexual abuse. *Child Maltreatment, 24*(1), 36–44. https://doi.org/10.1177/1077559518786821

Wiederman, M. W. (2015). Sexual script theory: Past, present, and future. In J. DeLamater & R. F. Plante (Eds.), *Handbooks of sociology and social research* (pp. 7–22). Springer International Publishing. https://doi.org/10.1007/978-3-319-17341-2_2

Wilson, E. K., Dalberth, B. T., Koo, H. P., & Gard, J. C. (2010). Parents' perspectives on talking to preteenage children about sex. *Perspectives on Sexual and Reproductive Health, 42*(1), 56–63. https://doi.org/10.1363/4205610

Wolak, J., Mitchell, K., & Finkelhor, D. (2007). Unwanted and wanted exposure to online pornography in a national sample of youth internet users. *Pediatrics, 119*(2), 247–257. https://doi.org/10.1542/peds.2006-1891

Index

U

V

W

About the Author

Brian Allen, PsyD, is a clinical psychologist, professor of pediatrics and psychiatry in the Penn State College of Medicine, and core faculty in the Child Maltreatment Solutions Network at Penn State University. He conducts research on the developmental impact of childhood trauma and maltreatment, the effectiveness and implementation of clinical interventions for maltreated children, and problematic sexual behavior among preteen children. His research is funded by the National Institutes of Health, the Children's Miracle Network, and other public and private agencies. He is the primary author of the Phase-Based Treatment for Problematic Sexual Behavior of Preteen Children protocol.